URBANIZATION AND MIGRATION
IN WEST AFRICA

Published under the auspices of the African Studies Center
University of California, Los Angeles

URBANIZATION
AND
MIGRATION
IN
WEST AFRICA

Edited by *HILDA KUPER*

UNIVERSITY OF CALIFORNIA PRESS

BERKELEY AND LOS ANGELES

1965

University of California Press
Berkeley and Los Angeles

Cambridge University Press
London, England

Library of Congress Catalog Card Number: 65-19248

Designed by Pamela F. Johnson

PREFACE

The essays published in this book were presented at the first of a series of interdisciplinary seminars held by the African Studies Center of the University of California, Los Angeles, in the fall of 1962. The broad topic of urbanization and migration was submitted to selected scholars in the fields of geography, history, linguistics, anthropology, political science, and economics. All had had fieldwork experience in Africa, and were asked both to indicate the methodology of their respective disciplines and to use factual data from their original research. Each essay was circulated in advance and then discussed at a seminar with faculty Africanists and graduate students. The papers were subsequently revised for publication.

The main points of the discussion are incorporated in the Introduction. I should like to acknowledge the contributions made by members of the UCLA faculty: Professors James S. Coleman, Wendell P. Jones, Leo Kuper, Wolf Leslau, M. G. Smith, Benjamin E. Thomas, Leonard Thompson, and William Welmers; and by the following student participants: Ukpabi Asika, Ernst Benjamin, Charles Bird, Naomi Brickman, Robert G. Brown, Ed Ferguson, Daniel Fine, Norman Gosenfield, Victor Low, Wyatt MacGaffey, Marian MacReynolds, Kenneth Rothman, and Charlotte Smith.

H. K.

CONTRIBUTORS

Michael Banton, professor of sociology in the University of Bristol, England, has done fieldwork in West Africa and Britain. Publications include *West African City: A Study of Tribal Life in Freetown; White and Coloured: The Behaviour of British People towards Coloured Immigrants; The Coloured Quarter: Negro Immigrants in an English City;* and *Roles: An Introduction to the Study of Social Relations.*

Elliot J. Berg is assistant professor of economics and research associate in the Center for International Affairs and the Center for Studies in Education and Development at Harvard University. He has done fieldwork in French West Africa, and his publications include "French West Africa," in *Labour and Economic Development*, edited by Walter Galenson; "The Economic Basis of Political Choice in French West Africa," *American Political Science Review* (June, 1960); and "The Character and Prospects of African Economies," in *The United States and Africa*, 2d edition, edited by Walter Goldschmidt.

John D. Fage, director of the Centre of West African Studies and professor of African history at the University of Birmingham, England, was on the faculty of the University of Ghana from 1949 to 1959. He has done fieldwork in West Africa. His publications include *An Introduction to the History of West Africa; An Atlas of African History; Ghana: A Historical Interpretation;* and, with Roland Oliver, *A Short History of Africa.*

Joseph H. Greenberg, professor of anthropology at Stanford University, did field research among the Maguzawa in Nigeria in 1938-39, and conducted a linguistic survey of Jos Plateau, Nigeria, in 1954-55. His publications include *Essays in Linguistics; Studies in African Linguistic Classification; The Languages of Africa;* and *Universals of Language* (ed.).

Hilda Kuper, professor of anthropology at the University of California, Los Angeles, has done fieldwork in southern Africa, and her publications include *An African Aristocracy; The Uniform of Colour; The Swazi;* and *Indian People in Natal.*

Horace M. Miner is professor of anthropology and sociology at the University of Michigan, and representative on the Governing Body of the International African Institute. His areas of fieldwork include North and West Africa. His publications include *The Primitive City of Timbuctoo; Oasis and Casbah: Algerian Culture and Personality in Change* (with G. DeVos); and "Social Science in Action in Sub-Saharan Africa," a special issue of *Human Organization* (ed.).

William B. Schwab, associate professor of anthropology at Temple University, Philadelphia, has done fieldwork in Nigeria and Southern Rhodesia. His publications include "Growth and Conflicts of Religion in a Modern Yoruba Community," *Zaïre* (October, 1952); "Kinship and Lineage among the Yoruba," *Africa* (1955); and "Continuity and Change in the Yoruba Lineage System," *Annals of the New York Academy of Sciences* (1962).

Elliott P. Skinner, associate professor of anthropology at Columbia University, has done fieldwork in French-speaking West Africa and British Guiana. His publications include *The Mossi of the Upper Volta;* "Mossi Trade and Markets," in *African Trade and Market Systems*, edited by Paul Bohannan; and "Labor Migration and Its Relationship to Socio-Cultural Change in Mossi Society," *Africa* (October, 1960).

Benjamin E. Thomas, professor of geography at the University of California, Los Angeles, has done research in East, West, and North Africa. His publications include *Trade Routes of Algeria and the Sahara; Transportation and Physical Geography in West Africa; Kenya and Uganda;* and "Railways and Ports in French West Africa," *Economic Geography* (January, 1952).

Immanuel Wallerstein, associate professor of sociology at Columbia University and chairman of the University Seminar on Africa, has done research in Ghana and the Ivory Coast. His publications include *Africa: The Politics of African Independence;* and *The Road to Independence: Ghana and the Ivory Coast.*

CONTENTS

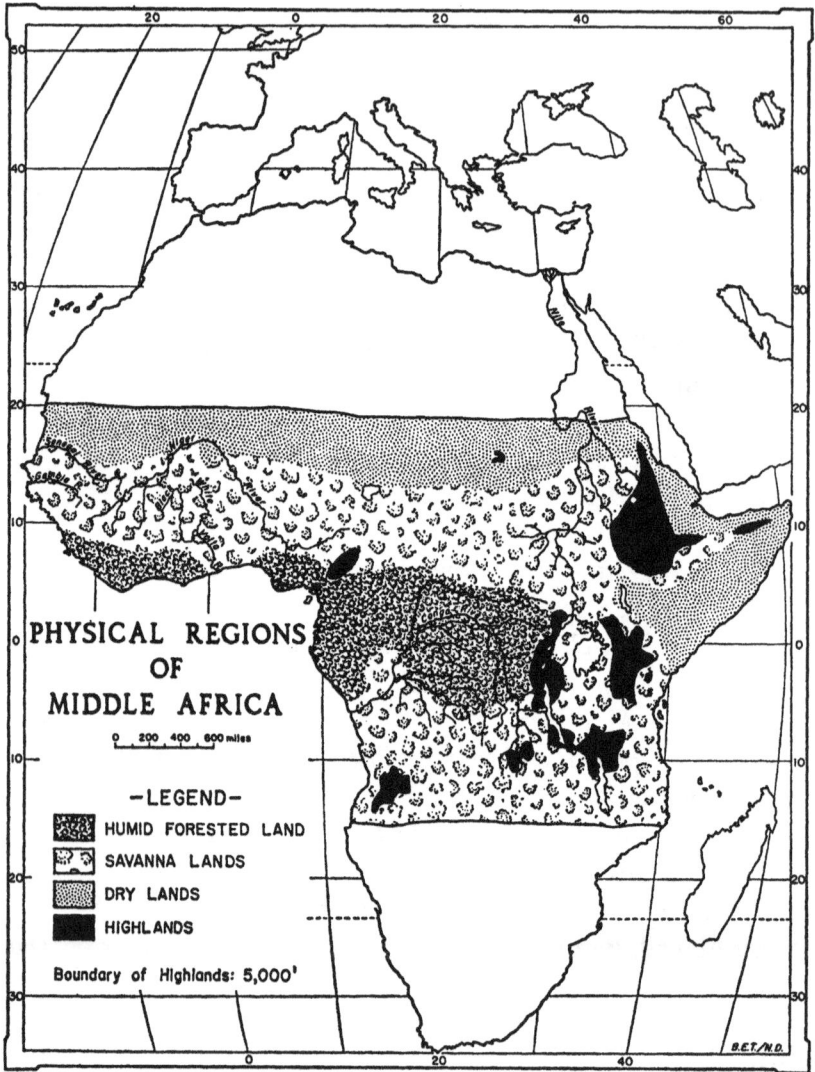

PHYSICAL REGIONS
OF
MIDDLE AFRICA

0   200   400   600 miles

—LEGEND—
HUMID FORESTED LAND
SAVANNA LANDS
DRY LANDS
HIGHLANDS

Boundary of Highlands: 5,000'

Map 1

1.
INTRODUCTION
by Hilda Kuper

The peoples of Africa are increasing in numbers and growing in political power; and the societies into which they are organized are industrializing on an expanding scale. The process of industrialization, generated by political policies and economic innovation, is widely associated with movements from rural areas to urban centers. This process has several distinctive characteristics: economically, the structure of production changes and an increasing proportion of workers are involved in non-agricultural activities and have unequal access to economic opportunities; politically, bureaucratic machinery and administrative control are becoming more extensive; legally, conflicting claims are expressed in contractual rather than in status arrangements.[1] Industrial urbanization is thus more than a shifting of people from country to city, from land-bound to urban occupations, and more than increasing population density and economic differentiation. It entails also changes in distribution of power, interests, institutional arrangements, norms of conduct, and social values, and, as a particular process of increasing complexity, cannot be isolated from the more general context of social growth.

The city has long been a subject of interest to students of different disciplines, and also of controversial approaches within disciplines. The concept of "city" exists in contrast with other types of community—especially in contrast with "village" or "town." As in many areas of the social sciences, where words of everyday usage are retained for social facts, there is confusion in this terminology. Village, town, and city have no fixed meaning, and are used differently in America and England, and even in different states in America, as well as in Africa. The community described as a village by an Englishman is spoken of as a town by a New Englander.[2] A city is defined in America by municipal privileges; charters granted by state legislatures raise towns and villages to the rank of cities; in England "city" is basically a title of dignity bestowed on

[1] For notes to chapter 1, see page 185.

towns in virtue of some preëminence, and does not confer any specific municipal functions. In West Africa any large settlement seems to be labeled "city" or "town," indiscriminately. In one of the main indigenous languages, Yoruba, there are basic terms distinguishing town and village, but no distinction is made between the metropolitan town and smaller towns.[3] In parts of North Africa, an Islamic city is defined by the presence of a mosque, public baths, and covered markets or bazaars.[4] Social scientists are less concerned with adventitious verbal usage than with principles of organization, and the linguistic confusion reflects in part the complexity of the subject. In the following pages "city" and "town" are used synonymously.

Migration, as a culturally patterned movement of people, generally interacts with modern urbanization when political regimes associated with technological developments expand labor requirements. In the past, many of the routes of trade were tramped by the feet of slaves—animate power required to produce surplus food or to build walls and dams, or to mine the ore for despotic rulers or masters. The colonial era, which introduced new focuses of control, a more extensive economy, and sources of inanimate power, forced or drew men to work in ports, mining towns, and factories. Towns, as strategically situated centers of innovations, have always received immigrants. At the rural end migration may be set in motion by negative pressures (land shortage, political oppression, family feuds) or by positive inducements (marketing of cash crops, new opportunities for achievement). But migration, coerced or voluntary, has also been directed to nonurban centers, more especially to plantations; and though migration is a key to African history, the town is not, and has not been, a necessary terminus, or determinant, of the migrant's route. Urban and industrial centers are spatially limited, and Africa, including West Africa, is still predominantly rural, producing mainly raw materials and foodstuffs. With the extension of industry, commerce, and administration, modern migrants have a wider choice of place of sojourn and employment.

West Africa has a long history of settlements that have been described as "urban."[5] In the past these settlements, though sufficiently advanced in cultivation to provide subsistence requirements, were restricted in size of population by the relatively simple technology, dependence on agriculture, limited, albeit diverse, functional differentiation, mediocre transport and storage facilities, and the slowness of communication between the central authority and its officialdom. At the same time, West African towns were politically centralized, and controlled institutionalized markets and long-distance trade. Their specific land-use pattern gave preëminence to the central area over the periphery, and particular spatial recognition was accorded to different ethnic or occupational groups. As in the preindustrial city described by Sjoberg,[6] the central governmental and religious structures dominated the urban horizon both physically and symbolically.

The period of Western colonial control placed a new stamp on existing societies, and though each Western power—British, French, or Portuguese—expressed a separate colonial policy and introduced something of its own national pattern of urban organization, the differences are probably less significant than between the precolonial and colonial periods. For colonialism was distinctive. "Peace," backed ultimately by new military techniques, was established in arbitrarily defined territorial regions, and the new politico-economic regime was characterized by a complex of innovations involving, over a number of years, modern transport facilities, more extensive communications, trade agreements, and a bureaucratic organization requiring formal paper work in a different legal framework. But every historical event has geographical boundaries. Arab influence in West Africa was confined primarily to certain northern regions; later colonial penetration did not automatically obliterate old types of settlements. In modern Nigeria there are "traditional" (pre-European) Yoruba kingdoms, such as Oyo and Ekiti, in which the metropolitan town (with its distinctive subsections) is large and centrally situated, with farm lands extending from 3 to 10 miles from the town;[7] and there are also the (Muslim) Hausa emirates of Kano and Sokoto which continue the traditional settlement pattern of compact walled towns, distinguished by market place and mosque and ringed around by bush hamlets;[8] there are also "modern" cities such as Lagos and Ibadan in which there is a sharp contrast between the "old" town and the "new," with the new section organized around Western administrative residential and commercial buildings.[9]

In West Africa the industrial and commercial complex is concentrated in cities that Europeans either developed from preindustrial "traditional" cities, or created themselves; these cities fall into political boundaries within which their relationship is both with other cities and with various types of peasant communities. The distinctions, which developed historically, in mode of control of preindustrial and industrial cities in Europe, may not apply in Africa or in other formerly nonindustrial colonial areas. In medieval Europe control was exercised from political capitals over the surrounding countryside; with the rise of indigenous industries new cities developed. These centers of economic diversity involved multiple control of labor and required new forms of governmental supervision. These controls, however, were built from within; they were organic correlates of economic growth. In Africa the development of industrial cities was accomplished by outside powers, and entailed a different order of city regulations, whereas the regulations that operated in traditional centers were submerged or changed their meaning.

Yet the acceptance and the rapidity of industrial urbanization challenge a widely prevalent assumption that traditional societies are impeded by "tradition" from making radical changes. Tradition is not necessarily conservative, and in the newly independent countries of Africa reaffirmation, and at times rediscovery, of tradition are used deliberately as an incentive to modernization and industrialization. But at the same time it is clear, even from West African material, that there is no single model of "the city"; and there are many mirrors through which it can be viewed. Not enough is known of urbanization in general to enable the student of a particular city to determine what is singular or otherwise. Social scientists are, however, striving to analyze the general principles of organization and social process underlying the variety of towns described in their uniqueness by novelists and poets.

In the following sections of this introduction I discuss briefly some of the approaches and problems raised by the participants in this interdisciplinary seminar. Social research in West Africa is relatively recent, and there was a constant awareness of major gaps in knowledge, the need for further research, and for more systematic comparison. The papers themselves reflect the thoughts and outlook of a geographer, a historian, sociologists and anthropologists, a political scientist, and an economist.

A geographer may delineate towns primarily by population distribution and the pattern of settlements—the functional areas. Cartography is a specific technique for conveying conditions observable on the surface of the earth at particular periods of time. For this purpose it is legitimate to isolate a town on a demographic basis, and then (*a*) to map the ecological areas (residential, commercial, and industrial) that provide the outer shell of interpersonal relations; (*b*) to draw the transport lines that indicate the design of communication; and (*c*) to locate the places of public assembly which serve as centers for worship, barter, or administration. A geographer may seek the intangible underlying network of social relationships as well as the organizational role of government and other sociological principles of association, mainly insofar as they explain the location and growth of cities.

Using accepted, but arbitrary, population figures, Professor Thomas focuses on West African towns, old and new, and derives a typology from the interaction of the physical infrastructure—climate, soil, water supply—with the social superstructure—communications, transport, trade, political development. The successive zones of rain forest, open woodlands, and grass and shrub profoundly influenced the patterns of settlement and the direction of migration. It is primarily in the savanna

belt that there developed the traditional centralized states with aristo-
cratic political cities, advanced agriculture, and specialized crafts. In the
forest regions such politico-economic expansion and the growth of
towns were stimulated by their position in relation to external contacts
in trade and war. As with other social sciences, there are many approaches to the geography of cities. The one chosen by Professor
Thomas is intended to serve as background for the later papers on social
aspects of urbanization and migration.

A historian, interested in what happened and when, adds the dimen-
sion of time to that of place and seeks a thread of continuity in social
phenomena. Thus Professor Fage questions the generally held assumptions (1) that the great states emerged first in the savanna belt, and (2)
that similar developments in the forest area were largely the result of
influences emanating along lines of contact from the west and central
Sudan.

The process of history is marked by such critical events as the development of trade, or conquest by aliens, or the introduction of a new
religion—in which instances migration may link different historical cultures—or by internal change through revolution or invention. In West
Africa the history of each society is unique, but dominant trends pre-
vail in different areas. Thus in some of the northern regions the growth
of early sporadic agricultural towns was stimulated by long-distance
trade associated in the tenth century with the introduction of Islam,
which religion became politically entrenched in the eighteenth century
by the jihad. At the same time there was, from the sixteenth century,
contact with Europeans, initially through sea trading and later through
colonial administration; finally, with rising nationalism came political independence.

In the relative absence of documents, the historian of early African
cities relies largely on the data of archaeology, linguistics, ethnographic
analysis of trait distribution, and current ethnographic description. As
archaeological research is still limited, Professor Fage considers that for
some time to come the historian will have to work more often with
oral tradition and clues suggested by material culture, confirmed at some
points by "historically recognizable" texts. With the available evidence,
Fage supports a hypothesis that two distinct types of urban settlement
developed in West Africa—one along the northwest axis, the other from
the northeast—and he relates each type to movements that gave different emphasis to trade or military and political interests. The northwest
pattern seems to have given rise to a "twin city," in which a Mandi-
Muslim commercial center arose alongside a royal-pagan capital, while
in the northeast, he suggests, the walled city came into existence for
protection against attack.

Professor Fage recognizes explicitly that this method of reconstruction, similar in some respects to the approach of the diffusionist school of cultural anthropology, results in hypothetical or conjectural history. This approach is always open to criticism.[10] A historian of preliterate societies may have to work without relevant facts about social organization, about trade, about status systems; in short, without relevant facts about the social context in which particular culture traits receive their meaning. Even such material remains as the walls of cities (Kano, Benin, Oyo) may have been built for different reasons and may have served different purposes at different periods. Wall building itself must be related to political and economic situations. With the techniques available in preindustrial states, large walls required a labor force that had to be controlled by some centralizing power, and at the same time wall building was a device that rulers used to help achieve political centralization. In parts of West Africa *corvée* rights and local concentration of control were associated with slavery, and in Hausa territory extensive wall building and extensive slavery were associated. On the other hand, in the early period of the Akan Kingdom, both the walls and the degree of centralization characteristic of the more Islamized districts were absent, and in the eighteenth century, when centralization occurred, it did not lead to wall building. Or again, the existence of twin cities in both West Africa and North Africa may be related to separate and distinctive societal conditions. Traditions of the origins of a city are difficult, if not impossible, to date, and legends may be created as retrospective justifications of city organization.[11]

Contradictory interpretations of events are frequent in history; in colonial countries this tendency seems to be almost inevitable. The attitude that "civilization" came to Negro Africa from outside, more especially from Egypt, persists in many European circles, and evidence to the contrary is underestimated. For the Africans who were denied their historic contribution in the colonial regime, the affirmation of indigenous cities and past glories is a necessary correlate of independence. Ancient names may therefore be revived to commemorate traditional achievements and stir modern loyalties. The academic question of the rise, and fall, of early African cities may become a current political issue.[12] In the battle between contending historiographies, it is difficult to remain a nonpartisan historian.

The method of hypothetical reconstruction of migrations and urban development lies between the approach of those historians who stress the particularism of specific events in time and place, and those social historians who have been concerned with the broad process of changing relationships and values underlying the rise of the city.[13] History provides material for comparison, though the principles for comparison, and the validity of the units that can be selected for comparison, are (and probably will always be!) debatable. Such historic reference concepts as the "medieval city" or "feudalism" are useful in bringing anthropologists absorbed in the uniqueness of difference to consider the more widespread occurrence of structural similarities and developments.[14] "Traditional" West African cities exhibit many of the political and economic features characteristic of medieval cities of Europe, in which resident burghers satisfied a large part of their food needs through cultivation and also produced food for sale, while at the same time the city was serving as a place of market traffic and typical urban trade and as the center of religious authority. On the other hand, West African cities are without sharp economic class distinctions or the military emphasis of medieval feudalism. The crucial problem is how to control comparison, how to isolate the variables, so that we can arrive at general explanations of the process of social growth.

A historian who uses language as evidence of diffusion or borrowing requires the assistance of both the formal linguist and the sociolinguist. Urban life is frequently characterized by peculiarities of language (slang, dialects, official languages), and the discipline of the linguist provides distinctive clues to understanding the logic of the complexity of social expression and communication. It does not follow that language is inherently logical, but that by reason of the unique character of language, a linguist is able to isolate the components (phonetic, grammatical, stylistic, and lexicographical) of different languages, draw formal comparisons, and suggest possible correlations between linguistic structures and social structures.[15] Distinct from this analytic approach is the situational approach selected by the sociolinguist who emphasizes social meaning rather than verbal form, and social rather than logical relations. These approaches are not mutually exclusive. Language embodied in oral tradition is a social document, and the linguist, in turn, requires historical and anthropological data for insight into the cultural meaning. Language, seen as a cultural tool that can cross geographical boundaries and endure historical revolutions, and as a mode of organizing behavior and ideas, is closely identified with institutions, structure, and values. When the linguist relates language to groups of people, he moves toward a sociological approach in which language becomes a symbol of social identity. It is this approach that Joseph Greenberg adopts in his particular discussion of language in relation to African migration to the cities. Elaborating this theme, Professor Greenberg points out that American sociologists have neglected to study the role of language probably because the United States is a monolingual country, despite its immigrant subcultures. The implicit assumption is that research itself is practically motivated; and in a country that is sufficiently powerful for the official language to be adequate, it is ethnocentrically valued as "the best." Stimulus to language research comes from the challenge to this self-sufficiency and superiority.

Africa presents the linguist with a monumental task: there are more than 800 languages, and virtually no area has a natural linguistic boundary. The language maps of Africa are all first-language maps, but especially in the towns migrants speaking different languages are frequently brought together, and in certain situations must communicate with one another. But how? What language will be chosen? Or developed? Is the cosmopolitan character of cities reflected in the variety of languages recognized in commerce, even when not spoken by many of the rank and file of the populace? What value is placed on differences in language or accent?

Professor Greenberg argues cogently that the choice of language made by an individual in a multilingual urban situation reveals not only his personal identification but more generalized principles of social alignment; that social identities are expressed in language loyalties; and that the persistence of the "mother tongue," or its rejection, the borrowing of terms for new concepts, and the adoption or creation of new languages are part of the complex structuring and process of urbanization. In the modern towns new language idioms are developing together with other cultural acquisitions. Language, like a flag, is a symbol of unity; when hostilities arise between different linguistic groups, the language of each serves as a rallying call. The members (protagonists) do not conceptualize this unity in rational terms; they do not say "our language is better than yours" for such and such a reason, any more than they say "our flag is better than yours because it has more stars." Urban languages have no inherent superiority. Similarly the question of the extent to which auxiliary languages are recognized is not answered by the logic of communication, but by the directions of politics or economics. Professor Greenberg distinguishes a lingua franca from other languages of contact (pidgin and Creole) by its social context, not its "linguistic nature," and considers that in contrast with a "mother tongue" a lingua franca evokes no deep emotion.

It would appear that in Africa linguistic unity is not so important a support of nationalism as in Europe. In Nigeria people can communicate in Hausa or in English, and the particularism that might endanger national unity seems to be based on factors other than language. If tribalism were prejudicial to national unity, a good many African languages would have to be sacrificed. But a lingua franca may coexist with tribal languages, and it has been argued that national sentiments might be enhanced if linguistic dominance was not imposed and if the languages of immigrants and minorities received more tolerance and respect.[16] A single official language may be required for administrative and commercial efficiency, but in some areas existing diversity cannot be obliterated without evoking passionate reactions. On the other hand, in South Africa, where language has long been a focal point of partisanship and divided loyalties, the battle of politicians has been carried into schools and universities, and the prohibition of participation in a universal language and of emphasis on the vernaculars has aroused deep antagonism.

The way people themselves evaluate languages and the precedence given to one or more must be sought in specific historical and social contexts. Professor Greenberg points out that colonial policies (and now national policies) have molded languages and have affected language choice. Dialects have become standardized by selecting one out of several and then building it up with a written grammar, dictionary, and so on. Though from the point of view of a typical dialect the choice may have been poor, the written form of language is associated with a power group and gives a positive prestige. Pidgins, on the other hand, are often connected with a master-servant relationship and have a negative value. In some instances, Professor Greenberg links the rise of a lingua franca with both numbers and local political dominance (Kanuri is an example); or, again, he discusses the extension of the language of traders in Fulani-Hausa contacts. From his examples he shows clearly that numbers alone are relatively unimportant in shaping the choice of language. Mossi who go to Ghana do not learn another language, a fact that can be related to their particular stereotyped pattern of seasonal migration relative to the limited requirements of the city and the status of the Mossi immigrant on his return; but we do not know which of these factors is crucial. The attachment of immigrants to their native tongue is generally assumed, but there are instances in Africa of group affiliation being deliberately changed by linguistic "passing," particularly in the towns, where old social bonds can be less easily traced, and individuals may wish to assimilate with a group that has superior prestige and economic possibilities.

It is common to read in ethnographic literature the bald statement that conquering migrants took over the language of the indigenous inhabitants, or that they imposed their own language on the conquered. The circumstances of retention, abandonment, or adoption in this situation require further sociological description in the context of religious, political, and economic systems. Isolated correlations with numbers, or "prestige," or commercial interest, or "conquest and defeat" cannot yield adequate theoretical principles of interpretation. It is true that empirical data on the existing situation are sparse, and statistics on language selection (e.g., by children of intertribal marriages in towns) are almost nonexistent, but such data must be set in a comprehensive and coherent framework of linguistic and sociological research.

Professor Greenberg's paper raises a fundamental theoretical problem —the definition of social identity in relation to language—and he indicates the extent to which the cities of Africa provide a context of situations for such a task. The context of situations includes a configuration of different immigrants in relation to one another and to things of the modern world, and organized in ways different from those of their more self-contained traditional societies. This type of linguistic analysis is, of course, not suggested as a substitute for the linguist's grammatical treatment of the languages of the city; it operates at a different level and requires different techniques.

The anthropologist, whose field itself is changing from preindustrial, small-scale, folk communities into industrial, large-scale, urban societies, is being forced to reëxamine his techniques of research and his theories of interpretation. At the same time sociologists, confronted with data from non-Western urban societies,[17] as well as from recent detailed studies in America[18] and England,[19] are querying previously accepted generalizations based on limited studies of Western cities.

The writers of the sociological articles contributed to this volume make no distinction between social anthropology and sociology, and they select from the same range of theory. The subject of their joint disciplines, in its basic formulation, is the structuring of social relationships—the ordered, complex interaction of individuals through kinship, locality, occupation, ethnicity, and other principles of association—and their cultural or symbolic manifestations. As in every social science, there are several ways (or schools) of interpreting and selecting from the recognized genre of social facts. In this volume each writer not only deals with different empirical material, but applies a selectively particular approach. The material itself gives some idea of the cultural variety as well as the social complexity of the situation. Professor Schwab discusses Oshogbo, a predominantly Yoruba town, under an *oba* whose people are grouped together by lineage ties. Professor Miner discusses sociocultural interaction between Zaria, a Muslim Hausa city centralized under an emir, and Kubau, a rural settlement. Professor Banton analyzes shifting alignments in the port of Freetown. Professor Skinner concentrates on the process of migration and its repercussions among the Mossi of the Upper Volta.

The writers are not concerned with the social-survey or the "social-problems" approaches which are engaging many urban sociologists. For the town planner and the welfare worker it is indeed essential to record such cultural features as the number of houses and of occupants, the distribution of income, sex and age ratios, rates of divorce, delinquency, and so on, and African cities may provide interesting comparative data. But at the descriptive (ethnographic) level, without a theoretical framework, they can only yield a compendium of elements "transparent to things and opaque to meanings."

The papers and discussions are more generally oriented. Sociological theories of the city stem mainly from the conspicuous contrast between modern complex urban societies and rural nonindustrialized societies. Studies of urbanization in modern Africa are directly or indirectly influenced by the classical works of Durkheim, Maine, Tönnies, and Weber, transmitted in part through Wirth and Redfield. It is in this broad tradition that Professors Schwab and Miner frame their contributions. The focus is on typology and causality. "Urban" and "folk" are conceptualized as contrasted ideal types, each viewed as an integrated social structure or mechanism with its own forms of equilibrium and its own social (largely demographic) and psychological attributes.[20] Until fairly recently more thought was directed to examining and refining characteristics of heterogeneity, density, permanence, isolation, secularization, individualization, and literacy than to analyzing structural process.

In 1940 Professor Miner, then a student of Redfield's, studied the Sudanese city of Timbuktu with a view to discovering what urban elements were present in this non-Western setting.[21] He found a high population density (some 6,000 people in an area of less than a square mile), marked social heterogeneity (a lingua franca was required for simple day-to-day transactions between distinctive ethnic groups), considerable status differentiation, and a diversified commercial economy with extensive trade. On the other hand, within each ethnic group, kinship relationships were strong and stable, and were sanctioned by sacred values. Only in the sphere of market economy were relationships secular, impersonal, and fraught with conflict—even among co-ethnics. Miner concluded that Timbuktu owed its urban density to its commercial functions, which both bound the various ethnic elements together and provided the logics of the marketplace in terms of which they could interact. Aside from such interaction and the conflicts resulting from ethnic differences, life was very "folklike."

William Bascom, also a pioneer in African urban sociology, shows in his studies of Yoruba cities in Nigeria that ethnic heterogeneity was no prerequisite for urbanism.[22] In ten of the twelve largest Yoruba cities, over 93 per cent of the population was ethnically and culturally homogeneous. Though specialization and commerce were important, 60 to 80 per cent of the working males in the more traditional cities were (in 1952) engaged in agriculture and, to a lesser extent, in fishing. Heterogeneity was expressed, however, in their social stratification and the elaboration of the political structure.

Later work in Africa has made it increasingly clear that such ecological and demographic features as heterogeneity, density, and mobility are not necessarily associated with urbanism, or with one another, or with such assumed sociopsychological attributes as secularization, anonymity, and individualism. Thus the formalized city government of the Yoruba is absent among the Ibo, some of whose settlements are comparable in population density but who are organized into congeries of villages. Again, there are dense settlements in Bechuanaland which fulfill entirely rural functions and must be excluded from the category of urban. Secularization no longer appears to be a city prerogative; new religious movements started in towns have reached out to the countryside. In West Africa, Islam is largely an urban religion, evoking wider and more active involvement than many traditionally sanctioned rituals; research in South Africa has demonstrated the efflorescence of Christian sects in urban and rural centers.

Anonymity and individualism, often related to the breakdown of kinship ties, are not inevitable consequences of urban living. In this volume Schwab shows that in Oshogbo the lineage remains the "primary focus of unity" and is, in fact, sufficiently flexible to accommodate different (nondescent) bases of authority and leadership. Even when there is a wide variety of groups recruited on diverse bases, and to which individuals can belong for particular purposes, kin identity need not be lost in other identities.

"Model" building does not claim to be, nor intend to be, identical with any real society; the aim is to provide a heuristic classificatory device, rather than any interpretive theory. By examining characteristics in the context of new empirical data, some will appear more general than others, providing a sort of urban core, an abstraction useful for classifying, rather than comparing, societies of similar type. The concept of "more urban" or "less urban" or "smaller-" or "larger-scale" is part of the "model" approach, and efforts are being made to introduce more statistical precision into the classifications.[23] As far back as 1912 Durkheim advanced certain indexes of social solidarity, and also distinguished clearly the relationships from the causes effecting changes in the relationships;[24] and in 1938 Wirth differentiated between industrial and nonindustrial cities, suggesting that social heterogeneity, secularization, and impersonality might be concomitants only of industrial urbanization.[25]

But the "model" approach has its weaknesses. There is the danger that models set forth as an analytical device are then "discovered" as empirical phenomena. In some instances ideological (populist) pressure may account more than empirical fact for characteristics of the model.

There is also an underlying semantic confusion in which urbanization is simultaneously a process and a measure. At the extreme end of the measure are the models as "ideal types," with the highest concentration of selected urban characteristics. But these may also be present in units not generally recognized as "urbs." Urban society may be made to appear as an assortment of varying negatives (disorganization, impersonality, anonymity), so that the urbanized individual is described as "detribalized," as marginal because he is without "roots" (land, chief, or kin), in a society characterized by a competitive money economy, full-time specialization, and an impersonal system of government. Conflict itself is interpreted as personal maladjustment, or as the result of inconsistencies in cultural patterns or of lack of adherence to cultural standards, and not as opposition between interacting and competing parts.

Heterogeneity, which, as we have seen, cannot be limited to tribal or ethnic origin, consists of the formal recognition given to different principles of organization (occupation, age, rank, locality, and so on). Their systematic interaction constitutes the essential structure of any urban society, and such an analysis provides sociological insights at a different level from discussions of how cities differ from other areas, or how urbanized rural areas differ from nonurbanized rural areas.[26] Analytically it is more purposeful to study the operation of principles of organization coördinating urban dwellers over a period of time, than it is to view new associations as replacements of traditional ties.

Economic, political, and religious changes widely associated with Western industrial urbanism cannot be treated as a single composite package. Beals pointed out in 1951 that "technological specialization and industrialization may be characteristics primarily associated with urbanized societies, yet not be necessary attributes of the city itself."[27] Certain societies may be more resistant to industrialization than others, but such incompatibility may be unrelated to urbanization.

Urbanization is part of the process of social change, and social change is not a mechanical accretion or accumulation of traits. It is not sufficient to recognize the functional interdependence of elements; in dealing with change it is necessary to recognize that different parts of a social system have different degrees of functional autonomy, and that a particular institution, a type of family, or an association may simultaneously become more specialized and part of a new total configuration.

Although city and village are conceptually distinct, their existence is interdependent. Interdependence is not a neatly closed circuit; other cities and other villages intervene, and the relation between them varies within boundaries that have not yet been conceptually defined. Professor Miner's article in this volume reveals the extension of interdependence beyond the city's need for agricultural produce, and shows how modernizing influences are channeled (through economic, educational, and political machinery) to satellite villages. Within this situation, new leaders both express and manipulate change at the same time as they are limited by the varying pressures of tradition. Their success depends in part on personal ability in maneuvering people representing conflicting interests. Thus Miner draws attention to the process of "modernization." Inherent in his approach are the acceptance of a continuum between "town" and "village" and the assumption that some natural relation exists among some or all of the characteristics, so that change with regard to some tends to bring about change in others.

In the Zaria-Kubau example, change is, as it were, held in check by the flexibility of the town-country network of relationships, and there is no sharp or irreconcilable break between the two centers. There are other societies in which such a cleavage does indeed exist, and town and country are kept together by political and administrative coercion. Such in fact is the position in parts of southern Africa where there is intense conflict and discontinuity in organization and values between urban industrial centers, founded and dominated by whites, and country areas, inhabited by Africans. Moreover, a particular city may have contradictory links with differently structured rural communities which in turn have no connection with one another. In such instances "interdependence" is opposition maintained within a total system of coercive control.

This problem is raised by Dr. Banton, who analyzes the structure of African towns through the process of alignments of inhabitants, old and new, host and immigrant. He considers that the situation has its parallels in America, where newcomers are given stereotyped identities which may not correspond with their own views of themselves or their groups, but which, in the initial stages, may regulate their place of abode and type of work. Cut off from home, and in separate social boundaries, the immigrants may have their attachment to tradition reinforced and seek to join or create associations in which they receive recognition through group alignments, which also mediate between them and "the others." Such an approach, which does not accept the premise that because groups are functionally interrelated the society is necessarily held together by "consensus," enables Banton to indicate the multiciplicity of cleavages—ethnic, economic, religious, and so forth—which make possible the comparison of social structure at different times within or between different societies. He follows through suggestions of Gluckman, Mitchell, and Epstein, social anthropologists who derived their conclusions from detailed fieldwork in southern Africa and were not interested in "model building." [28]

These scholars showed that identities shifted with particular situations, and that the emphasis placed on any particular principle of allegiance or coöperation might change in response to new situations. The dominance given any particular identity was related to the pervasiveness of the cleavage separating its members from others. In the towns of Northern Rhodesia, the dominant and most persistent cleavage was derived from "race," and racial (or rather color) identity was preëminent. Banton posed the question why cleavage should be, or appear to be, more acute in urban centers in Southern Rhodesia than in those in West Africa, and sought the answer in historically shaped structural alignments. And here it is useful to digress, drawing together discussions interspersed throughout several meetings, indicating major contrasts between cities in South and West Africa.

In the south, Africans, though they organized powerful centralized states, have no traditions of specialization beyond the activities of rulers, medicine men, priests, and smiths. The towns were created by whites, and they controlled the entry of Africans for their own security and interests. At the same time they moved as masters into African-occupied areas, permitting in some parts landless Africans to remain as labor tenants, and in others containing Africans in reservations. Growing industrial demands led to increasing pressure on Africans to move from an economy embedded in familiar institutions into a monetary system, but at the same time the racist policy of the white settlers prohibited Africans from settling in the towns established by their labor.

In West Africa the wage-earning population is a relatively small proportion of the total, whites are few and preponderantly transient, there is little land alienation, migration is seasonal, occupational opportunities are less restricted, and political participation is less conspicuously prescribed. Between the "city" and outlying villages there may be a "symbiotic and ecological attachment." An extended family may own a compound in the city and may also have sites for farming in the village, and members may live alternately, for varying lengths of time, in both places and, in some instances, commute between them daily.

In the south, urban centers created by industrialization and controlled by the alien Westerner conflicted in power, organization, and economic interest with traditional rurally based capitals. Traditional leaders (chiefs) not only lost their subjects to white employees, but depended for recognition on the white government which sanctioned and encouraged industrialism. The chiefs were forced to give their support to, and even to recruit labor for, the new centers of power. At the same time, urban industrial centers with their growing numbers of people, usually drawn from several traditional ethnic groups, provided a larger and more powerful base for new African leaders interested in labor organization and in political control. These leaders tended to concentrate in urban areas and to be both antiwhite and antitraditionalist. The new racially plural societies developed in the south required for their maintenance periodic demonstrations of physical force by white-settler governments; validation for the system of African subordination was imminently as well as ultimately coercive. The cities, centers of wealth, were and remain the white strongholds, while Africans are forced by law, backed by penal sanctions, to reside in "reserves" or in large peripheral townships ("locations") which are not urban, as they lack specialized economic activities and incapsulate mainly unskilled and semiskilled labor.

In Freetown, as Banton shows, the Creole "host" is not so distinctive a power group, and even in the mining towns of West Africa the populations are relatively small and workers from the surrounding territories are more readily incorporated. In many other towns the relationship of colonial domination is mediated through metropolitan officials coöperating with traditional leaders. With the coming of independence under an urban-oriented African leadership, the dominant emerging cleavage in the towns appears to be along lines of the "indigenous" versus the "stranger" or the "foreigner" (the new migrants).

It would seem that each society has structural and ethical antecedents of its own which interact with the introduced physical and social attributes of cities associated with modern industry, and so create distinctive types of urbanism.[29] Industrialization cannot be treated as a given change which then produces uniform consequential changes. This approach to society as an integrated social system functionally attaining a new balance after a temporarily disturbing innovation in a vital sector of social life—the economic—is unrealistic. Such a "before" and "after" approach ignores the dynamics of simultaneous change, the complexity of uneven sequence, and the nature of structural conflict.

From West African as compared with South African data, at least two major distinguishing sets of related facts emerge in the sociohistorical process of urbanization. The first set relates to the general problem of stratification. In both societies stratification is associated with economic and political pluralism, but in South Africa pluralism is overt racism backed by force. The industrial cities, centers of power and wealth introduced by whites, are as much military fortifications of white privilege as any medieval fortress. In West Africa, even in the colonial period, stratification was based less on race and economics, and power was more widely bureaucratic (perhaps because many of the cities developed from traditional urban settlements). The period of independence, marked by a removal of white administrators in the upper echelons, gave an already existing African upper stratum greater authority and wider opportunity, and extended its organization within a newly defined national framework. At the same time, urban industrial development stimulated the rise of the new economic elite.

The second set of distinctive facts pertains to identification—the coalescence of the individual with socially defined groups in specific situations. A wider range of identification is available in West Africa through the commercial and religious complexity of traditional urban centers, as well as through the relative freedom from political restraint over new associations. These points have already been suggested, and space does not allow me to deal with them more fully.

Migration, which I have described as a patterned movement of people not necessarily related to urbanization, is the main focus of the remaining papers. It is discussed both as part of a general process of change and also as a complex of variables, including the nature of absence—seasonal, temporary, nonseasonal, recurrent, continuous, and permanent—and the relative numbers and prestige of migrants. The two aspects are distinct, but complementary. As a process migration is never haphazard; routes become established and behavior becomes formalized. The effects of migration as a complex of variables may be compared in diverse types of society. Some types of migration may be found to be more compatible with some forms of economy or social organization than others. In the process of adaptation, different structural systems might be shown to exist at the beginning and end points of migration. Migrations through economic pressure or struggles for power are part of the history of most African peoples, but the present problem is largely the changing rate and scale of movements and the forces behind them.

Professor Skinner, as an anthropologist, stresses the difficulty of isolating the effects of migration from other complex forces of change. He presents a careful analysis of Mossi society in which migration was initially a response to pressure for taxation by a colonial power and then gradually became accepted and stereotyped. New experiences away from the home areas were mediated by the retention or resumption of traditional ties under traditional chiefs, and continued association with Mossi speaking co-workers. But though some 80 per cent of Mossi migrants work under these conditions, Dr. Skinner considers that even seasonal migration has produced new tensions or has accentuated old and potential tensions in the family (between parent and child, husband and wife) and has weakened the ties built by the traditional economy; the coöperative work party is falling away, and some hand skills are lost and some cash crops are neglected when they interfere with migration.

The economist, Elliot Berg, applies a selective argument that contrasts with the more general sociological outlook represented by Professor Skinner. Dr. Berg deals exclusively with the economic aspects of migration, explicitly excluding social implications. His argument is carefully mounted within the classical framework of demand, cost, and supply. The seasonal demand for labor is dovetailed with the migrants' rural economy and does not seriously interfere with the production of traditional crops. West Africa is described as the "perfect market" in which the migrant is a commodity for which there are many buyers. Without migrant labor as an alternative to permanent emigration, neither the wide dispersal of income to African villages nor the efficient expansion of production in the forest and coastal zones would be possible. The alternative of full-time emigration would demand higher wages as inducements for the worker to leave his village and vast expenditure by employers in providing adequate housing for the entire family. To minimize the higher production costs, the employer would be encouraged to introduce more capital-intensive methods, ultimately resulting in less real income for the African economy and a greater concentration of paid earnings in the hands of a few workers. Coöperative work systems and seasonal rotation of the migrant workers (who leave only after needed productive work in the village is completed) offset expected declines in the village output. Although cash crops and handicrafts may substantially suffer, the greater efforts of the coöperative work parties that remain at home will ensure prosperity for the subsistence economy. The success of the system depends on three variables: the proportion of men absent; the technical conditions of production; and the nature of village social structure and kinship arrangements. Migratory labor becomes economically unattractive to the migrant laborer only when income-earning possibilities in the village increase (which is unlikely). It remains attractive to employers as long as the costs of recruiting are not prohibitive, there is only a minimal growth of secondary industry, and wage rates do not increase too fast.

It is important to recognize the limitations of this economic thesis. In effect, Dr. Berg shows that for parts of Africa, if villagers leave integrated societies which have firmly based coöperative work patterns in order to perform seasonal agricultural labor which complements home production (provided the numbers of migrants are sufficiently limited to avoid disrupting village organization), then migratory labor has economic advantages. This argument cannot be extended to many societies. Moreover, even in West Africa, we need to be better informed on the social and psychological costs of a complex process which cannot adequately be measured by tangible goods. It is also debatable whether or not the categories of classical economics, developed in societies structurally and ideologically different, can be applied cross-culturally. Even in West African societies where developed markets exist, the market principle itself is not so central as in Western capitalist economy. Economic functions of labor reciprocity and noncommercial gift exchange are embedded in noneconomic relationships and are difficult to offset by cash returns. The situation is complicated by the simultaneous participation of African societies in an industrial revolution in the midst of modern international economic and political developments.

We do not know the psychological concomitants of African migration, with or without urbanization; but working from analogy it is generally a difficult, if not disturbing, experience, particularly for adolescents and adults. Behavior learned in childhood acquires deep emotional and moral qualities, and migration, particularly to urban centers, requires an individual to act in ways different from those accepted as custom and unconsciously internalized as "good" and "moral." Even differences that appear to the "host" to be specific and morally neutral (a "mere" change in clothing or etiquette) are frequently charged with emotion. We do not know the depth of African alienation—powerlessness and normlessness associated with living in a mass society—and can only surmise if it exists at all. On available evidence we can, with equal uncertainty, state that "city air makes one free," and that the individual finds greater "satisfaction" in the city. The fact that migration and urbanization are social processes does not mean that their psychological effects can be regarded as insignificant, but that we need to study them more deeply.

As a politically oriented sociologist (or a sociologically oriented political scientist), Dr. Wallerstein is primarily interested in the structure and distribution of power. He interprets migration as serving "the elementary function of widening the political perspective of increasingly large numbers of people." New, supertribal "loyalties" developed and associations formed by migrants become training grounds for participants in movements of national independence. By incorporating countrymen into a more inclusive money economy, and in some instances widening their religious perspective, migration generates increased urbanization. He considers migration in three periods: precolonial, colonial, and postcolonial. In each period boundaries—frontiers—were redefined, and the local bases of competition and stratification shifted with inclusion, or exclusion, of different groups. Modern cities became centers from which the new political elite exercised control, but the leaders were aware of the political implications involved in the unrestricted admission of "foreigners." In a competitive struggle for status, in situations of forced coexistence, the tribe is the most obvious reference group, but effective nationalist leaders requiring urban support often come from smaller tribal groups which traditionally have not threatened other groups in the emergent nation.

Migration may influence, as well as be influenced by, the structure of political power. In much of West Africa the rate of educational development has not been equivalent to the rate of economic growth. The demand for educated personnel has opened the door to "foreigners," and at the same time there has been local unemployment of unskilled workers. These have been two major factors in cross-frontier migrations, which in turn have threatened interstate lines. The use of migrant labor and the expulsion of aliens are alternative responses to changing conditions. Frontier control is largely a political device, which need not promote economic and social development, the avowed aim of the leaders.

Politics are characterized by shifting alliances, competitive struggles for office, manipulation of minority groups. These situations are not new in West Africa, but the points generating conflict may vary and may be intensified in the urban setting. In the traditional Sudanic towns, struggles for power were associated with trade and the proselytizing demands of Islam; in Benin, struggles occurred between palace chiefs and town chiefs, and between rival claimants to each. Migration is an additional complicating factor, for immigrants may be used to build up force or to consolidate opposition. The process, which may be labeled the "strategy of migration," is not restricted to cities; analogous movements have occurred in certain cash-crop areas where complex local structures developed, broadly polarized along lines of "stranger" versus indigenous farmers. In some instances the immigrants may be considered as having traded political status for economic gain.

Obviously, social structure cannot be reduced to considerations of power; many other influences, formal and valuational, affect the fate of migrants. But in the emerging nations of Africa decisions may be more explicitly political than in America or in Britain. The status of immigrants, rights over property, avenues of access to power, and occupational qualifications involve conflicting legal principles which require direct political intervention; in America and in Britain these issues fall within the established legal system. Political intervention may be politically justified in terms of "national unity" (nationalism), but national unity is not a legal framework. Like loyalty, it is an emotionally charged concept which, for sociological purposes, needs to be related to such factually delineated trains of events as are evident in urbanization and migration.

African societies are no longer the pawns of outside powers, but the selective recipients of their culture. Just as they are struggling to develop their own variations on given political themes, so they are struggling to express and contain new economic and cultural forces within national boundaries. As the social pattern of emerging African cities is not fixed, there is little reason, except the pessimism of human uncreativity, to predict that industrialization and urbanization inevitably spell standardization to given models. To do so would be to accept a technological destiny, a denial of man's freedom in his social character. We have banished the illusion of Utopia, but is it not possible to recognize the reality of diversity and the potentiality of social experimentations accompanying revolutionary innovations in material goods and scientific knowledge?

The new African states are in the singularly fortunate position of being catapulted through the industrial revolution without a philosophy of antiurbanism, so marked in the writings of recognized and influential Western philosophers—Jefferson, Emerson, and even Santayana and John Dewey in America; Ruskin and Carlyle in England.[30] Modern African leaders do not consider the towns necessary evils, nor do they lament their "bigness and hollowness"; they appear, on the contrary, to welcome new towns as centers of progress and symbols of participation in an expanding world.[31] In America the frontier was not associated with poverty, but with independence; in England land was associated with the aristocracy, the city with work and slums. In Africa, land formerly dominated man; land in the city becomes, in the hands of new planners, a product of a growing society, and the city becomes an instrument for extending new relationships. But if a city is to express the interests of its inhabitants in ways compatible with their own interpretation of social relationships, the imposed plan of a Western city may be unsuitable and dysfunctional, erecting new barriers and creating conflicts.

Town planning is related to a prevailing social ideology. Planners of emerging cities have a better chance to build a physical environment more in keeping with present ambitions and hopes. New leaders who move into residences (or palaces) of former masters, or who turn these buildings into museums, symbolize different approaches to the future as well as to the past.

In his prefatory remarks to Weber's study, *The City*, Don Martindale, arguing from the fact that Weber considered fortification and political autonomy essential components of the fully developed urban community, writes: "The modern city is losing its external and formal structure. Internally it is in a state of decay while the new community represented by the nation everywhere grows at its expense. The age of the city seems to be at an end."[32]

Using different criteria, other urban sociologists have also shown that there is a tendency for metropolitan society (in which all communal aspects are controlled by large specialized organizations, including the main political parties) to dominate the traditional city. Regulations governing commerce and industry have shifted from the city to the regional, national, or international level. In West Africa the cities are locally bounded units with relative autonomy and specific structural and cultural attributes of their own. As centers of new political development, they control the direction of modern rural developments and migrations. In America and in England the "age of the city" may be at an end; in Africa, the age of new cities, cities that have connotations different from those generally associated with "urbanism," appears to have begun.

2.

THE LOCATION AND NATURE OF WEST AFRICAN CITIES

by Benjamin E. Thomas

One of the striking features of West Africa is the rapid growth of urban centers, a growth that is accompanied by many economic and social problems. It is true that there have been a few centers of note for hundreds of years—places like Timbuktu and Kano near the southern margin of the Sahara, and Ibadan and other agricultural towns in the Yoruba country of southwestern Nigeria. But in recent decades some of the older centers have grown from villages to cities and have been joined by new ports and inland trade centers. The purpose of this essay is to describe the distribution and general characteristics of West African cities, to analyze the locations of selected centers, to point out a few urban economic functions and their relations to resources and trade routes, and to consider some of the potentialities for further growth.

Some Urban Features of West Africa

Compared with industrialized Western Europe or the United States, West Africa is decidedly an underdeveloped area, with only a few dozen moderately large urban centers rather than hundreds. Compared with the West Africa of earlier decades or with present-day central or eastern Africa, however, these dozens of urban centers and their rapid growth impress both the casual visitor and the African scholar. West Africa (south of the Sahara and west of Cameroon) has almost forty places with a population of 50,000 or more, whereas Central and East Africa combined have only about twenty (see accompanying table).

The comparatively dense concentration of agricultural people in southern Nigeria and at spots along the coast of West Africa provide one of the potentials for urbanization. These concentrations, in turn, are related to historical and cultural factors which favor agriculture and the

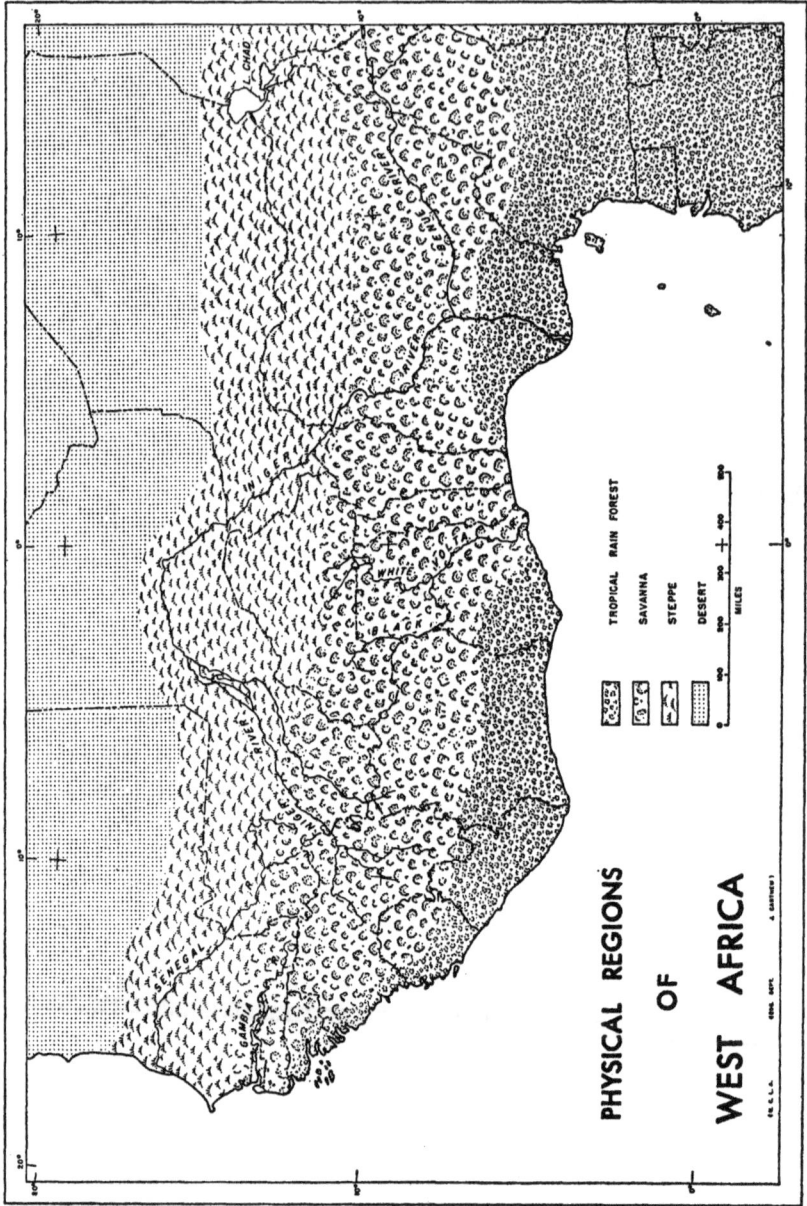

PHYSICAL REGIONS
OF
WEST AFRICA

TROPICAL RAIN FOREST
SAVANNA
STEPPE
DESERT

MILES

Map 2

Country	Over 200,000	100,000 to 200,000	50,000 to 100,000
Senegal	Dakar		Kaolack
			Rufisque
			St. Louis
			Thiès
Mali		Bamako	
Guinea			Conakry
Sierra Leone		Freetown	
Liberia			Monrovia
Upper Volta			Bobo-Dioulasso
			Ouagadougou
Ivory Coast		Abidjan	Bouaké
Ghana	Accra	Kumasi	Takoradi
Togo			Lomé
Dahomey			Cotonou
Nigeria	Ibadan	Ife	Aba
	Lagos	Iwo	Abeokuta
		Kano	Benin
		Ogbomosho	Enugu
		Oshogbo	Ilesha
			Kaduna
			Katsina
			Maiduguri
			Onitsha
			Oyo
			Port Harcourt
			Zaria

formation of villages, as well as to natural conditions of climates and soils which can support large numbers of farmers.

In the savanna belt there were trade centers in precolonial days where camel caravans from across the Sahara unloaded imported goods and collected gold, leather, and other savanna products for the return trip. Some towns were also political capitals of Sudanese empires, residences of local chiefs, seats of Muslim learning, or centers for local crafts and the exchange of agricultural for pastoral products. There were also a few small places in the forest belt farther south which were political capitals; examples are Abomey in Dahomey and Kumasi in Ashanti, now a part of Ghana. Thus the historical and cultural tradition for urbanization, in at least a limited form, has existed for centuries, and is considered in more detail in later papers. Some of the important centers of the eighth to the sixteenth centuries probably had populations of 1,000 to 20,000. The present focus is on the towns, old or new, which have recently grown to populations of 50,000 or even of several hundred thousand.

The Location and the Appearance of Cities

The reasons for the location and growth of large towns are complex. In order to understand them, it is necessary to know something of the social organization and the needs of the people involved, the history and geography of the region, the forms of transportation and communication, and the economic and political policies that bear upon the movements and activities of the population. Several of these factors are involved in the rise of trade centers at places where there is a break in transportation, such as a transfer from one form of conveyance to another, a regrouping of goods that require handling and storage, or the unloading of goods and a transfer of ownership. Workers and organizations that perform these duties may form a new settlement or add to the size of an older one, and additional people find employment serving these primary workers.

Most of the large towns of West Africa are located on the coast. Except for the inland republics of Mali, Upper Volta, and Niger, each country has a port as its most important trade center. A second group consists of interior trade centers located at junctions of important routes, such as roads, railways, or navigable rivers. A number of these places, especially in southern Nigeria, have farmers and craftsmen who add to the population and the importance of the center.

In matters of exporting and importing, which are vital to many forms of economic development, the coast has a double advantage over the remote interior. Some imported goods cost twice as much in the far interior as at the coast because of the added cost of transport from the port. On the other hand, agricultural products for export are often worth much less in the interior, because they must bear the cost of transport before they can command the market price set at the port by international trade conditions.

Some of the towns in West Africa have become attractive to rural Africans for both economic and social reasons. Ports were also often selected as colonial capitals, and the combined political and economic functions resulted in the concentration of Europeans at these places. The demands of the Europeans and of employed Africans for various goods and amenities caused some ports to rise as markets for imported items, domestic produce, and locally fabricated materials.

West African cities have characteristics that are derived from indigenous cultures, as well as from colonial cultures and policies. Some of the cultural influences are revealed by even a brief glimpse of an urban center. Traditionally, the larger African towns had sections that were occupied by people from different African communities. People tended to associate with and live near others of the same language and customs who had come from the same village or tribe. These people brought their techniques of house building, their food preferences, and other traits which, although gradually modified, often gave each section a distinctive appearance and atmosphere. Most towns still have several quarters that are identified with specific African communities, or with residents from other continents. As a striking example, some towns in Mali have round huts with thatched roofs, built by migrants from savanna farming areas, which contrast with the rectangular, flat-topped houses of migrants from desert areas.

The Europeans also brought their attitudes and certain items of material culture with them, and these, combined with colonial policies, have given many African towns their "colonial French," "colonial British," or "colonial Portuguese" atmosphere. Automobiles drive on the left of the street in areas of British tradition, and on the right in the others. Buildings and railways, factories and port equipment, and urban construction in general show British and French influence in their respective areas. Hotels in former British areas often serve morning and afternoon tea, and some towns have cricket fields. The sidewalk café, the French pastry shop, and shuttered windows are features of some French towns. The full list of indirect colonial influences, extending through language, administration, economic policies, and educational systems, is a long one.

Some general Western or European urban characteristics have also been built into the newer and larger West African centers: commercial districts, railway freight yards, port or factory areas, civic centers, and residential quarters, as well as school grounds, parks, and airports. Many of these features, associated with city planning and with the concept of urban zoning, are comparatively recent introductions into West Africa. A few of the older African towns with residential, commercial, and manufacturing functions mixed together in the same area are gradually being rebuilt with separate zones. More commonly, however, the old town has remained and a new city with specialized areas has developed beside it.

Urban Geography

Urban areas, as important places in human affairs, are of interest to all the social sciences, as well as to several of the humanities. As man-made features of the surface of the earth, they are an important element in the study of geography.

Urban geography deals with the forms and patterns of villages and towns, their growth and spread over the earth's surface, the size and distribution of cities, and the human and natural explanations for these features. It may include a study of present patterns, an investigation into the origins and evolution of settlement forms, or an attempt to forecast the changes to come.

For describing an individual town, some of the items of geographical relevance are the appearance, character, and arrangement of districts within the center; the functions of different urban areas; and the relations of these areas to one another, to the natural environment, and to the economic and human geography of the region. Many of these relationships can be studied by examining the forms and functions of earth features which facilitate trade and transportation: streets, commercial areas, roads, port facilities, market places, railways, and so on. Maps of urban districts, flow charts of traffic within the city and between the city and other areas, and diagrams of harbor approaches and port layout are devices which are commonly constructed and used by urban geographers.

Most of these items, of course, are also included within the range of investigation of workers in other disciplines; it is more the approach and the viewpoint rather than the data examined which distinguish one field from another. In studying the location of an urban area, for example, geographers distinguish between "site" and "situation." The site of a village or town is the local feature upon which the center is located, such as a peninsula, a river flood plain, an island, or a hilltop, together with the relation of this feature to the shape of the settlement, its internal arrangement, and its functions. A comparatively minor item—a well, a ford on a stream, or a clump of trees on an open plain—may be a critical feature in the selection of the original site for a city. But as the settlement evolves, the site is often reëvaluated in terms of new conditions. A scarcity of well-drained level ground for new buildings, or the difficulty of finding an additional local source of water, may be a problem associated with the site of a growing town.

The situation of a center refers to its relation to external features, such as rural population and the resources and trade routes of the associated regions. Studies of situation vary from historical investigations of the rise and fall of cities with changing regional conditions, to statistical investigations of the physical and economic bases for urban growth, the flow of traffic through the city, and the expansion or contraction of the trade area served by the city.

Studies of site and situation are often combined with work on the internal characteristics and functions of an urban center. A study of the rise of industrialization in African towns from the viewpoint of economic and urban geography, for example, might involve the site and layout of the factories, as well as the sources of workers, power, and raw materials, and the market areas and the flow of goods to them. The differences between a study of industrialization by an economist and one by an urban geographer often lie in contrasting objectives. The purposes of the economist might be to determine the possibilities for investment or expansion, or the effect of industry upon the national economy—aims that are economic in nature. The purposes of the geographer might be to discover the origin, nature, and growth of industrialized portions of cities and their relations to agricultural and mining areas, thus giving a better picture of the patterns and functions of both urban and rural portions of the African continent—aims that are primarily geographic.

All major towns of West Africa, and most of the minor ones, have been studied to some extent by geographers. Arab travelers and scholars, as well as European explorers, often wrote on geographic subjects. Heinrich Barth, the famous explorer of Timbuktu and other Sudanese towns, was a professor of geography at the University of Berlin, and every European colonial power had academic geographers who studied trade centers along with general physical and human geography of the African colonies. A score of geographers have worked on West African towns since World War II. Some of the earlier work is immature, fragmentary, or obsolete, and investigations on some of the new trade centers have hardly begun. Nevertheless, the total amount of published information on West African urban centers is surprisingly large, and it would be impossible to cover many topics or many cities in this brief paper. The concentration here on the site and the situation of selected ports and interior towns, and on the patterns of routes, is a limitation imposed by restricted time, not by the scope of the field of urban geography.

West African Ports

The coast of West Africa is notoriously poor in natural harbors. The coastline has few indentations, and even river mouths are likely to be obstructed by islands, swampy deltas, or submerged bars. The comparatively straight shore line is explained by the geological history; much of the coastline is a fault, a line along which the earth was cracked when the continent was uplifted. The uplifted interior is drained by rivers that fall over the edges of plateaus on their way to the coast. Rapids and falls at the plateau edges obstruct interior navigation on the rivers. The rivers flow swiftly over these rapids, pick up sediment, and usually drop it near the river mouths when the gradient and the velocity of the river decrease. Ocean currents, waves, and tides cause the sediment to be formed into deposits of varying shapes which often make it difficult or impossible for ships to enter the river.

A few examples will show some of the varied conditions of site and situation for West African port towns.

St. Louis, founded in 1638, lies at the mouth of the Senegal River. This stream was not a good route to the interior, but was the best in the area. The river has its sources in the Guinea highlands. It runs down the northeastern slopes toward the interior, and then swings northward and westward through the margins of the Sahara to the coast. The alternating wet and dry climates give the river a pulsating flow, with a high level only during late summer and fall. Sediment is deposited at the mouth, and has been formed into an offshore bar, many miles in length, which separates the river from the open sea. At one point there is a sand bar in the river, and St. Louis is built upon the long outer bar, the inner bar, and the adjacent mainland. Shallow water, shifting sand, and a stream with an intermittent flow are serious navigational problems. Neither the site of St. Louis, nor its situation with respect to interior trade, is very favorable in the light of modern requirements. St. Louis now has a population of only about 50,000, and has been surpassed by nearby Dakar as well as by other West African ports.

The site of Dakar on the Cape Verde Peninsula was originally even less favorable than that of St. Louis. But in recent decades, piers and breakwaters have improved the site until the harbor is far better than that of St. Louis. The growth of Dakar has been further stimulated by the development of peanut-producing areas nearby, as well as by the extension of a railway to Bamako and the Niger River. Dakar has served as the economic outlet for a vast region of interior French West Africa. It is also a strategic crossroads for air and ship traffic from North America to South Africa, and from Western Europe to South America. With a population of some 375,000, Dakar is the largest African city west of Nigeria, and has economic advantages and amenities which are attractive to both Africans and Europeans.

The peninsula on which Conakry, Guinea, is located is somewhat protected by islands, and the harbor has been improved by the construction of piers. The hinterland, however, is less productive than that of Dakar. The railway to the Niger taps a segment of the Niger Valley which is comparatively unproductive, and difficult to navigate. Conakry lacks the strategic advantages of Dakar, but has better access to the interior than St. Louis. The discovery of bauxite and iron near Conakry, and the city's political activities, have recently given it a boost. It now has a population of about 80,000.

Freetown in Sierra Leone has the best natural harbor in West Africa.

The mouth of the Sierra Leone River is broad and deep, large enough to hold 150 vessels at one time. Tidal currents cause some difficulty for berthing a ship, but their movements scour the channel. The excellent site has served as a base for British naval forces and as a commercial port. But the interior trade region is restricted by the modest size and resources of Sierra Leone. Freetown has a population of about 100,000.

Monrovia, Liberia, was merely an open roadstead—a place where ships anchored near the shore—until an artificial port was built during World War II by the United States government. It serves only part of Liberia, but the export of iron ore and rubber has led to increased activity since the war. Monrovia is now a growing center with about 50,000 inhabitants. The buildings and other features with a somewhat American atmosphere give Monrovia what might be termed an Americo-Liberian urban style.

For a long time Abidjan, Ivory Coast, with a bar separating the town and bay from the open sea, was comparatively unimportant. After World War II, however, the French opened the harbor by cutting a canal through the bar. This improvement, plus a further extension of the Abidjan railway from Bobo-Dioulasso to Ouagadougou in Upper Volta, was a factor in the rise of Abidjan from a small town to one of the largest and fastest-growing cities in French Africa. The immediate hinterland of Abidjan has a productive and varied economy, and the port serves both the Ivory Coast and Upper Volta. The population of Abidjan is now estimated at more than 100,000.

Accra, in Ghana, is an open roadstead where ships are anchored off-shore and unloaded by boats that travel through the surf between ship and shore. The growth of Accra is largely due to its productive agricultural region, communication with the interior, and its administrative functions; the population has grown to more than 200,000. As a seaport it has been surpassed in activity by Takoradi Harbor to the west and the new port of Tema to the east, both with artificial harbors and rail connections to the interior which equal those of Accra.

Cotonou, Dahomey, has been an open roadstead like Accra. The hinterland served by the railroad from Cotonou is far less productive than that of Accra, however, and despite harbor improvements now being made, the port is likely to remain a secondary one. The population is about 70,000. The French atmosphere of Cotonou contrasts with the colonial English aspects of Accra and Lagos.

Lagos, Nigeria, has a harbor somewhat similar to that of Abidjan, but with the big difference that the bay and the island are naturally open to the sea. Further improvements have been made, and Lagos, with a densely populated productive locality and a railroad extending to northern Nigeria, ranks next to Dakar among West African ports. It

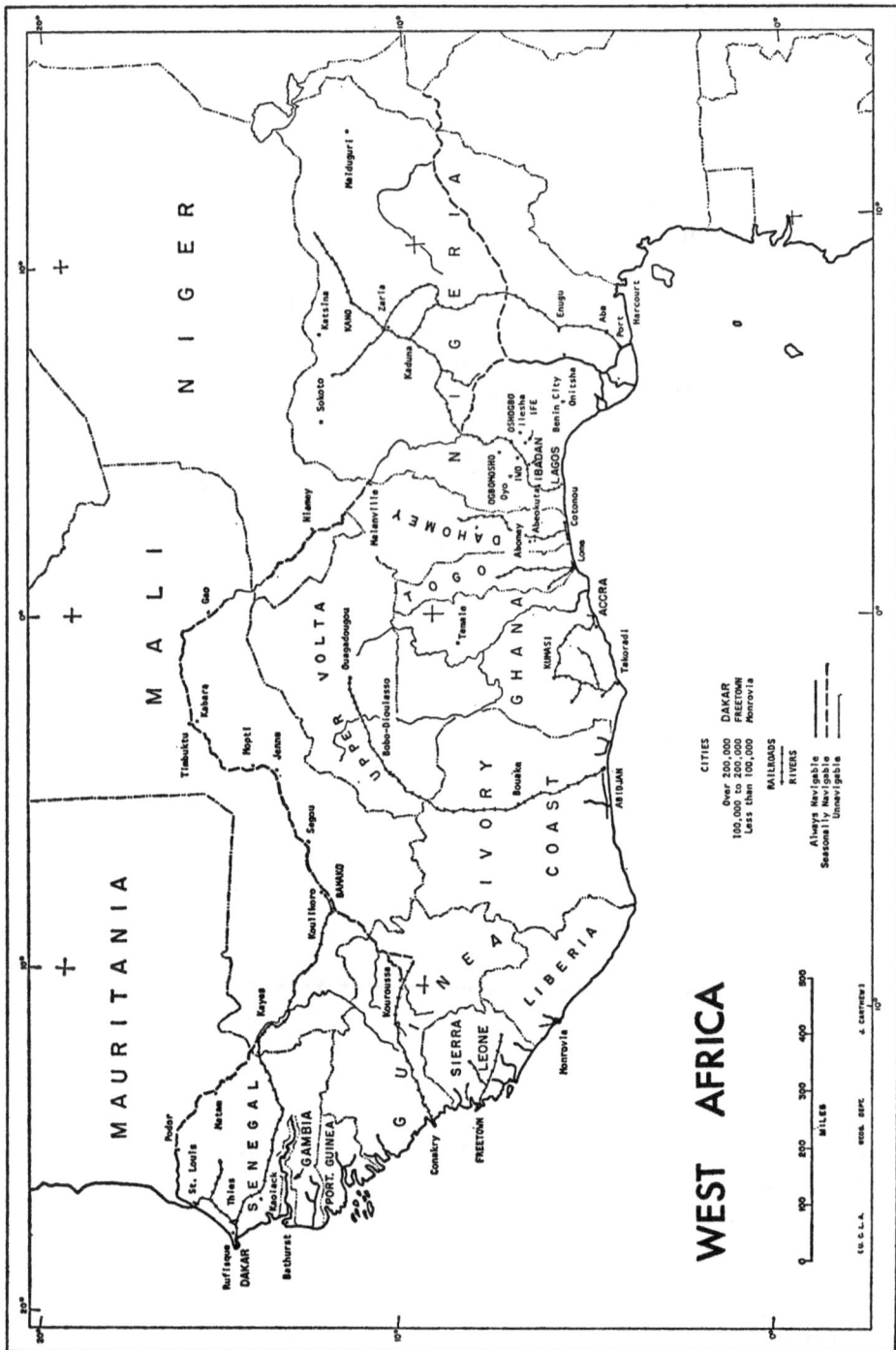

WEST AFRICA

Map 3

MAURITANIA

MALI

NIGER

SENEGAL

GAMBIA

PORT. GUINEA

GUINEA

SIERRA LEONE

LIBERIA

IVORY COAST

UPPER VOLTA

GHANA

TOGO

DAHOMEY

NIGERIA

Ruffisque
DAKAR
Thies
St. Louis
Podor
Matam
Kaolack
Bathurst
Kayes
Kaedi
Kouroussa
Kankan
Koulikoro
Segou
BAMAKO
Jenne
Mopti
Kabara
Gao
Timbuktu
Niamey
Conakry
FREETOWN
Monrovia
Bouake
ABIDJAN
Bobo-Dioulasso
Ouagadougou
Temale
KUMASI
ACCRA
Takoradi
Lome
Cotonou
Abomey
Porto
Kandi
ABEOKUTA
IBADAN
LAGOS
Oyo
IFE
Ilesha
OSOGBO
OGBOMOSHO
Iwo
Benin City
Onitsha
Enugu
Aba
Port Harcourt
Sokoto
Katsina
KANO
Zaria
Kaduna
Maiduguri

CITIES

Over 200,000	DAKAR
100,000 to 200,000	FREETOWN
Less than 100,000	Monrovia

RAILROADS

RIVERS

Always Navigable
Seasonally Navigable
Unnavigable

MILES
0   100   200   300   400   500

(G. C. L. A.   GEOG. DEPT.   F. CARPENTER)

has a population of more than 300,000. Lagos has sections with old buildings of varied styles and functions which, as in Accra, are being cleared and rebuilt in more orderly fashion.

Three Inland Urban Centers

In inland areas of West Africa the junctions of important routes are often favorable centers for trade, although other factors must also be considered in a complete analysis. Bamako, Bobo-Dioulasso, and Kano illustrate the influence of the pattern of trade routes.

Bamako is sited on the Niger River where rapids interrupt trade between two navigable segments of the river. A railway has been built at Bamako to join these two waterways, and a longer railway runs from Bamako to the coast at Dakar. Trade to and from Dakar from both river segments therefore passes through Bamako. The town is an important road junction, has an airport, and lies in a moderately well-developed agricultural region. It has grown as an administrative center for both France and independent Mali. For many decades Bamako has been the largest and most important town for a large part of the interior. Although rail traffic has recently been interrupted between Mali and Senegal, Bamako still benefits from its commanding position as the main commercial center of Mali.

In past centuries the northwestern bend of the Niger River, linked by camel caravans to Morocco, was a more favored location, and it was here that Timbuktu developed. Canoes brought goods downstream to Timbuktu from the southwest and upstream from the east. It was "the port of the Sudan in the Sahara." The development of a railway to the coast, instead of caravans across the Sahara, was one reason, among many, for the rise of Bamako as compared with other inland centers. Timbuktu now has a population of about 6,000, but Bamako has more than 100,000.

Bobo-Dioulasso, one of the major centers of Upper Volta, lies at the junction of a route running eastward from Bamako toward northern Nigeria, and another road running southward to the port of Abidjan in the Ivory Coast. The French built a railway northward from Abidjan, and for many years its northern terminal was at Bobo-Dioulasso. An airport was added, and Bobo was the major center of rail, road, and air traffic in Upper Volta. The railway was pushed on to the capital of Ouagadougou after World War II, and this latter center is now growing at a faster rate. Bobo-Dioulasso and Ouagadougou each has a population of about 50,000.

Kano, in northern Nigeria, has many trade advantages, and surpasses even Bamako as an inland center of West Africa. It lies at the southern end of one of the famous camel-caravan trails, but this route is still in use as a trans-Saharan automobile trail and as a highway linking Kano to the peanut-producing areas of the Republic of Niger. Other roads lead to the east and south, and the western one continues on to Bobo-Dioulasso and Bamako. Northern Nigeria is the best developed interior agricultural region of West Africa, with many functions that center in Kano. And Kano is served by railways that give access to two harbors on the Nigerian coast, Lagos and Port Harcourt.

Truck traffic is increasing in importance in West Africa, and waterborne traffic on the Niger is of consequence for certain local areas. It should be emphasized, however, that railways carry the bulk of exports and imports for the interior, and that there has often been a correlation between rail service and the rise of inland towns, as well as of ports. Bamako, Bobo-Dioulasso, and Kano are well placed to benefit from rail traffic.

One factor hindering road and water transportation has been the alternating rainy and dry seasons which affect most of the interior of West Africa. Dirt roads are often impassable after rains, and many streams become unnavigable during low water. In places, road traffic is suspended during the hottest part of the summer. This seasonal nature of road and water traffic gives added importance to railways, which can operate at all seasons.

Interior Roads and Waterways

An example of the seasonal problems of interior transportation is provided by the savanna zone of former French West Africa, the area now included in independent Senegal, Mali, Upper Volta, and Niger. Comparable data are available for this area,[1] and a brief summary of the seasonal patterns is much more complicated than one might expect. These changes are of great importance to the situations of interior towns with respect to both trade and, as mentioned above, the availability of rail connections to coastal ports. Note that the discussion in this section is restricted to the savanna zone formerly controlled by France; rivers and roads in areas like Gambia and Nigeria are not considered.

Interior West Africa has a tropical savanna climate, with rainfall in the warmer months and drought in the cool season. The month of May is at the end of the dry season, and roads are usable almost everywhere. They extend into the Sahara north of Nigeria. Farther west they extend from Timbuktu to Kayes on the Senegal River and connect Kayes with areas to the south and to the west. River navigation, however, is at a minimum. No part of the Niger in the savanna zone is navigable for large boats or steamers, and only the lower portion of the Senegal, from St.

[1] For notes to chapter 2, see page 187.

Louis to Podor, is usable by steamers. Canoes can operate locally on certain ponds and rivers throughout the year, but do not form part of the long-distance freight system.

In mid-June the situation for river navigation is the same as in May; in the area of former French West Africa only the short lower segment of the Senegal is navigable. Summer rains have started in the south, but the rivers have not risen to navigable levels. The rains, however, are sufficient to make many roads impassable. Kayes is isolated insofar as road transport is concerned; there are no usable routes to other regions. Only the railway gives Kayes commercial land transport to the coast and the interior. Other examples of flooded roads are found to the east of Bamako. The Sahara is so hot by June that road traffic stops. North of Nigeria there are few usable routes. The wet areas are impassable, the dry areas are too hot.

By mid-July the Senegal has risen until it is navigable as far upstream as Matam. The upper Niger River fills until it is navigable to Bamako, and water pours over the rapids at Bamako to bring the river to navigable levels as far as Mopti. Additional roads are flooded in many areas between Dakar and Bamako, and east of Mopti. Summer heat discourages travel into the Sahara.

In August the rivers continue to rise. The Senegal is navigable upstream to Kayes, and the Niger is usable as far as Kabara, the port for Timbuktu. The northern roads are still impassable because of flooding in the Sudan, and heat in the Sahara.

In September the Senegal is still navigable to Kayes and the middle Niger has risen as far as Gao. The road pattern is about the same as in August. This is the season when the combined Senegal and Niger waterways come closest to providing an east-west route. It should be noted, however, that navigable depths started at the mouth of the Senegal and spread upstream, but that navigable levels started near the headwaters on the Niger and spread downstream.

Before World War I the French had one railway that reached from Conakry, French Guinea, to the upper Niger, and another that connected the Senegal at Kayes with the Niger at Bamako. These facilities, of course, were not satisfactory for the months when the upper Niger was not navigable, and when the railway from Kayes to Bamako connected two almost dry stream valleys. The railway was later completed from Kayes to Dakar, providing a rail line from Dakar to the middle Niger and avoiding some of the navigational problems of Senegal, as well as those of the upper Niger River.

By October water has drained from the upper Senegal, making it unnavigable from Kayes to Matam. But water is still draining into the downstream part of the Niger River, which becomes usable from

Niamey to Malanville. North of Nigeria it is cool enough for desert motor traffic, and the southward retreat of the rains leaves additional segments of usable roads east of Niamey and southwest of Mopti.

November and December are dry months, and many roads, including those to the south and east of Kayes and to the southeast of Mopti, become usable. The lack of rain permits the channel of the upper Niger to drain almost dry, and in December it becomes unnavigable from Kankan to Bamako. Along the north side of the Senegal River, however, the roads are flooded by water from the river.

By January the Senegal has fallen until it is navigable only to Podor. An additional segment of the Niger, from Bamako to Mopti, drains until it is unnavigable. Roads are usable almost everywhere. But the middle Niger, from Timbuktu to Gao, has received so much water from the upper Niger that, in places, it floods the nearby roads and makes them difficult to use or impassable.

The February patterns are about the same as in January, but by March the level of the Niger falls until only the short segment between Niamey and Malanville is navigable. This situation continues in April. It is now a long way indeed from the usable segment of the Senegal to the usable part of the Niger.

In May, as indicated earlier, even the segment of the Niger downstream from Niamey becomes unnavigable, and only the Senegal near St. Louis is usable. Soon afterward, the rains start moving northward again, and another cycle begins.

These complicated and changing patterns of usable roads and waterways in the savanna zone are a hindrance to economic development. In addition, there are many problems related to infertile soils and agricultural practices which restrict agricultural production. The patterns of routes, of course, also condition the effectiveness of sites for trade centers, and the situation of ports and inland towns in relation to trade with the interior.

Climate, it may be noted, plays a dual role in handicapping interior West Africa; rainfall for agriculture is often scanty, seasonal, or unreliable, and both heat and seasonal rains give a rhythm, rather than continuity, to usable roads and waterways.

Conclusions and Future Prospects

One of the reasons for the attractive appearance of many French towns is their newness and modern style. Much of the growth was made during the period of heavy French investment after World War II. British towns like Accra, Lagos, and Ibadan started their central growth earlier, and some older sections show deterioration and urban blight, as well as obsolescent styles. The many African stores in former British areas are often unattractive in comparison with European shops. The British towns may therefore be ugly by some standards, but they are often solidly based upon African production and commerce; Ibadan is an outstanding example. It should also be noted that city planning and urban renewal are improving the appearance of all the major cities.

Taking a long view of the site and the situation of West African ports, it appears that local site factors have often been outweighed by the factors relating to interior development. The West African coast has a generally strong surf, but violent storms are rare. Open roadsteads have therefore been used when the value of the interior made it profitable, as at Accra and at numerous small ports. And, if the situation warrants, artificial harbors can be built.

The rising cost of harbor improvements and equipment, and the great increase since World War II in traffic to ports served by railways, have caused a concentration of effort upon the main ports; many small ones are in decline or have been abandoned. This concentration of investment, plus the varied activities that are attracted to a major city and port— often a capital as well—accounts for much of the recent expansion.

One activity of modest but rising importance is modern manufacturing. Often it starts with the processing of raw materials—the hulling of peanuts, the extraction of palm oil, and so forth. These raw material-oriented industries will be joined by power-oriented industries when power plants on the Volta River and elsewhere come into operation. Market-oriented industries, however, are now making the greatest advances in the modern category. Almost every town of size has its bakeries, breweries, soft-drink bottling works, and furniture factories. These market-oriented industries, plus service industries, add to the growth of urbanized areas, especially the larger ports. Nevertheless, one should not be led to believe that handicraft industries have been equaled or surpassed in monetary value produced or in number of people employed. There are many towns where crafts like weaving, dyeing, tanning and leatherworking, wood carving, sewing, and sandal making are still very strong and contribute to urban activity.

West Africa is basically agricultural, with mining of secondary importance. For the present and the immediate future the potentialities for extensive urban growth are probably closely linked with the rural spots where agricultural products or minerals have been developed for commercial sale, export, or manufacture. These are the places where the sale of goods, cash incomes, and trade centers are possible. These areas— resulting from both human activity and natural resources—cover only a small part of West Africa. Such islands of development are found in coastal Senegal, near Bamako, near ports like Freetown and Conakry, in southern Ghana, Ivory Coast, and Dahomey, and in both northern and southern Nigeria.[2] The continued growth of towns serving these islands is likely; the rise of towns in other areas is unlikely.

3.

SOME THOUGHTS ON MIGRATION
AND URBAN SETTLEMENT

by John D. Fage

In the present stage of West African historical studies, two major assumptions are commonly made: (1) Towns, and polities sufficiently developed to be labeled "states" and "empires," and having an international exchange economy, all emerged in the savanna lands of the Sudan before they appeared farther south, in the forest lands which may generally be labeled "Guinea." (2) The development of these phenomena in the Guinea area was largely due to influences emanating from farther north, from the western and central Sudan.[1]

The first of these assumptions could be an illusion resulting from the nature of the sources available. Absolute data, with some approach to an absolute chronology, for the earliest manifestations of these phenomena in West Africa are really to be expected only from archaeology. But the achievements of men like Fagg, Mauny, Thomassey, Willett, Davies, and Shinnie, though individually considerable, are, in relation to the size of the archaeological problem, as yet totally inadequate to enable any firm conclusions to be drawn even for the comparatively small areas in which they have been active. At the present time (and probably, indeed, for some time to come), therefore, the history of West Africa over the last two thousand years or so must primarily depend (apart from such historical clues as may be suggested by the study of West African languages and by physical and social anthropology) on the interpretations placed on the surviving oral and written texts.

West Africa is rich in oral traditions, but these take many forms of widely varying value to the historian. This is not the place for a formal discussion of the problems involved here.[2] But formal traditions that have the character, if not quite of history, at least of reliable chronicles, rarely penetrate back into time for more than about five centuries from the present. Moreover, if these traditions are to have survived to permit

[1] For notes to chapter 3, see page 187.

their recovery and use by the professional historians of the present, it is necessary that the societies that harbor them should have evolved a formal and continuing mechanism for their perpetuation. Such a mechanism is most obviously effective when it is part of a polity, that is, of a state (or township) artificially created by men to transcend more natural biological or social human groupings. It is indeed the existence of a state and the need to perpetuate it which seem to give rise to the idea of history and the demand for its perpetuation. If a state has ceased to exist, its tradition, or parts of it, can survive at best only in an elastic, changing, and eradicable folk memory. Furthermore, such a folk memory is all the oral evidence there is apt to be, not only for the times before the state existed, but also for the circumstances that brought it into being.

Oral tradition, therefore, is unlikely to provide unequivocally historical data for the origins of towns, states, and significant trade in West Africa; this statement is as true of the Sudan as it is of Guinea. The situation with regard to written sources, however, is not identical in these two areas. There are no written sources for Guinea before the advent of Europeans to its coastline in the fifteenth century, and they do not really begin to deal with its interior in meaningful detail until the eighteenth century. For the western Sudan, on the other hand, external Arabic references begin nearly a thousand years earlier. It is true that these references are extremely exiguous before the eleventh century, but there are two ways in which they may be supplemented and filled out. In the first place, by the sixteenth century at least, literate Sudanese were themselves compiling retrospective chronicles of their peoples and lands in Arabic. Second, it is possible to correlate the earliest external Arabic writings with clues from classical sources which, if they do not deal directly with the Sudan proper, at least say something relevant about the Sahara desert which linked it to the Mediterranean world.

With all their defects, it is still possible to use the early Arabic sources as a basis for at least an outline picture of the general development in the western and central Sudan from about the eighth to eleventh centuries onward, and this outline can at times be supplemented by clues from archaeology, oral tradition, and so forth. Urbanization, state formation, and long-distance trade form part of this picture, at least in certain areas, from the outset. Furthermore, the nature of some of the evidence enables us to conjecture that these phenomena, as revealed by Arab authors, stretch back for at least a thousand years.

It is against this background that one must consider the evidence available for Guinea. At the time of the European arrival in the fifteenth century, the territory between the Ivory Coast and the Cameroons seems to have been the most advanced area. The European evidence shows, for example, that by about 1500 Benin was already a considerable town and that the coastlands of modern Ghana were commercially linked with the middle or upper Niger. On this basis modern commentators are inclined to push the origins of international trade, urbanization, and statehood for this part of Guinea back to about the twelfth and thirteenth centuries.[3] This approximate date is not far beyond the acceptable horizon of the oral traditions of the area as historical evidence. Although one is entering the mythical stage of these traditions, account must be taken of their widespread belief that the states and the towns encountered by the Europeans from the fifteenth century onward were the product of movements that originated farther north, in the Sudan or even farther afield.

At this point the historian seeking an overall reconstruction of the major movements of West African history is bound to take into account the broad views that have been developed, from the strands of evidence available, to explain the beginnings of trade, towns, and states in the western and central Sudan. Essentially there are three views.[4] One school of thought would maintain that these developments were the natural outcome of a more or less independent neolithic revolution among the Sudanese Negroes, which was proceeding from about 5,000 to 3,000 B.C. onward.[5] Most historians, however, while not denying this neolithic revolution (though perhaps placing less stress on its independence), would give greater weight to two other opinions. One is that the growth of trade, towns, and states in the western Sudan was stimulated by a continuing commercial contact across the Sahara with the Mediterranean world, a contact that goes back to at least 500 B.C. and probably into prehistory. The other is that towns and states in the central and western Sudan, but less obviously trade, were stimulated by influences spreading westward from the area of mixed Negro and Egyptian culture in the upper Nile Valley, associated with ancient Kush or Meroe (from *ca.* 800 B.C. to A.D. 350).

These opinions are not mutually exclusive; indeed, they may well be complementary. The trans-Saharan commercial influences would seem to have been most effective in the west, from the western Maghrib to Mandeland, and to have led, among the Mande, to a type of civilization in which commerce played a major role. The Nilotic influence would seem, naturally enough, to have been strongest in the east, in the central Sudan, and to have produced a civilization in which trade was less developed than political organization, and in which divine kingship and tightly knit urban centers were important. For both civilizations an advanced agriculture would be a necessary base.

The relevance of this Sudanese argument to the Guinea situation is that whether we look to the western Sudan, to commercial Mandeland, or to the central Sudan and the more politically oriented states of Kanem and Hausa, it is logical to believe that civilization was advancing, at least in part, following the stimulus of external influences. There is thus every reason to suppose that these influences, once established in the Sudan, might seek to penetrate farther into West Africa. This supposition is strengthened by the fact that the legends and myths of origin of states in Guinea, at least between the Ivory Coast and the Cameroons, seem to say that such penetration did occur.

Fundamentally, in the west of this area, these Guinean clues seem to point back toward the Mande heartland in the upper Niger Valley, whereas to the east they point back to the region of Lake Chad and the upper Benue. We would seem, in fact, to have here two major axes, which one may call the "northwestern" and the "northeastern" axes, respectively, linking this part of the Guinea forest land with the Sudan.[6]

The identification of these axes as lines of historical migration was begun long ago. The northwestern axis led eventually to the adoption of the name "Ghana" by the former colonial territory of the Gold Coast, and Kimble has traced this particular identification back to at least the end of the nineteenth century.[7] Few modern historians would contend that these axes were lines of mass migration, along which the bulk of the present Guinean peoples moved to their present habitat. But perhaps too little attention has been given to the question of exactly what kinds of movements may actually have taken place among them. The purpose of the present paper is to suggest that an examination of the types of urban settlement which have developed in each of the two areas astride these axes may afford useful evidence of the nature of these movements. Very roughly, the boundary between the two areas would seem to be a line running from the Niger, between Jenne and Timbuktu, to the vicinity of modern Accra. In recent times, that is, immediately prior to the colonial period, the two regions thus demarcated are fairly readily recognizable as a western area in which Mande traders and trade were dominant, and an eastern area dominated by Hausa traders and trade.

Historically, indeed, the northwestern axis appears primarily as an artery of trade developed by the Mande Dioula. The origins of Dioula commercial expansion go a long way back. In fact, it does not seem unreasonable to associate them with a southward and eastward dispersion toward Macina of Islamized Soninke at the time of the collapse of ancient Ghana. This interpretation, which seems to have originated with Delafosse (1912), is often derided today because of the somewhat fanciful myths that have been developed to connect modern Ghana with its ancient namesake. It should be noted, however, that it has recently been seriously advanced by Trimingham,[8] and, as he says, the history of the dispersion of the Soninke from ancient Ghana certainly merits investigation.

As has been noted by a number of commentators, the development of trade from Macina to the southeast is closely connected with the history of the town of Jenne. Jenne's situation on the Bani River suggests most strongly that its emergence as a commercial metropolis was not connected with west-east trade along the Niger, but with the development of trade to the south. It has been said that Jenne was founded in the eighth century.[9] The conversion of its rulers to Islam in about the twelfth century is, however, probably more relevant, marking the achievement of dominance by its Muslim Dioula community. A twelfth-century date for the beginnings of Dioula penetration to the southeast is consistent with Mrs. Meyerowitz's interpretation of Techiman tradition[10] that Mande merchants reached Bono (equivalent to modern Techiman) in the middle of the fourteenth century. Furthermore, Wilks has recently reminded us (1961, 1962) that there is evidence that Mande traders were actually on the coast of modern Ghana at the time of the Portuguese arrival there toward the end of the fifteenth century. The impetus for this Dioula drive to the southeast was the desire to gain access to sources of gold, and possibly also of kola nuts.

Between Bono-Mansu, the Bono capital, and Jenne, the centers of Dioula settlement include Begho (the principal town of Banda before its destruction in about 1640), Bonduku (which by about 1740 had taken Begho's place as a Dioula trading center), Kong, and Bobo-Dioulasso (note the occurrence of "Dioula" in this name). But Dioula commercial expansion does not seem to have been the origin of these towns. It seems rather that the merchants were attracted to already established pagan political centers. Initially at least, the typical pattern of urban settlement along this route seems to have been one of twin cities, a separate Mande and Muslim commercial center arising alongside a royal pagan capital. Both Bono-Mansu and Begho are said to have conformed to this pattern, and it may not be entirely fanciful to suggest that its original prototype in West Africa was the capital of ancient Ghana described by al-Bakri in 1067.

Political influences, however, as well as trade, seem to have penetrated southward along this road from the northwest. Probably the most famous example of this development is the creation of the state of Gonja by the great folk hero, Jakpa, about the beginning of the seventeenth century. Jakpa is represented in tradition as a soldier-adventurer coming from Mandeland. But some Mande were already in Gonja; Jakpa or his family may have been among them.[11] It is conceivable, therefore, that the creation of Gonja represents a new Mande initiative in the chaos following the Moroccan invasion of the Niger bend. Later examples of Mande traders seizing the political initiative in regions where they had long been settled are well attested. This happened in Kong in 1730, and in Bobo-Dioulasso as recently as 1860.[12]

There would also seem to be some evidence of Mande influence in the formation of the Akan states in what is now southern Ghana. Meyerowitz (1952) claims such influence for Bono, and Wilks (1957, 1961), for Akwamu. All that need be said here is that the nature of this political influence coming down the northwestern trade route merits very serious investigation.[13]

If we turn now to the northeastern axis (southern Ghana–Chad–Benue), a quite different pattern of urban settlement seems to be apparent. Along this axis we commonly find states whose core is a walled capital city after which the state is named. As Forde (1951) has remarked of the Yoruba, "The government of the capital was that of the state also."

Walled cities are characteristic of the Sokoto of the swampy Logone and Shari valleys and, on a more extensive plan, of Kanem, Bornu, and Hausa. Historically at least, the same pattern would seem to be traceable through the Nigerian Middle Belt along the line Jukun-Nupe-Borgu-Bussa. (It may extend farther west also; Nalerigu, the seat of the Nayiri of Mamprussi, has the ruins of a large encircling wall.) The pattern is quite manifest in Yorubaland, whence it extends to Benin in the southeast. Archaeologically there is some evidence that it also once extended westward from Yorubaland, along a line running parallel to the coast and about 60 miles inland. At Tado on the river Mono, and at Nuatsi, about 50 miles north of Lome, there are the vestiges of extensive earthworks. It is probably significant that the line Ketu-Tado-Nuatsi is recalled in Ewe (and in some Ga) traditions as the line of emigration of their ancestors; Tado was the dispersal point for the Aja, and Nuatsi, for the Ewe.

The urban centers along this line would seem to have a number of features in common. Their areas may be very extensive (and sometimes there are, or have been, more than one concentric circle of walls enclosing them). Thus the circuits of the walls of Kano and Katsina are both of the order of 14 miles around; of Ibadan, about 10 miles; of Ife, about 7 miles; of Benin, apparently about 15 miles. According to Willett (1959), the total area of Old Oyo (now ruined) was about 20 square miles, which would suggest a circuit of some 16 miles. Second, the area within the walls is often appreciably larger than the area actually built up with habitations. This circumstance seems to have been normal. For example, Barth's observations in Hausaland in the 1850's suggest that some 30,000 citizens of Kano occupied only about one-third of the area within the city walls, whereas at Katsina some 8,000 people took up only about one-sixth of the available space. Much the same is true today of those Yoruba cities (e.g., Ife) that have not undergone a dramatic modern expansion. Third, where the configuration of the ground permits, the walls often contain within them a rocky eminence or eminences, as, for example, in Kano, Old Oyo, Abeokuta, and Ibadan. According to Bivar and Shinnie (1962), N'Gazargamo (Bornu) originally had an apparently artificial mound. (One might also notice that the So towns, in swampy country liable to inundation, are built on earth mounds which Lebeuf (1950) believes to be artificial.)

There is as yet very little exact evidence as to the antiquity of these towns or of their walls. Few of them have been subject to systematic archaeological investigation. A beginning was made in this direction at Old Oyo by Willett, whose preliminary conclusion was that the site could not be older than the early sixteenth century, as maize impressions were found on pottery at all levels.[14] But among the Yoruba settlements, Ife at least must be presumed to be appreciably earlier (though not necessarily on its present site, of course) because of its formative influence on Benin history and art. Benin's wall, as described at the beginning of the seventeenth century,[15] was "a very high bulwark, very thick, of earth, with a deep broad ditch within." In Benin tradition,[16] the building of the wall is ascribed to Oba Oguola, who was probably a fourteenth-century king. Farther west, Tado and Nuatsi would seem to have been deserted in about the sixteenth century. If the conclusions of this paper are acceptable, the walled cities of the country north of Yorubaland ought to be of earlier origin. At first sight, Hausa tradition would not seem to bear out this idea, as many Hausa walls are ascribed to a legendary heroine, Amina, who is probably to be dated about the fifteenth century. The Amina stories suggest affinities with the west, with Borgu, and even with Mandeland. This period was certainly one of pressures from the west, first from Mali and later, and perhaps more forcefully, from Songhai, and it is therefore possible to believe that Hausa wall building was a response to these pressures. But Hausa traditions[17] also aver that city walls existed before Amina's time.

Some of these towns developed as great commercial centers, especially in Hausaland and later in Yorubaland. But by and large the traders were natives, not immigrants, and in the whole area there is virtually no reflection of the twin-city pattern seen in the west.[18] The pattern seems most obviously to be one of political and military settlement. It is known that this pattern was followed at Abeokuta and Ibadan, new foundations consequent upon the political and military upheavals in nineteenth-century Yorubaland. But, in building large walled enclosures around natural eminences, it would seem possible that the founders of Abeokuta and Ibadan were repeating an older tradition. It is here contended, indeed, that this pattern of settlement originally derived from the political and military bases established by immigrant conquerors entering from the northeast into a potentially hostile new country. The first settlers would establish themselves on such high ground as was available, and would then encircle it with a wall. In normal circumstances the inhabitants would sally forth daily to cultivate their fields, but in an emergency the extensive area within the walls would afford protected cultivation and, no doubt, shelter for the people of outlying settlements.

Such a hypothesis needs to be supported by evidence that the northeast axis along which these towns lie was indeed a route of migration in a generally southward direction. Traditions are explicit that the southerly ramifications are linked to the northeast axis. Thus both Benin and Yoruba traditions agree that the modern kingdom of Benin was founded from the Yoruba dispersion center of Ife. It has already been noted that Ga and Ewe traditions acknowledge as a route of emigration the line from Nuatsi through Tado back to Ketu and Yorubaland. (The nature of this emigration, however, is not clear. It could be that the migrants were refugees from the movement that set up the Yoruba states, and the abandoned earthworks might be evidence of Yoruba penetrations in their wake. Certainly today there are islands of Yoruba colonization westward in this direction.) It may also be noted that there are acknowledged links[19] between Borgu tradition and that of Mamprussi (and Dagomba and Mossi) to the west and Yoruba to the south. What needs to be considered here, therefore, is the myths and traditions of origin of the states along the main line of the axis. It seems possible to discern evidence of some continuity of movement from the northeast.

In Kanem-Bornu there would appear to be two separate traditions of the state-founding activities of immigrants. First of all, there are the traditions of the So, a term that may mean no more than "the (autochthonous) people." As set out by Lebeuf,[20] these tell of the coming of "Whites" into a land first inhabited by Negro giants.[21] The Negro king drew a large circle on the ground (town walls?) with his bow, and gave the "Whites" permission to settle within it. Later, by trickery, the "Whites" overcame the Negroes. Lebeuf also states that the walled towns of the Logone-Shari country are all attributed to the So, and that they contain evidence of two distinct cultures, distinguishable by round houses and prone burials, and by rectangular house compounds and contracted burials.

Second, there is the tradition of the Sefawa,[22] who provided the ruling line, first in Kanem and then in Bornu, from probably the tenth century until 1846. The Sefawa were so named because they claimed descent from the historical Sayf ibn Dhi Yazan of sixth-century Yemen. In strictly historical terms this descent is doubtless not very relevant. It is worth noting, however, that the historical Sayf had connections with northeastern Africa and also with Sasanid Persia. He called upon the Sasanid king Chosroes I for aid in ridding his country of Ethiopian conquerors. It seems probable that the Sefawa were in reality members of that Zaghawa "nation" that so interested Arabic writers of the ninth to fifteenth centuries, that is, nomadic pastoralists of the eastern Sahara who had probably been subject to some degree of influence from the Kushitic kingdom of Meroe. Urvoy's interpretation of their tradition is that these Sefawa began early to infiltrate into established agricultural and urban Negro society, but that they did not begin to weld it into a hierarchical kingdom much before the fourteenth century.

In Hausaland there would seem to be a comparable duality of legends of origin. The key source is the so-called Daura *girgam* printed by Palmer,[23] which gives two quite separate stories. The first claims that the Hausa states (i.e., the rulers of the states) descended from Daura, one of the daughters of Abduldar, a man who came from the north. This story apparently relates to an early matrilineal, even matriarchal, state of Hausa society. Second, it is said that the Hausa states descended from Bayajidda, who came from the east via Bornu and Biram to Daura, where he killed the snake that was preventing people from getting water from the well. He then married the ruling queen of Daura, and their six sons became the kings of the Hausa states.

Yoruba tradition also retains two distinct stories of origin.[24] One is a creation myth. God sent his son Oduduwa to Ife where both earth and man were created. The other is a story that the Yoruba (or perhaps, more properly, their kings) descended from Lamurudu, who came from the northeast (he is said to have been a king in Arabia). One of his sons was Oduduwa, the first king of Ife; two others became kings of Gobir (the most northerly Hausa state) and of Kanem-Bornu.

The possible interpretations of stories like these are legion. But two points are worth noting. First, they all suggest a picture of two successive stages of political development. The first apparently was one of small-scale agricultural and, it would seem, urbicentric communities; the second involves the imposition on these of a more forceful concept of kingship and government.[25] (Benin tradition[26] states this explicitly: the period of the small and quarreling Ogiso kings was ended by the intervention of Oduduwa from Ife.) Second, on their own showing, the second versions of Kanem, Hausa, and Yoruba origins link up together. Thus Bayajidda is said to have come to Hausa from Bornu, while Oduduwa had "brothers" who became kings in Hausa and in Kanem-Bornu, respectively.

A further linking element may exist in the Kisra tradition ascribed to the Middle Belt of Nigeria—Jukun, Nupe, Bussa, Borgu.[27] Although this story presents a difficulty in that its exact relation to Nigerian political realities is not always easy to assess, it has the advantage of putting the other references to Near Eastern places and people into a valid and datable historical situation. The central story seems broadly as follows:

Kisra (Kisara), king of the Persians, was at war with Egypt and Byzantium. He occupied Egypt, but was later forced to flee up the Nile to Nupeta, where he asked to settle. The king of Nupeta consulted his spiritual adviser, who recommended that Kisra be asked to conquer to the west and that the king of Nupeta should follow. Kisra eventually got as far as Borgu. The king of Nupeta followed as far as Gobir, where he married and had a son from whom all the people (rulers) of Gobir are descended. Kisra conquered the three areas around Bussa, Borgu, and Yorubaland (though, according to some variants, the kings of the latter area were established by the king of Nupeta). Kisra died at Bussa (soon after the beginning of the Muslim era), but his work was continued by one of his generals, who was the first founder of Nupe.

The first part of this story is historically recognizable. Kisra is the Sasanid king Chosroes II (Khusru Parviz), whose troops invaded Byzantine Egypt in A.D. 616 (though there is no evidence that Chosroes accompanied them in person, and he certainly did not die in Africa). The Persians were later expelled from Egypt by Heraclius. But some of them had previously made an expedition against Nubia, and it is by no means impossible that some of them were marooned there. Nupeta is presumably Napata, the capital of Kush before Meroe. It seems possible that the Kisra story recognizes that the Nubians were now Christians, for some versions of the story give their king the name "Mesi" (Messiah) and his spirit the name "Issa" (Jesus). The validity of the rest of the story is at present conjectural, but there would seem to be a growing body of scraps of archaeological evidence[28] for the extension of some kind of Nubian (and possibly Christian Nubian) influence as far west as the Chad region.

The question arises as to which of the two levels of political development the Kisra migration should be related to. Biobaku (1955) has suggested that it should be related to the first. If he is right, northeast Africa's contribution to the agricultural Negro communities of the west-central Sudan would seem in fact to have been less that of Christian Nubia than of an earlier tradition of divine kingship, emanating specifically from Meroe, but perhaps also possessing overtones suggesting a relationship with southwest Arabia, Axum-Ethiopia, and conceivably even Persia. Furthermore, it would seem to follow that the northernmost communities, at least, were later penetrated by people from the desert, whom we may call Zaghawa. These may already have been influenced by Meroe, but in any event they seem to have taken over the kingship concepts of the local rulers with whom they merged. In Kanem their activities ultimately resulted in the fusion of the smaller units into a large state (as well as the immigrants' own fusion with the local rulers). Here, incidentally, perhaps because of the proximity of the invaders to their territory of origin, the idea of the state as an extension of its walled capital seems to have been least applied. Elsewhere the result would seem to have been, either directly or by a process of chain reaction, to superimpose upon the earlier agricultural communities aristocracies, which, from their walled cities, ruled them as determinate states. The Afro-Asiatic character of the Hausa language suggests that in Hausaland this process must have been direct. Farther south it may have been various kinds of reflections of, or reactions to, what was happening in Hausa.

Such an interpretation is conjectural and could well be wrong. But even if it is, there is still enough in the traditions of origin of Kanem-Bornu, Hausa, and Yoruba, and also in the Kisra legend, to give substance to the hypothesis that the walled towns of West Africa, east of modern Ghana, resulted from a political impulse coming from the north-east.

4.

URBANISM, MIGRATION, AND LANGUAGE

by Joseph H. Greenberg

Introduction

Among the most conspicuous phenomena noted by observers of the present-day African scene are the large-scale seasonal migrations and the related growth of urban centers. For, although most of the workers return to the rural tribal areas and not all migrate to urban centers (many work on farms), it is nevertheless true that the urban centers of Africa are growing at a significantly faster rate than rural areas. This expansion of population is a result not only of natural increase, but to a considerable extent of recruitment of immigration from the countryside. In other words, permanent urbanization of a substantial and increasing part of the population is now a continent-wide phenomenon.

Urbanism and migration are, of course, not exclusively colonial and postcolonial events in Africa. In particular, the historical record discloses the existence of large-scale agglomerations, especially in the western Sudan, the present Western Region of Nigeria, the east coast Swahili-speaking ports, Ethiopia, and perhaps even in Bantu Monomotapa in present Southern Rhodesia. Moreover, in some instances at least, the ethnic heterogeneity bears witness to the role of migration in the formation of such cities as Timbuktu, which even in the precolonial period contained Arab, Tuareg, and Songhai elements, to mention the most important.[1]

Still the present movement toward urbanization differs in both quantity and quality from that of the precolonial period. In sheer size and number the cities are usually of a different order of magnitude. Moreover the functions they serve, directly or indirectly, result from the impact of the West. Formerly largely commercial, or even raising their own food, as did the pre-British Yoruba cities, they now perform industrial or service and administrative functions that are of relatively recent and exotic origin. The link with the past can be seen, however, for these cities, particularly in West Africa, are often older communities, not new

[1] For notes to chapter 4, see page 189.

foundations, and inevitably the preëxisting conditions continue to exert their influence. It has been pointed out, as a further historic connection, that the routes and the destination of migrants display, in many instances, the persistence of pre-European patterns.[2]

Lingua Francas

It is obvious that such large-scale movements of people as are now taking place must inevitably have repercussions on the most basic aspects of the societies involved; among these is the communication system, or language. In the present paper I attempt to give some notion of the nature and scope of these changes. I believe it will also appear that communication is an area in which we are short of basic information, no doubt because the problems are by their very nature interdisciplinary. It is only recently that linguists have begun to talk seriously about an area of research which they call sociolinguistics, and its very existence is probably unknown to many workers in other social sciences.[3] I have attempted to discover the pertinent data from a fairly full, though not exhaustive, study of the literature on urbanism and migration, and to supplement these with my own personal observations. The inadequacy of the data will be sufficiently obvious. It is to be hoped, then, that by pointing to questions that cannot be fully answered on present evidence, this study may make a modest contribution toward outlining the problems of sociolinguistics in an African setting and toward sharpening the awareness of practitioners of social sciences, other than linguistics, to a set of problems that I believe to be relevant to their own research interests.

The most obvious, one might say elemental, problem of communication which arises for the migrant is that of a common language with his employer and others with whom he comes into contact, whether in an urban or a rural situation. The overriding sociolinguistic fact about Africa is simply its vast language diversity. The conventional number of 800 separate languages for the continent is certainly an underestimate. These languages are for the most part the primary spoken languages in relatively restricted areas. Hence migrations of more than local scope are bound to bring populations with divergent native languages into the same urban or rural areas. With the addition of European employers and administrators, as well as clerical personnel who, if not Europeans, are likely not to be indigenous to the area in which they carry on their work, the existence of linguistic heterogeneity tends to be the rule. Among the few exceptions are the Yoruba-speaking cities of the Western Region of Nigeria which, as we have seen, existed in precolonial times. The Yoruba-speaking area is sufficiently extensive for these cities to have retained in large measure their linguistic and cultural homogeneity. Yet even here the necessity of dealing with Europeans and, in certain cities, with a significant influx from the Eastern Region, mainly of Ibo-speaking people, creates a communication problem of the usual type, though of less significant proportions.

The usual solution to this problem is the so-called lingua franca. Terms in this area are not very well standardized. In the present context nothing is being asserted about the linguistic nature of this lingua franca. It may be a standard form of some existing language, or a "pidginized" form, or even, conceivably, a new creation. All that is meant here by a lingua franca is a language used for purposes of communication between people; it is not the first language of both communicating parties, but on occasion may be the first language of one party or of neither party. A given area might thus have more than one lingua franca, as so defined, and this situation occasionally exists.

Most frequently, however, there is a single lingua franca which tends to be dominant over a substantial area. This solution is rational, in a sense. Particularly if the lingua franca is the first language of the numerically largest group, it is the solution that requires the least amount of second-language learning. There is a further psychological advantage, for a single lingua franca is likely to be, in many instances, a language foreign to both speakers. Thus neither has to make the compromise of speaking the other's language. That this element is important in interpersonal and intergroup relations may be seen from the fact that in most instances Europeans, who were in the dominant position, did not learn the African language. It was the African who had to make the linguistic adjustment, a situation that sometimes produced resentment on the African side. In other instances, the use of an African language or, even more, of a pidgin is viewed as "talking down" to the African, and likewise causes resentment.

The single lingua franca tends to become the dominant solution not because anyone plans it that way, but because, once a language has a head start by being the language of a numerically important group, particularly the locally dominant one, others discover the advantage or even the necessity of learning it. Once it becomes at all widespread, it has an advantage over other possible lingua francas so that its expansion continues. There is thus a dynamic quality to the spread of a lingua franca. It tends to accelerate after the initial stage is passed. Once well established, it is likely to be the subject of certain policy decisions making it an official regional language, for example, or a language of school instruction. Such adoption gives the lingua franca a further impetus. The only thing that is likely to arrest its spread is a rival lingua franca. A lingua franca, however, may spread very slowly when it encounters a language with a large number of speakers in a compact area, particularly if there is relative isolation from developing urban-industrializing trends. An example is Kanuri, dominant in Bornu Province in the Northern Region of Nigeria. Itself not expansive—it is rarely spoken by non-Kanuri—it has offered solid resistance to Hausa, the dominant lingua franca of the Northern Region. The demographic and economic factors are obvious. The Kanuri are a substantial population occupying a fairly large area, relatively undeveloped in the modern sense and hence with relatively restricted contacts with non-Kanuri speakers. A historical-psychological factor, however, also plays a definite role: Hausa was the language of the Fulani-dominated Muslim empire of Sokoto, which fought for supremacy with the Kanuri empire of Bornu in the pre-European period. This traditional attitude of hostility still finds expression in an unwillingness to recognize the dominant position of Hausa and to accommodate to it.

Along with urbanism, lingua francas existed in the precolonial period. In the well-attested instance of Timbuktu, for example, Songhai functioned as the lingua franca and was known as a second language by the resident Bella Tuareg and Arabs. Indeed, it was largely preëxisting lingua francas that spread as the result of repression of internal conflict and of the expanding trade and industrialization of the colonial period. In the pre-European period, languages spread in response to political and commercial needs. The large Muslim empires were always ruled by an elite from a particular ethnic-linguistic group. Other groups learned the language of the dominant group, just as more recently they have learned European languages. The expansion of internal and external trade tended to favor traders of the dominant group. It thus became expedient to learn their language in order to carry on trade. The empire of Mali, for example, which flourished in the Middle Ages in the western Sudan, had a dominant core of Malinke speakers. It seems reasonable to attribute the wide spread of the very closely related Malinke-Bambara-Dyula complex to its dominant position in this empire. Malinke was widely employed by traders, and is today the dominant lingua franca over extensive areas of West Africa, particularly of Mali, which takes its name from the old empire. Again, Hausa spread over an extensive area as a lingua franca in the pre-European period largely through its linguistic dominance of the vast Fulani empires of Sokoto and Gwandu. Together with trading, the mechanism of large-scale slave raiding, followed by linguistic and cultural assimilation of the diverse pagan groups, was a dominant factor in the precolonial spread of Hausa.

While several African languages thus became established as lingua francas through political and commercial factors in the interior of West Africa, in the centuries preceding the explorations and the colonial expansion of the nineteenth century quite different lingua francas developed on the coast. Here the contact of Europeans and Africans led to the development of "pidginized" forms of European languages, mainly English, French, and Portuguese. The manner in which these languages were formed still presents important, and as yet unsolved, historical problems. It does seem safe to assume that these pidgins were widely disseminated in Africa before being brought to the New World.

A pidgin that becomes the first language of a population is called a Creole. Such Creoles became the dominant local language in a number of Caribbean Islands—Haiti, Curaçao, and Trinidad—and on the South American mainland. Taki-Taki is the English-based Creole of Surinam. The repatriated slaves who formed the original population of Freetown at the end of the eighteenth century likewise adopted their own common tongue, pidgin English, which in Africa itself thus became the first language of a population. Events of the colonial and postcolonial periods have fostered two major developments in the communication situation as thus outlined. The suppression of intertribal warfare and the establishment of rail and road communications have led everywhere to the expansion of indigenous lingua francas. These have usually been languages that had performed these functions in earlier times, such as Hausa, Malinke, and Swahili. Some African languages, however, usually in modified, pidginized form, have arisen in the European contact situation. Examples are Sango, the lingua franca of the Central African Republic; a pidginized form of Ngbandi; and Lingala, a similarly modified form of Bangala, spoken in the Middle Congo. Such new lingua francas do not seem to have originated in West Africa. I believe that the reason is the preëxistence of urban centers whose heterogeneous populations already had well-established lingua francas, in contrast with the situation in most of central and eastern Africa.

The spread of lingua francas has been so extensive under the impact of Westernization that there is now hardly an area in Africa which does not have a dominant lingua franca. All our existing maps are first-language maps. There is a great need for precise information on the areas of dominance of lingua francas. We need to know not only the geographical area embraced, but the extent to which the lingua franca is known, the degree of its command, and its distribution in relation to social stratification.

A second major result of European contact has been the introduction of European languages themselves as lingua francas. For example, the dominant lingua franca of both the Western and Eastern regions of Nigeria is English. The introduction of European languages was partly on the level of the "picking up" of more or less pidginized versions of European languages by the illiterate, who in the beginning, at least, used the traditional pidgin of the slave-trade period. At the same time languages such as English and French were being taught in mission and governmental schools, and have been in undisputed use for university-level education. These dual forms of European languages led to the denigration of pidgins, which became associated with illiteracy and, above all, with the colonial master-servant relationship. On the other hand, a full spoken command of standard English, French, or Portuguese is the sign of the African elite. Though nowhere, except in Liberia, is any European speech the first language of Africans, the ability to speak a European tongue becomes a supraregional, supratribal, even supranational mark of a new elite whose badge of membership is education, as proven by fluency in the European language employed in higher education.

Statements concerning the language situation of migrants are not very common in the literature. In general, it would seem, the migrant acquires a reasonably practical command of the dominant language of the area to which he comes. Thus, Abdoulaye Diop informs us that of ninety-six Toucouleur (linguistically Fulani) in Dakar, ninety-one had learned Wolof, the language of the African inhabitants of the city.[4] Again, Audrey Richards found that a knowledge of Luganda was sufficient in interviewing most of the migrants in Uganda.[5] There are, however, exceptions. Skinner and others report that the Mossi migrants in Ghana normally do not learn the local language (usually one of the Akan group).[6] The migrants from the north have a common linguistic bond in their own regional lingua franca, Hausa, and therefore tend not to associate much with the Ghanaians. This linguistic insulation, so to speak, considerably restricts the effect of migration on traditional tribal life. According to Skinner, "Even when the loud-speaker trucks of the various Ghanaian political parties visit the farm areas where most of the migrants work, the Mossi seldom understand the language being used."[7]

Language and Sociopolitical Groupings

Thus far, language has been considered mainly from the utilitarian point of view, as a means of communication. It is, however, more than that. Language is perhaps the most important single criterion of group identification, at least among groups sufficiently large to play a political role. For example, in Africa "tribe" is defined, with very few exceptions, in terms of first language. If a common language did not have this important function, we might expect that people who had learned a foreign lingua franca of wider usefulness than their tribal language would forthwith abandon their first language, or at least not bother to see that their children learned it. Of course, there are sources of tribal cohesion other than language, but Africans themselves are aware that the loss of their linguistic heritage would almost inevitably follow their loss of tribal identity. In interviews I conducted in the Plateau Province of the Northern Region of Nigeria, a highly multilingual area in which Hausa is the undisputed lingua franca, practically all informants with children said that they taught them their tribal language as their first language, and Hausa somewhat later. In the words of one informant, "If we abandoned our own language, we would become Hausa just like the rest." Pagans said that their ancestors would be greatly angered by the abandonment of their language. Several illiterate informants ventured the opinion that the language itself had a positive aesthetic aspect. There was, however, no hostility to the learning of Hausa. In fact, my informants expressed a unanimous desire for their children to learn Hausa because it was the medium of instruction in the lower grades and because ignorance of Hausa condemned a man to a restricted and economically marginal traditional agricultural existence.

We can think of linguistic continuity of a group in the urban environment as most perfectly maintained by group endogamy and the teaching of the tribal language to the children. Concomitantly, a lingua franca may be current in the group without producing any evident movement toward assimilation. Such a situation, called by linguists "stable bilingualism," has apparently existed in Timbuktu, as previously noted. The Tuareg and the Arabs have been bilingual for centuries, employing Songhai and their own language without loss of ethnic identity or serious impairment of group membership. Tribal intermarriage on a wide scale, of course, tends to undermine this continuity. The evidence seems to show that up to now tribal endogamy has prevailed markedly over tribal exogamy in the urban centers of Africa. Systematic data seem to be lacking in regard to the language or languages spoken by the offspring of intertribal marriages, and in regard to the relationship of this question to tribal identification. As most people in West Africa are patrilineal, and as the bride price is interpreted as implying possession of the children by the father's group, we may conjecture that in most instances the child learns the language of the father, along with the language of the mother and sometimes an external lingua franca. Skinner describes the reluctance of the patrilineal Mossi to marry women of the matrilineal Ashanti, presumably because both groups would claim the children under native law.[8]

The phenomenon of "passing" is a more direct mechanism for changing group affiliation than is the use of children. The situation in Africa is quite the opposite from the passing of Negroes in the United States, where physical type, not language, is the problem. There is occasional evidence in Africa of such passing by the adoption of language, dress, and other distinguishing marks of tribal membership. Audrey Richards describes migrants in Uganda whose Luganda is good enough for them to pass by claiming ancestry in some other district and thus becoming members of a group with superior local prestige and economic possibilities.[9] Banton describes how in Freetown, where non-Creole Africans are ranged in prestige in order of degree of adherence to Islam, members of the still largely pagan Temne tribe joined Mandinka and Aku (Yoruba) associations, and acquired the appropriate languages competently enough to pass into these groups. As Banton points out, however, an "African does not lightly renounce his tribe for another,"[10] and a countermovement led to the formation of a Temne young men's association to avert further depletion of Temne tribal strength in Freetown. Although instances of this kind have no doubt occurred more widely in Africa than has been reported in the literature, in neither of these two, nor presumably in others, was the phenomenon of sufficient scope to result in the complete absorption of a tribal group.

The attitude toward the tribal language as against the lingua franca is very different. The former is connected with a sense of group identity, of loyalty to traditional ways and to ancestors; the latter is a utilitarian instrument important—indeed, often absolutely essential—to getting ahead in the world, but not as yet setting up a real bond of solidarity.

It does not follow that the indefinite survival of tribal languages is thereby assured. Innumerable languages have become extinct in the course of the world's history. The preponderance of existing evidence from Africa, however, is that exceedingly few languages are in danger of immediate extinction, and any political or social planning that would count on the loss of tribal identity through the universal use of a lingua franca in the next generation, at least, is not realistic.

It is useful to draw a distinction here between tribalism as a political form based on a territory and marked by traditional customs and by political organization in terms of chiefly office, and the wider notion of group identity which, for want of a better term, I will call "ethnicity." Thus the Welsh are an ethnic group but not a tribe. It is entirely possible that the traditional tribal groupings of Africa are evolving toward ethnic groups of this kind, although it is clear that traditional tribal organization has, on the whole, shown remarkable resilience and adaptability. The tribe, as has been pointed out, may, through the medium of associations or tribal unions, re-create itself in urban centers and strengthen and maintain its ties with the rural hinterland.[11]

Africans seem quite conscious of the mechanisms necessary for the maintenance of group identity. Rouch aptly compares the behavior of some tribal groups, with migrant members in cities or on farms elsewhere, with that of expatriate Europeans.[12] If indeed there is group endogamy, if the children are sent back to the villages after a certain age to learn the traditional customs and if the language is maintained, then, in effect, the emigrant groups become "colonies" in the original Greek sense. As long as distance is not too great for fairly continuous visiting and intermarriage, the prediction is that linguistic unity can be maintained indefinitely. Once the ties of fairly continuous communication weaken, the emigrant's language will diverge and ultimately become unintelligible to the home group. This process has often taken place in the past in Africa, as elsewhere, but it requires centuries, not decades.

Finally, it should be noted that language may be the subject of conscious planning and policy. Until now, decisions on matters of language in Africa have been made either by missions or by colonial governments. The former, by choice of specific dialects as standard forms of a language, and of certain languages rather than others for use in instruction in mission schools, as well as by the orthographies they introduced, exercised a very real, if haphazard, influence. The very act of creating an orthography and using a language for literary purposes gives it a certain prestige and an attendant advantage in other situations. The influence was haphazard because decisions were habitually made without sufficient knowledge of the degrees and the kinds of dialectal variations, or of the attitude held toward the various dialects by those who spoke the language. The form of speech current near the mission station was normally chosen without any understanding of the long-term consequences. Mission influence on language may be called haphazard also because of the lack of overall interdenominational planning. Consequently we even have Protestant and Catholic forms of orthography for certain languages (e.g., Ibo).

The other important policy agent is government. The French policy of using French exclusively in education and administration has tended both to facilitate the spread of French as a lingua franca and to bring loss of prestige to African languages; the latter is a factor still to be reckoned with in areas of former French rule. On the other hand, the official recognition and use of Swahili in East Africa, particularly in Tanganyika, and of Hausa in the Northern Region of Nigeria, under British administration, have strengthened processes already at work tending to the spread of these languages.

The question of language, then, has more than local import. Because tribalism, as a basic political factor in Africa, is tied to the question of the survival of communities, each with its own peculiar linguistic heritage, the question of language becomes a fundamental one for the newly independent African states. A degree of linguistic unity is a presupposition of European nationalism, occasionally violated but then always with some derogation of the feeling of national unity, as in Belgium, for example. In Africa, outside Somalia and the Malagasy Republic, this linguistic unity is lacking and, if the present analysis is correct, unattainable in the reasonably near future. Here I propose merely to point out that there is a problem of language in relation to nationalism, for it has ramifications that would take us far beyond the present topic.

Sociolinguistics

This brief review of what I believe to be the salient problems regarding the role of language in the urban and migratory situations of contemporary Africa should serve to emphasize the point made earlier, that relevant data on a good many essential topics are scarce. It may prove useful, in summary, to indicate the main aspects of the "language situation," the basic topic of investigation of sociolinguistics.

These aspects may be enumerated by means of a rough division on the basis of the disciplines that seem best equipped to handle particular problems. The purely linguistic factors include the classification of languages and dialects, judgment as to whether a language is to be considered a pidgin or a Creole, extent of vocabulary development, linguistic complexity as a factor in ease of learning for nonnative speakers, and information regarding the existence of standardized literary forms and their relation to existing spoken dialects. The purely demographic aspect concerns the distribution of speech forms in the area under study, and the extent of multilingualism and of literacy in one or more languages. Ideally, such information should be included in censuses. Until now, only first-language information has been available, but, in my experience, it has seldom been even reasonably accurate. Sociocultural facts concern the distribution of first and other languages in relation to occupation, social stratification, ethnic origin, and religious affiliation, as well as types and frequency of language choices for offspring from mixed marriages. The social-psychological aspect includes attitudes toward and prestige ratings of languages as might be indicated by attitude tests, semantic differential, and so forth. Of more individual psychological import are the motives for learning new languages, and the manner in which they are learned. Africans pick up new languages without formal instruction, but we know almost nothing of the processes involved. Finally, a political aspect may be recognized. We may include here the policies of governments and private agencies in language matters, and the relation of language questions to political parties, national aspirations, and so on.

This essay is intended, of course, merely as a rough outline. It should be evident, however, that the language situation, taken in a broad sense, is a substantial part of what economists call the "infrastructure" of development. As such it is, I believe, at once one of the most important and the least studied factors in the contemporary African situation.[13]

5.

LABOR MIGRATION AMONG THE MOSSI
OF THE UPPER VOLTA*

by *Elliott P. Skinner*

Labor migration in Africa is most properly seen as a modern phenomenon, first stimulated by the presence of Europeans, and now sustained by changing socioeconomic conditions the Africans themselves fostered. True, Africans did move about the continent in aboriginal times. Small kin groups constantly left their parent stocks to find and occupy more fertile lands; cattle herders migrated in search of better pastures, or traveled in transhumance cycles; and warrior groups left one polity and moved off to establish their rule and dominance over neighboring populations. Merchants and traders also traveled extensively throughout the more complex societies of western Africa, often establishing special wards or *zongo*'s in the larger towns. These movements, however, based as they were on local conditions, did not have the characteristics of modern labor migrations. The latter, geared to a highly developed foreign industrial system, were fostered by Europeans to obtain African labor for their mines and plantations and later for their industrial, transportation, and urban complexes. Nevertheless, like other sociocultural phenomena, labor recruitment and labor migrations were made possible only by supporting features in the cultures and societies of both Africans and Europeans. As African societies changed under the impact of European institutions and values, labor migration, which formerly had been an imposition upon the Africans, became an important part of their own sociocultural systems.

Today vast areas of Africa are free from European rule, but labor migration continues. In this attempt to understand labor migration among the Mossi of the Upper Volta and its impact upon their society,

*The fieldwork on which this paper is based was made possible by a Ford Foundation African Studies Program fellowship during 1955-1957. Additional data were collected during brief visits to the Upper Volta in the summers of 1960 and 1962 under the auspices of Operations Crossroads Africa. I bear full responsibility, however, for the contents of this paper.

attention is focused upon the historical aspects of the phenomenon, upon the development of forces within Mossi society which stimulate it, and upon the relationship of labor migration to other factors that are causing changes in the society.

The annual exodus of thousands of Mossi laborers to the mines, plantations, urban centers, and transportation complexes of Ghana, of the Ivory Coast, and to a lesser extent of Mali and Dahomey, constitutes one of the chief migratory patterns in contemporary West Africa. Albert Balima, deputy director-general of labor and manpower in the Ministry of Social Affairs, Republic of Upper Volta, states that for his newly independent country

> ... the most vital problem—and the one on which the entire future of the nation depends—is that of migration. Every year the population increases by two percent. And every day thousands of citizens of the Republic, believing that living conditions are better in the rich lands to the south—in Ghana and the Republic of the Ivory Coast—following in the footsteps of earlier generations and attracted by the vision of paid employment, voluntarily migrate. . . . There are believed to be somewhere between 300,000 and 400,000 emigrants in Ghana, and between 200,000 and 250,000 in the Republic of the Ivory Coast; but these figures are based on no more than guess work.[1]

Most authorities believe that 50,000 Mossi workers migrate annually to Ghana, and some would put the figure closer to 100,000.[2] Mossi men also constituted the majority of the 50,000 workers officially recruited each year in the Upper Volta (until quite recently) to work in the coffee and cacao plantations of the Ivory Coast.

Mossi society has managed to remain viable while producing so large a number of labor migrants because of several important geographical, historical, and cultural factors. The Mossi live in the Volta region of West Africa, a relatively poor and infertile 105,900 square miles of territory bounded on the south by Ghana, the Ivory Coast, Togo, and Dahomey; on the east by Niger; and on the west and north by Mali. Mossi society itself developed as a result of the northward expansion of the Dagomba people of Ghana, who conquered and partially assimilated the autochthonous populations. The resulting population continued to move northward into the bend of the Niger River, where, according to local traditions, they raided Timbuktu and fought the ancient Malian and Songhai peoples until they were driven back to their present location.[3] Here they developed four important kingdoms and lesser principalities under a number of chiefs, all joined together by bonds of kinship, ritual, and military power. The chiefs of the larger kingdoms, the *mogho nanamsé* (sing., *mogho naba*), ruled over provinces, districts, and villages headed by members of the royal lineage. The village populations in Mossi

[1] For notes to chapter 5, see page 189.

country were divided into noble, commoner, serf, and slave, and organized in segmentary patrilineal groups. The people lived virilocally in polygynous, extended-family households.

The Mossi marriage system was based on the exchange of women between lineages linked by long-term reciprocal relations. Because the older men were the ones who controlled most of the lineage resources, they obtained most of the wives. The young men either had to wait until their elders died to inherit wives, or sought wives *(pogsiouré)* from chiefs against the promise of providing goods and services to their benefactors and giving them their first daughter to serve as a future pogsiouré.[4] Lineage heads also supervised the economic activities of the people under their charge. These activities included the cultivation of staples: several varieties of millet, sorghum, and maize, as well as rice, okra, sweet potatoes, and cotton and indigo used in the making of cloth for export. The Mossi also herded livestock, which they traded on local markets, along with grain and cloth, and exported to Timbuktu and the forest zones of Ashanti and Togoland. The early Mossi traders were well known around Timbuktu as men who did not waste their money, but who "departed as soon as their business was concluded."[5]

Although they had been in contact with Islam since the fourteenth century, the Mossi resisted all attempts at conversion, whether by jihad or by peaceful proselytizing, until conquered by the French. Traditionally, their religion included veneration of the ancestors, belief in an omnipotent but otiose high god, Winnan, and worship of an earth goddess, Tenga, by means of sacrifices at earth shrines *(tengkouga)* by earth priests *(tengsobadamba)*.[6] Annual sacrifices to the ancestral founders of the Mossi nation joined all the people behind their chiefs, the earthly representatives of these ancestors.[7]

Traditional Mossi society was sufficiently well organized economically, socially, and politically to withstand the vicissitudes of Sudanese history and warfare which destroyed the other contemporary kingdoms and decimated their populations. Even before the country had been conquered, the Mossi aroused the interest of European travelers as a potential source of labor. Crozat, who visited Mossi country in 1890, declared that the Mossi population "is surprisingly dense for a Black country. There is here an enormous capital, immediately exploitable."[8]

The Mossi first began to migrate for work in order to earn money for the taxes introduced by the French in 1896, immediately after the conquest, and demanded in francs rather than in kind or cowries. Some Mossi tried to meet the new obligation by intensifying their dry-season trade to the forest and northern Niger River zones, but since French conquest had largely destroyed the northern trade, they concentrated on the south. They soon found that working in the Gold Coast was more profitable than trade, because they were paid in coins that could be exchanged for French currency. The taxes were raised gradually, however, and more and more Mossi men had to migrate for work. According to Tauxier, who served as one of the early administrators in Mossi country, the tax was raised from 311,000 francs in 1906 to 656,000 francs in 1910, and "exacted with such rigor and on such short notice that it was exactly as though the amount of the tax had been tripled."[9] To make matters worse, those Mossi who remained at home could not obtain the silver 5-franc pieces that were demanded of them, because the Europeans who had this money withheld it from the market in order to profit from the need of the people. Mangin states that at taxpaying time the Mossi were compelled to pay from 10,000 to 15,000 cowries for a coin that was worth only 5,000 cowries at the official rate.[10] Those men who were unwilling or unable to obtain European money with which to pay taxes had their goods sequestered and sold by chiefs and by administrative officials. Those who had neither taxes nor goods were compelled to migrate in ever-increasing numbers to the Gold Coast to work, or face punishment by the administration.

By the beginning of World War I the Mossi people had gradually developed a pattern of seasonal migration which enabled them to obtain money for taxes, fitted into their traditional economy, and compensated for some of the economic benefits they had formerly derived from trade. As soon as the young men had harvested the crops, in November and December, they moved south to the Gold Coast along routes formerly used by traders. From Ouahigouya and points north the migrants went through Ouagadougou and Po, or through Koudougou and Léo, to the Gold Coast; from points south they went straight down through Po or Léo; and from points east they moved through Tenkodogo, crossing the Gold Coast border at Bawku and then heading south. Most of these laborers remained in the Gold Coast until the end of April and then made their way north over the same routes, except when news of stiff customs tolls at certain border points caused them to seek other ways.

This migratory pattern of the Mossi was disrupted after World War I by the labor demands of the French administration and of private colonial interests. In 1919, when the Upper Volta was created as an administrative territory, an official, M. de Beauminy, made the significant statement that "the principal riches now available in Mossi country are its numerous laborers."[11] When, in 1921, the French minister of colonies, Albert Sarraut, began to implement the postwar plans expounded in his *Mise en valeur des Colonies Françaises (Development of the French Colonies)*, the Mossi people bore the brunt of the labor demand. Mossi chiefs were made to recruit tens of thousands of their subjects both for public works and for private commercial enterprises in the Upper Volta, the Sudan, and the Ivory Coast. In 1922 the Upper Volta officially furnished

... 6,000 workers for the Thiès-Kayes railway, replaceable every six months, and under the same conditions furnished 2,000 laborers to build railroads in the Ivory Coast. Similarly, with the consent of the chief administrator of the colony, it was possible to recruit a thousand workers in the regions of Ouagadougou and Bobo-Dioulasso for private corporations in the Ivory Coast.[12]

Buell states that

Between 1921 and 1925, the Upper Volta furnished the Thiès-Kayes and Ivory Coast railroads with nearly forty-nine thousand men. In 1924, the Upper Volta Colony in addition employed men for a total of 318,814 man-days not including prestation labor and other local labor.[13]

Albert Londres, who visited French West Africa in the late 1920's, reports that the Upper Volta was then considered a

... "reservoir" of manpower: 3 million Negroes. Everyone comes here to get them as one would go to wells for water. For the building of the Thiès-Kayes and Kayes-Niger railroads, the Mossi were tapped. For the railroads of the Ivory Coast, Mossi country is tapped. The [French] woodcutters leave their lagoons [coastal areas] to tap the Mossi.[14]

Robert Delavignette, who served in the Upper Volta as a young district officer during this period, and who was to become director of political affairs in the French Overseas Ministry, wrote in 1932:

In the course of ten years, 93,000 men were thus sent far away. They came back, but without having learned a trade; having, on the other hand, lost touch with their families, which had suffered by their absence and which could not be made whole by their return. Fields had been neglected, betrothed girls had not been married, wives had become undernourished, children had been poorly cared for. The recruiters paid no heed to local labor customs. The young leaders of the age associations and of the rural cooperative organizations were not acknowledged [in their true roles] as monitors of peasant life and agriculture, but were seized as ordinary laborers and in preference to others because they were stronger. French Africa has lived on Voltaic labor in the Sudan, and notably in the Ivory Coast.[15]

When, in 1932, the French administration decided that the Upper Volta should be dismantled as a colony because it was insolvent, the planters of the Ivory Coast successfully lobbied to have Mossi country attached to the Ivory Coast so that they might have unrestricted access to Mossi labor. Only in 1937 did the French administration recognize that a "grave injustice had been done to the Mossi people simply to further the interests of a small group of coastal planters and foresters," and only then did it stop the recruitment of Mossi laborers for private concerns.[16] Recruitment for public works was continued until 1946. The recruitment of soldiers did not stop until the Upper Volta became independent, but by this time many Mossi, including the late Mogho Naba Sagha II, had lost sons in Indo-China and Algeria.

The Mossi displayed little or no opposition to the initial demand for laborers, in part because they had a tradition of rendering *corvée* labor to their chiefs. They accepted the fact that they had been conquered fairly in warfare ("had become women," in their terms) and that they had to obey their new chiefs. According to Labouret, the "initial recruitment [of Mossi laborers] which took place in 1912 was carried out without any difficulty, thanks to the unexpected afflux of volunteers."[17] As the demand for labor increased, however, the Mossi people resisted. Labouret ascribes the reason for their resistance to the Mossi belief that "the Europeans were carrying off the most robust youths to sell them to the Men of the Sea [mythical cannibalistic beings]."[18] The truth is that the Mossi were appalled at the death rate of the migrants, and said, "Nansara toumdé di Mossé" ("White man's work eats [kills] people"), a not dissimilar idea. Buell states that after a while the Upper Volta government "had considerable difficulty in recruiting these men because of the low wages and high death rate,[19] particularly on the Ivory Coast railway. As a result of the intervention of the Governor of the Upper Volta, wages were raised to one and a half francs a day and rations were improved."[20] He adds, in a footnote: "Another dispute between the Upper Volta and the Ivory Coast governors was over the refusal of the latter to pay one hundred francs to the family of every man who died on the way home, the governor interpreting the *arrêté* concerned to mean that it should be paid only for men who died at work. The governor-general finally intervened, and required payments to be made in the former case."[21] Delavignette states that the low wages paid to the Mossi who had been drafted for work in the French colonies did not provide enough money:

. . . in order to pay taxes and earn money in this colony which should have been enriched by its cotton fields and civilized by its "imperial roads," the natives who were not held back by what remained of the family economy or sent back to the European sector of work depots and concessions, left on seasonal migrations to the Gold Coast where they worked on cacao plantations and on the roads under much better conditions than in the Volta and for better pay than in the Ivory Coast. There were years when 80,000 men left to contribute to the fortunes of the Gold Coast.[22]

These migrants, together with the thousands of men who fled to the Gold Coast in order to escape unprofitable forced labor, were joined by others wishing to evade the control of chiefs who often used their role as labor recruiters to extract goods and services from their subjects; and by others who wished to escape the police, the reprobation of lineage members and of the local community for violating customs, or the anger of husbands from whom they had stolen their wives. Those migrants who could return without fear of being apprehended did so, and later went off again; others, fearing imprisonment or abuse, stayed away or returned surreptitiously for brief visits.

The end of World War II marked a new era in French colonial policy, and forced labor was abolished altogether. By this time, however, seasonal and other types of labor migration had become so much a part of their economic system that the Mossi continued to migrate for work, and have retained this practice even now that independence has come to the Upper Volta. In fact, labor migration has become so institutionalized among the Mossi that its characteristics are familiar to everyone, and there is a consensus as to why, how, and when certain persons should migrate. When one asks either the migrants or their relatives why young men leave home to work, the answers are similar and extremely repetitious: "I am poor, I need money to pay taxes and to buy clothes" is the standard reply of young men. Another may declare, "I want a bicycle, clothes for myself, and clothes for my wife and relatives." The relative of an absent migrant replies with the statement, "Men go off to find money," or says, of a specific man, "He went to get money to pay taxes." The Mossi place so much emphasis on the economic motive for labor migration that none of my respondents among the migrants stated that he had gone to the Gold Coast or to the Ivory Coast for any other reason.

Nevertheless, Mossi families do not encourage their young men to migrate for work. On the contrary, most families try to persuade them not to leave even when it is obvious to all concerned that migration offers the only means whereby men can obtain money to satisfy their needs. Significantly enough, almost all the Mossi queried stated that if they were able to find work in their own home areas, they would not migrate. A number of men from the districts where I did my fieldwork went to the Gold Coast because they had "stolen" from their husbands the women they took with them, and a number fled after being accused of theft or rape, or after being caught in the act of adultery. As a number of these persons were not expected to return, however, they cannot be considered true labor migrants. On the other hand, no one reported that men had migrated because of quarrels with the traditional chiefs or with lineage members; the Mossi have always been able to leave their district or village and render allegiance to another chief, and have always been sure of finding haven with their mother's patrilineage if they experience any difficulty with their own. The Mossi women, rather than the men, are the persons who now run off to neighboring territories either because of dissatisfaction with an arranged marriage, or because of a difficult domestic situation. Women are even heard to warn the judge at court that if their husbands do not reform, they are likely to run off with "any stranger on his way to Kumasi." Attempts to find out whether some of the migrants were led to travel by a desire for adventure or for amusement often prompted the response, "One does not go to Kumasi to give one's money to the movies or to women." When I called the attention of respondents to the fact that there were Mossi men who had resided in the Gold Coast for several years, and who might have been seduced by city pleasures, the immediate response was, "Perhaps, but the hearts of such men have changed" (meaning that they have lost their heads).

Mossi migrants are usually men in the 16-to-30 age group. Prepubescent boys or married men who have taken on the responsibilities of family life are discouraged from migrating. Those men who contemplate migration prepare for it as inconspicuously as possible so as not to arouse the attention of their relatives, who would try to persuade them to remain at home. They save money and collect small livestock for sale in order to pay for their transportation. Of course, these preparations often come to the attention of their relatives, but the Mossi sense of decorum is so strong that nothing is said. The main concern is often that the man should remain at home until the end of November, when most of the crops have been harvested and the short but exacting agricultural period is nearly over. When the migrants do leave, they usually slip out of their compounds "at the first crowing of the cock" (about 3 A.M.) and take to the road where they meet with friends at prearranged places, or go on alone until they encounter other migrants along the way. Migrants travel mostly in the early morning hours, buying breakfast from women vendors along the road before setting off. They rest during the hot part of the day and travel again in the afternoon until sundown. They customarily sleep on the outskirts of villages near clumps of trees called *kumasi kakanga*. They avoid the village centers for fear that they may be accused of theft if some villager loses his property. But they stay close to villages and away from wooded areas and rivers so as to avoid encounters with marauding beasts. They travel in this manner until the money they carry is sufficient to pay their fare to Ghana or to the Ivory Coast; if they have no money, they proceed on foot or do odd jobs along the way in order to get the funds to pay for transportation.

Mossi migrants try to ascertain whether more jobs are available in Ghana or in the Ivory Coast before they leave home, but few of them know exactly where they will go or what kind of job they will obtain. Of course, most of these men are prepared to take any kind of job, "even women's work," provided that they can earn money. Some men are fortunate enough to meet Ashanti truck drivers at border towns such as Po, Léo, or Tenkodogo, who are commissioned by Ashanti cacao farmers to procure laborers and give them free transportation. Others meet similar truck drivers who transport them to coffee and cacao fields in the Ivory Coast under the same conditions. A few migrants may head for areas where they have heard that their relatives are working, and others may seek out Mossi chiefs who have established themselves in foreign countries, and try to get work through them. Most migrants, however, simply inquire from other Mossi and strangers they meet along the way as to where they might obtain jobs.

The largest number of migrants who go to Ghana or the Ivory Coast ultimately find work as laborers on cacao, coffee, and vegetable farms. Of 9,518 Mossi migrants who were interviewed at the Yeji Ferry in Ghana in 1954, 7,783, or 82.6 per cent, worked on farms. The others worked in mines, on roads, or as town laborers.[23] Regardless of what kind of work these migrants find, however, they all state that they make every effort to save as much money as possible so that they will not have to stay away from home for more than five or six months, the duration of the dry season in their home country. The percentage of seasonal migrants who earn 15 Ghanaian pounds, which most of them seem to regard as their goal, is unknown. Most of the men who return say that they have done so. Obviously, there is no way of checking their statements except by querying employers. The 20 per cent or so of those migrants who do not return at the end of the season may be men who have not realized their economic goal or who have decided to earn more money.

The 80 per cent of the annual migrants who return home for the agricultural season try to leave their places of employment in April, when they observe such signs as the flowering of certain trees and the orientation of the Pleiades, indicating that the rains are not too far off. They collect their wages and head for the markets where they buy the goods they desire: zinc buckets, kerosene lamps, long robes, cotton shirts, pants, head scarves for women, Muslim-type fezzes, mirrors, sandals, mosquito nets, wooden bedsteads, eating utensils, cement for plastering walls and floors, and, most important of all, bicycles. They usually place these goods in wooden trunks to which padlocks have been attached, and after exchanging the remainder of their Ghanaian pounds for CFA francs at the market stalls of African money changers, they board trucks and head for home. Migrants returning from the Ivory Coast did not have to pay custom tolls, but those crossing the border from the Gold Coast (Ghana) were often severely taxed by French officials, so much so that they hesitated to return home until they had enough money to pay taxes on their belongings. In 1953 alone migrants paid more than $1,027,000 in tolls to the Upper Volta government.[24] The value of the goods they brought back in 1955 amounted to more than $3 million,[25] but no one knows how much cash migrants actually bring back.

The migrants try to arrive home during the night, as quietly as they left. This custom developed at the height of the colonial period, when a migrant seen returning either by the spies of the chiefs or by those of the administration was deprived of his goods and possibly shipped off to do forced labor. The custom is still followed, even though these abuses have disappeared. What has not changed is the Mossi dislike of the emotion-packed scene. Doubtless migrants will continue to return by night. They like nothing better than to be able to greet their relatives the following morning as though they had never left. The relatives, in turn, with the possible exception of mothers, assume an equally nonchalant air when they see the returning migrants at their "accustomed" places. This fiction does not persist for long, however, as news of the migrant's return soon spreads among his many friends, who come to greet him.

A returned migrant is commended for his journey, and this commendation serves to validate labor migration both in his own eyes and in the eyes of the community. He is expected to pay a visit to the chief, who welcomes him home and to whom he gives a present and brings news of the Mossi in the areas he has visited. The migrant also visits the market places, the centers of Mossi life, and here he shows off his new clothes, is welcomed by his friends, and in return gives them gifts of money, kola nuts, and native beer. He also distributes largess to the minstrels who accompany him on his tour of the markets, singing his praises and those of his ancestors. The relatives of the migrant show by their new clothes and presents that they too have benefited from his absence. Nevertheless, migration is too common in Mossi society for the returnee to occupy the center of the stage very long. As times passes, the migrants are reabsorbed into the life of the community. The clothes they have brought grow ragged; their new bicycles are exchanged for older ones plus some money or livestock, and their hard-earned cash is used up. They become indistinguishable from Mossi men who have not been away, and like them, dream and plan to migrate the following year or sometime in the future.

The effect of labor migration on Mossi society is not easy to isolate among the effects of other forces.[26] True, some consequences of migration are readily discernible, but they are also allied to other changes caused by the presence of Europeans and by the expansion of Mossi society. The migration of men has certainly affected the agricultural practices of the Mossi and the types of crops they produce. Traditionally, Mossi families cleared land for bush farms in uninhabited areas by calling upon their friends and marriage partners for aid in the form of *sissosé* ("work begged for"), or work bees. In return for this aid, the families provided food, drink, and kola nuts for the workers, and reciprocated when other families asked for help. Most of this work took place during February and March, leaving the families with the less difficult task of clearing their homestead plots toward the end of April, just before the rains of May or June heralded the planting season. Families also asked for and received help to clear the sprouting weeds during late July or early August. The problem of many contemporary families is that, with many young men still away during February and March, they are unable to obtain workers for sissosé. Families need all their workers to clear their own bush farms, and thus there has been a decline in the number of sissosé, and a corresponding decrease in the acreage of bush farms. During my period of active fieldwork (1955-1957), it was more common to see family units than sissosé groups clearing bush farms or clearing weeds on these farms.

Labor migration has also contributed to changes in the work patterns of Mossi family units. Formerly the extended family worked as a unit under the control of the *yirisoba* (household head), from about 6 A.M. to about 1 P.M., on the collective fields whose produce fed the family and provided for its socioeconomic and political obligations. In the afternoon, family members tended individual crops which the men exchanged for goods in the market place, while the women used this time to help feed their children. Today, however, the absence of men usually means that individual family members do not have as much time to cultivate crops for their own use. Every hand is needed to work the collective fields. The result is not so harmful to the economy of the Mossi household as one might expect, since labor migration itself makes up for the losses. The men get the goods which they formerly obtained through individual cultivation by going off periodically on labor migration, and many women now obtain extra money for their individual needs by selling cooked food to the migrants who stop in the various villages along the migratory routes.

Mossi officials in the Upper Volta government, believing, like the French officials before them, that labor migration has adversely affected the production of basic food crops, would like to reduce it. But in the absence of systematic studies of crop production in Mossi country, especially in areas heavily influenced by migration, the true facts are unknown. There is little doubt, however, that the desire of the men to migrate for work has affected the cultivation of some crops. For example, during the 1920's and early 1930's the French administration tried but failed to induce the Mossi to grow more cotton. The reason was that cotton production did not harmonize with labor migration. The Mossi never prepared fields exclusively for cotton, but mixed this crop with the growing of millet during the month of August. Millet was harvested in late October and early November, but cotton could not be harvested until December. As that would usually be too late for men planning to migrate, they refrained from planting cotton. Other factors were involved, however, in the decline of cotton production. It was, in fact, more profitable to migrate for work than to grow cotton. Furthermore, families who were short of men owing to migration or to forced labor devoted most of their energies to the cultivation of food crops rather than to the weeding of cotton plants. And, finally, the Mossi need for homespun cotton clothes was changing. The migrants were bringing back European clothes and fabrics judged more desirable by most of the people.

The French administration could not understand the relationship among cotton production, labor migration, and the Mossi need for money and goods, but Albert Londres, who visited the Upper Volta in the late 1920's, saw this relationship quite clearly and was surprised that the administrators should be "astonished that the Sudan and the Upper Volta no longer produce cotton."[27] There is perhaps a relationship between the decline of cotton production in Mossi country and the decline in the production of local staples. Some observers have shown for the Ivory Coast and for other areas that where there is an increase in the production of export commodities there is a corresponding increase in food production,[28] leading one to suspect that the reverse may also be true. Unfortunately, there are no data to indicate whether or not the Mossi reduction in cotton acreage is related to the reduction in food crop acreage. If, as it appears, labor migration and forced labor prevented the Mossi from enlarging their fields, the amount of food available to them is now less than before because medical help has increased the population. Labor migration, in conjunction with the sale of food for cash to urban centers such as Ouagadougou and Po, was held responsible for the famine conditions that prevailed in the southern districts of Mossi country in 1961.

The exposure of Mossi subsistence farmers to the cultivation of cash crops in the Gold Coast and the Ivory Coast has changed their attitude to agriculture. Men who have worked for wages on cacao, coffee, and vegetable farms learn to view farming in a new light; it must not merely provide subsistence, but bring a profit to its practitioners. One very articulate young man complained, "When I was born, I was told that to hoe [agriculture] was the occupation of the Mossi. But today the hoe is nothing. In Ashanti, you work on cacao under the shade trees; you find yams for food; and the Ashanteneba [Ashanti people] give you money. Here, you work hard on hard soil in the hot sun, and then you have to sell your millet to pay taxes. You have nothing!" As a result, many migrants tend to give up agriculture when they return home. Some resort to local trade; others trade between their home communities and the northern areas of Ghana; and a growing number migrate to Ouagadougou where they add to the ever-increasing urban Mossi population.

The migration of men to foreign areas has also had an effect on other aspects of Mossi material culture, especially on those aspects that formerly depended on labor performed during the dry season. It was during this period that the Mossi not only cleared new bush farms, but also wove cloth for home use and for export, cleaned wells, and repaired huts damaged by the rains. The high incidence of migration has been accompanied by a gradual loss of skill in cloth weaving among the youths of Mossi country. The growing shortage of skilled weavers is not viewed too seriously by most of the people because they now prefer European fabrics and clothes. Nevertheless, the old people declare that they prefer garments made of local cloth, and they are especially concerned about the possibility of not having Mossi cloth for their burial. The absence of men to clean wells during the dry season did present a problem to the rural population of the Mossi districts in former years. Now, however, this need has largely been met by the government of the Upper Volta, which has taken charge of opening and maintaining wells. In the past, the absence of men during the dry season resulted in the deterioration of huts and compound walls, because there were few individuals available to make the sun-dried bricks necessary for repair. People even took to building huts and compounds completely of grass and sticks and living in them for extended periods of time, much to the annoyance of Mossi elders who declared that it was a disgrace to live in a straw hut and compound longer than the year traditionally needed to build the structures out of brick. Now, however, more and more migrants bring back cement which they use to plaster not only the floors of their houses but also the walls. The result is that they do not have to be concerned with the need to make bricks during the dry season, because plastered walls resist rain much better. Many migrants even try to make their huts conform to patterns they have seen in other countries. Some men have built square huts like those they have seen among the Ashanti and the Baule; others have opened windows in the walls of their round huts, use curtains as "room dividers," install wooden bedsteads, and have even papered the walls of their huts with pages of old illustrated magazines. In many homesteads kerosene lamps have replaced the traditional shea-butter lamps, zinc buckets have replaced pottery jars, and lounging chairs have been added to the mats that formerly were the only furniture. Labor migration is thus changing the economic and material life of the Mossi people, but not all observers, especially among the Mossi elders, agree with a French economist that it is contributing to a "rise in the standard of living of the population."[29]

Labor migration has had an effect on the social institutions of the Mossi people, but here again it is only one of a number of forces making for change in their society. We have seen how in aboriginal times Mossi lineage elders secured wives from one another for their groups as the result of a whole nexus of relations among lineages which included, among other things, mutual economic aid. When young men began to leave on labor migration, lineage heads began to lose the personnel that had enabled them to maintain the relationships that brought wives both to them and to their charges. Some of the larger lineages, especially those of chiefs and nobles, did manage to maintain their "wife-bringing" relationships, but the others continued to exchange wives more out of inertia than as the result of effective structural factors. Occasionally a prosperous migrant returns and attempts to obtain a wife by being very generous to a lineage head. But the Mossi, who do not have the bride price as an institution, deplore this practice, and if there is no long-term relationship the elder is accused of attempting to "sell" a woman. The elders themselves are caught in a serious dilemma. They still retain the young wives they receive for themselves (with the alleged expectation, of course, that the wives will ultimately be inherited by sons and relatives), but now they justify retaining them by declaring that the young men of today do not deserve wives because they do not remain at home to help their elders perform the tasks that ultimately bring wives. As one district chief declared when questioned about the Mossi marriage pattern, "Nowadays, young men do not want wives; they want clothes and bicycles. If they wanted wives, they would stay home and help their relatives work the soil. No! They all go off to Kumasi, and then come back and steal other men's wives." But the very ability of young men to "steal" other men's wives is related to the fact that labor migration now gives them resources of their own with which to entice these women away from their husbands, and that they are no longer beholden to elders who at one time controlled all lineage resources.

Mossi chiefs and elders have found to their dismay that labor migration contributes to the loosening of the traditional sanctions against the disruption of their marriage system. Even previous to labor migration, the Mossi had serious difficulties with runaway wives for two interrelated reasons: the dislike of many women for their older husbands, and the efforts of younger, wifeless men to obtain the wives of other men. In those days, however, a husband was usually able to regain his wife through the simple expedient of having his lineage recall the women married to men of the "abductor's" lineage, and thus forcing the return of his own wife. Barring that, a husband could always petition the chief to secure his wife's return.

Nowadays, Mossi women have alternatives to staying with a husband they dislike. Gone are the days when a Mossi woman accepted resignedly an intolerable ménage with the statement, "What can I do? My father sent me to sit here!" Now a woman simply runs away with a migrant. Her paramour's lineage is free from the traditional pressures that would force her to return. (Even if her family recalled all women married into the abductor's lineage, this policy might not ensure the woman's return if she is out of the country.) Rather than break up the marriage of innocent people without any hope of gaining their objective, the relatives of a deserted husband often take no action. The deserting couple stay away for a few years until tempers cool, and then they return and live openly as man and wife. This practice has been supported by a French law and now by an Upper Volta law stating that a woman cannot be forced to marry or remain with a husband against her will. Furthermore, the returning couple are allowed to keep any children born to them regardless of what the former husband says, because neither the French nor the present administration has accepted the Mossi notion of sociological parenthood by which a man was able to claim the child of his wife whether he was the genitor or not.

Ironically enough, marital relations among the Mossi are often jeopardized by the attempts of husbands to provide for their families by migrating for work. Men whose wives complain about not having the same clothes as their peers often go off to work in order to buy the desired articles. Yet these same wives, needing male companionship, sometimes desert their households to live with other men. If the migrant does not remain away too long and the wife is not too knowledgeable about her "rights of citizenship," he is able to get her back through family pressures and promises of gifts. In such instances the husband also claims and obtains sociological parenthood of any child she might have conceived or borne in his absence. If, however, a man encounters difficulty in finding work or is seduced by the foreign area and does not return for two or three years, and his wife leaves his relatives and establishes another household, he has a great deal of difficulty inducing her to return when he finally comes back. Questioned about this problem, an older woman declared, "These men ask for trouble! They go to Kumasi, and expect the woman to sit down and eat *varda* [leaves or herbs which are the main source of food during the hungry period]. If a woman is not clever and does not sell *samsa* [fried bread] at kumasi kakanga, then she would have nothing. But the women are not going to sit any longer." Mindful of the effect of migration and modern life on Mossi marriages, the present administration of the Upper Volta is attempting to establish a new marriage pattern. During the early months of 1962 it conducted a survey of the changing attitudes of the people toward marriage, but so far the data have not been processed and no decisions have been made about the institution.

In general, Mossi women have a fairly good idea of the life led by women who run off either to Ghana or to the Ivory Coast. They believe that the "wives" of migrants do not have to perform the rather difficult agricultural work that is the lot of women at home, and, judging from what I have seen of Mossi women abroad, this belief is substantially correct. The only Mossi women observed working in fields alongside their husbands in Ghana or the Ivory Coast were the wives of men who had become sedentary farmers or who had planned to spend most of their working life outside the Upper Volta. A few of the wives of migrants who remained in the urban areas sold foodstuffs at the urban markets, but the rest remained at home and took care of their households. Mossi women in the Upper Volta, and the men too, believe that Mossi women abroad are treated better by Mossi men than those who stay home. The reason they give for this opinion is that the men fear that mistreated wives would run off and become the wives of more affluent and more sedentary Mossi men. Such men are allegedly always on the lookout for Mossi women as "wives" because they hesitate to marry foreign women whose matrilineal kinship systems would preclude them from owning the children and taking them back to Mossi country if they ever decided to return home. Some wealthy Mossi men in Ghana are so anxious for Mossi wives that they have even succeeded in obtaining pogsiouré from chiefs in Mossi country.[30]

The beliefs of Mossi women about life outside their country are not unjustified. They are constantly reinforced by the reports of women who occasionally visit migrant relatives in foreign areas, and by the behavior of Mossi women who have lived for a long time in those areas and who, when they return, not only wear luxurious clothes but refrain from cultivating. Even so, in the absence of serious domestic problems, Mossi women do not willingly migrate. Like the men, they are tied to their kin, their chiefs, and their country by strong bonds, and, given the opportunity, would rather go to Ouagadougou than elsewhere if circumstances forced them to leave home.

Those Mossi men who migrated to foreign areas have had expatriate Mossi chiefs to take care of many of their needs and help them adjust to their new situation. These men were often relatives of the traditional Mossi chiefs or of other officials, and had joined the ranks of migrant workers either as escapees from forced labor or as fugitives from French or Mossi justice. Some of these men or nobles, called *nakomcé*, worked alongside the migrant commoners and became indistinguishable from them.[31] Other nakomcé took advantage of their political status and established chiefdoms among the migrants. They were able to do so because of Mossi political beliefs and British colonial practice. The Mossi have always believed that men must have chiefs or life would be intolerable,[32] and while Father Mangin may have overstated the case when he wrote, "The power of the chiefs and the submission of their subjects are characteristic traits of Mossi country. The spirit of submission permeates the whole Mossi mentality,"[33] it is nevertheless true that the Mossi prefer to work under chiefs rather than as isolated individuals. Second, Mossi chieftainship was not tied to land, and the Mossi say, "A chief does not control land; he controls people." The nakomcé were able to establish themselves as *serkin* or headmen of their compatriots in the zongos of the larger towns, and in the villages of the cacao-producing areas of the Gold Coast. In time, many of the more than forty-two Mossi serkin in the Gold Coast made contact with the Mogho Naba of Ouagadougou and the other Mossi potentates, and obtained from them the *nam* or symbol of sovereignty over the migrants.[34]

The British government of the Gold Coast, with its penchant for in-direct rule, facilitated the establishment of Mossi chiefs and other "strangers' chiefs," for their presence made administration easier. The traditional chiefs of the Gold Coast, having lost ultimate power, either made alliances with the strangers' chiefs or simply tolerated them. The nature of French rule in the Ivory Coast, and the fact that the Mossi who went there were forced laborers rather than voluntary migrants, pre-cluded any serious development of Mossi chiefs in that country. Never-theless, there were a few Mossi chiefs in the Mossi settlements that the French tried to create in the Ivory Coast, and there were a number of them in the larger towns. But these men neither had the status nor played the role of their fellows in the Gold Coast.

The Mossi chiefs in the Gold Coast played an important mediating role between the migrants and the local population. Very often they functioned as labor recruiters for Ashanti chiefs and cacao farmers, since many migrants sought them out in order to find food, lodging, jobs, protection, and companionship. Even when most Mossi migrants found jobs on their own, they established relationships with Mossi chiefs so that they might have someone to protect them and look after their welfare in the event of trouble, sickness, or death. The migrants visited the chiefs whenever they could, giving them a few shillings and occa-sional help if the chiefs had cacao farms. The Mossi chiefs in turn were expected to—and did—come to the aid of migrants who had disputes over wages with their employers.

Of greater importance to Mossi society was the role that these ex-patriate Mossi chiefs played in maintaining affective ties between the migrants and their homeland. The chiefs created an affective community which made it possible for the migrants to work on the farms, in urban areas, and in the mines of the Gold Coast without coming into close contact with the local populations, or learning their languages or customs. Some mines even became known as "Mossi" mines because they were worked almost exclusively by Mossi migrants. Under these conditions, the seasonal migrants and even some, but not all, longer-term migrants were able to retain most of their traditional attitudes and values. The chiefs working in this context found it easy to police any deviants and even to impose sanctions on those who had fled prosecution in Mossi country. Many a migrant who had run away from the Upper Volta taking someone else's wife with him found to his dismay that the woman was to be seized by the local Mossi chief and returned home. Some of the chiefs of Mossi districts with large migratory populations were so closely linked to expatriate chiefs that they even sent them pogsiouré and local goods. The recipients of pogsiouré did not send their daughters back to the Upper Volta, but gave them to other Mossi, thus extending the nexus of relationships between the chiefs at home and their people abroad.

As a result of the close relations between the expatriate Mossi chiefs and the labor migrants, the latter introduced few if any political ideas into the Upper Volta. Returning migrants were so apolitical during World War II that they discarded in the woods the propaganda leaflets that agents of the Free French had persuaded them to carry across the border into their homeland. Moreover, prewar French rule was so different from that of the British that it was impossible for any political ideas that the migrants had absorbed in the Gold Coast to have any effect either on the French administration or on the traditional political organization of the Mossi. Those migrants who went to the Gold Coast during the postwar period of rapid political change were aware that something was happening when they saw posters in the towns and villages, observed political rallies, and heard sound trucks proclaiming the virtues of the various political parties. For the most part, however, the migrants took little interest in these things because they did not understand the languages involved. Those migrants who returned to the Upper Volta in 1956 and early in 1957 did speak of having heard of the "fight" between Kwame Nkrumah and the Asantehene of Ashanti, but they could not understand it. They could not understand, for example, how Nkrumah, a commoner, could aspire to control the Gold Coast government, as he was not a member of the royal family of Ashanti. But many migrants spoke quite seriously of Nkrumah's strength, saying that he was "stronger than a devil because he had no wife and did not have to eat" (he is given to long periods of fasting). A few of the long-term migrants who returned to Mossi country from the Gold Coast during this period spoke of having voted for "Islam," that is, in support of the Moslem Association Party. I encountered only one returnee who had voted for the Convention People's Party (CPP) of Nkrumah, but this young man had decided to live in the Gold Coast and had returned to Mossi country only because his elder brother had died and he had inherited his property. Interestingly enough, this young man, although a nobleman, had a history of being antichief before he left for the Gold Coast, and he continued to express opposition to the chiefs after his return. Nevertheless, he was powerless to act against the local chiefs because they had the support of the politicians and in turn supported them.

The Mossi political leaders of the Upper Volta took a special interest in the political events of the Gold Coast, not only because thousands of their people were there as labor migrants, but because their country faced somewhat similar problems. The Mogho Naba of Ouagadougou and the other traditional chiefs were quite concerned over the struggle between Nkrumah and the established chiefs, because the majority of the Mossi representatives in the French governmental bodies were commoners. One perceived the nature of these chiefs' concern when listening to their discussions of whether or not people without the nam should rule a country. The commoner elite, especially those who were members of the Rassemblement Démocratique Africain (a political party of West Africa headed by Félix Houphouet-Boigny of the Ivory Coast) saw in Nkrumah a prototype in the struggle against the chiefs as well as a model in gaining national independence. This struggle soon became of more than academic interest to all the Mossi, when Nkrumah, starting in 1956, expelled a number of Mossi serkin or expatriate chiefs from the Gold Coast. They had been caught in a political cross fire between Nkrumah and the Ashanti chiefs, and they were forced to leave the country. Behind this episode lay the fact that the Mossi chiefs, like most of the permanent and semipermanent residents of the Gold Coast, had become involved in the postwar nationalistic movement. They had supported Nkrumah in his "positive action" against the British, voted for the "Boys in Jail" when he was imprisoned,[35] and helped to elect Nkrumah "Leader of Government Business." But the split between Nkrumah and the Ashanti (with whom the Mossi chiefs had not only political but also important economic relationships based on their own relations with the labor migrants), led them to "Vote for Cacao," the rallying cry of the separatist National Liberation Movement. As a result, when the CPP won, Nkrumah deported such Mossi chiefs as Amama Moshie (Mossi), head of the Mossi community in Kumasi, even though this man claimed to have lived in that town for thirty years.[36] The Gold Coast (Ghana) government continued to deport Mossi chiefs who opposed it, and in a white paper the government accused them, among others, of "covertly participating in partisan politics," and defended its action in deporting them "on the grounds that their presence is not conducive to the public good." The government added its hope that by taking this drastic step it would make "Non-Ghanaians residing in this country . . . realize that their participation in political activities is unacceptable to the Government." [37]

The Mossi traditional chiefs and politicians in the Upper Volta found themselves in a dilemma over the expulsion of the chiefs of the migrant laborers. They disliked this attack on their fellows and on the institution of chieftainship, but they did not criticize Nkrumah openly for fear of being accused of joining the French administration of the Upper Volta in its disapproval of the pace of political evolution in the Gold Coast. The younger politicians saw the expulsion of the chiefs as an attempt by Nkrumah to break up an anachronistic alliance of chiefs—barriers to independence and parliamentary rule, as these young politicians saw it— but they said nothing for fear of antagonizing the French, the traditional Mossi chiefs, and the families of migrants whose relatives seemed to be left without support in the Gold Coast.

Political change in the Upper Volta between 1956 and 1959 sharpened the latent conflict between the Mossi chiefs and the commoner politicians. Both groups sought support among elements of the Upper Volta population, including the migrants in Ghana. The traditional chiefs had strong political relationships with those who controlled the migrant groups, but, as soon as the commoner politicians moved into administrative positions, they sent representatives down to Kumasi to safeguard the rights of the migrants. The young politicians used their position to full advantage. They said that the Mossi chiefs had had useful connections with the Ashanti chiefs, but that these connections were no longer useful, and reminded the migrants that Mossi chiefs had been expelled. The representatives of the migrants said that nowadays governments deal with governments, and that they were in Ghana to seek the interest of all Voltaics, Mossi and non-Mossi alike. Then, when commoner politicians of the Upper Volta finally wrested complete control from the chiefs, they invited the expatriates in the Gold Coast to send representatives to the Independence Day celebrations in Ouagadougou in August, 1960. There the visitors were entertained by the elected representatives and not by the chiefs, as had still been the custom as late as 1959. They saw how the newly elected president of the Upper Volta, though a Moaga (sing. of Mossi), ignored the Mogho Naba of Ouagadougou at receptions given in honor of the representatives. The traditional chiefs were chagrined by their treatment, but realized that in any power struggle the migrants would most likely side with the politicians. The latter, for their part, took pains to assure the expatriates and migrant leaders that the Upper Volta would come to their rescue if they were persecuted. "No longer," said one minister, "will persons of Voltaic origin be defenseless in foreign countries. Your rights will be guaranteed, by international treaties if need be." Both official and migrant representatives stressed the unity of Mossi and non-Mossi populations at home and in foreign areas, and spoke of the mutual responsibilities of these people and of the government of the Upper Volta.

The desire on the part of the Upper Volta government to ease the lot of the migrant workers in Ghana certainly contributed to its agreement with Ghana to abolish the customs barriers between the two countries, which had become independent but whose customs procedures had not changed since the colonial period. Many migrants, wishing to visit or return home, still saw their life savings and property reduced by punitive tolls. As a result, many of these persons continued to remain in Ghana longer than they wished, or tried to slip across the frontier, running the risk of being caught and punished. When the sentiment against customs barriers coincided with the wish of Ghana's president to foster bonds of unity among West African countries, action was taken. In May, 1961, the presidents of Ghana and the Upper Volta announced that "immediate effective measures will be taken to improve communications between their two countries and [that they] are considering the necessity of removing Customs barriers and any other barriers which impede contact between their people."[38] Hundreds of Mossi among the Voltaics working in Ghana journeyed to the frontier to acclaim both presidents when the protocols concerning these measures were finally signed in June, 1961.

The relationship between labor migration and changes in Mossi religious beliefs is quite clear, even though here again many forces were at work. The Mossi had adhered to their religion for several centuries, despite attacks by Islam, primarily because it supported their political structure.[39] Changes in one, they felt, would bring changes in the other. When they were defeated by the French, however, both Islam and Christianity were free to make converts among them.[40] Christianity came in as the religion of the conquerors, whereas Islam, long held at the gates by the Mossi political system, came in promising liberation from the whites if all the people became Muslims. In their struggle to convert the Mossi, the Muslims had more factors in their favor than the Christians. When labor migrations developed among the Mossi, more of them came into contact with Muslims than with Christians. The drivers of the trucks that took them to the Ivory Coast or to the Gold Coast were often Muslims, and Mossi pagans felt left out of the impromptu groups of strangers joined by religious bonds who shared their water supply. They were certainly left out of the groups that descended from the trucks to pray, and they were often made the butt of jokes by the Muslims. Pagans also were the prey of thieves who would not take the goods of coreligion- ists, and the migrants discovered that Muslims, whether Mossi or not, often received jobs from African Muslims looking for laborers. More- over, they saw that Muslim foremen included Muslim workers in their prayer groups and often invited them into their homes, and that these workers made more economic progress than their pagan fellows. Finally, the Mossi pagans were impressed by the fact that the Muslims, and often the Christians, took care of ill migrants, whereas an isolated pagan was not cared for when ill; if he died he was often unceremoniously buried in an unmarked grave.

The labor migrants' experiences with Muslims while out of the country made them highly susceptible to conversion. Interestingly enough, how- ever, few Mossi migrants became Muslims while away from home, pri- marily because they feared the wrath of pagan relatives if they should return with a new faith. Nevertheless, once they had returned with an awareness of the usefulness of Islam to migrants, many of them became willing followers of Mossi hadjis who had made the pilgrimage to Mecca and had returned as active proselytizers for their faith.

In contrast with Islam, Christianity made few inroads among the Mossi as a result of labor migration. The Mossi saw the missionaries as Euro- peans and as part of the colonial complex, even though the French administrators in the Upper Volta, when not altogether neutral to mis- sionaries, seldom gave them much support. As the Mossi had no notion of the true relationship between the administration and the Catholic missions, however, they fearfully turned over their children to the mis- sionaries who asked to educate them, regarding the missionaries as "recruiters" of children in the same sense as the administrators were recruiters of forced laborers. Some of the missions did not help their own cause by taking advantage of the political situation in which the Mossi found themselves. Delavignette[41] reported that under the guise of con- verting the Mossi to Christianity, many missionaries coerced them into making bricks for churches, with the result that many of the migrant laborers had the same negative attitude toward the missionaries as they did toward the administration. The relations of the migrants with Christians in the Ivory Coast and the Gold Coast were not conducive to changing these attitudes. First of all, the only Christians with whom the migrants came into contact in the Ivory Coast were the French planters for whom they worked, and the regime of forced labor was not likely to foster warm personal relations. The situation in the Gold Coast was different but had the same results. Here, according to Rouch, the concept of the *catholique-crapule*, or debauched Catholic, was so strong that pagan Mossi migrants avoided Catholics as much as possible. Further, he reports, so strong was the hostility toward and the suspicion of Catholics that when "they are in the Gold Coast, Mossi Christians, rather than tolerate the vexatious ridicule of the coastal Muslims, prefer to side with the Muslims and follow Islamic rituals for appearance's sake."[42] Thus, in contrast with Islam, which was seen as a religion conducive to the establishment of wider contacts for the migrants, Christianity, in this instance Catholicism, was regarded as detrimental to the forging of helpful ties. The Catholic missionaries in Mossi country became aware of these problems, and in about 1955 began to imitate the Muslims in many ways. For example, they began to encourage Catholics to migrate together and to pray alongside the road in the manner of Muslims, but with their faces turned toward their church. Catholic missionaries also reported the existence of—or plans to establish—reception centers for Catholic migrants both in the Ivory Coast and in the Gold Coast. By so doing, they hoped to prevent their converts from joining Islam, and also to provide for Mossi pagans an alternative to Islam as a source of help and comfort while away from home. It is perhaps too early to say whether or not the Catholics will be successful in their attempt to gain as many converts as Islam among the Mossi migrants.

Summary and Conclusions

The phenomenon of labor migration among the Mossi does not differ fundamentally from that found in other parts of Africa. The Mossi, like many other African populations, first went to work in the mines, plantations, and urban and industrial centers outside their homeland because of the need to pay taxes imposed by the French after conquest. In contrast with many other populations, however, including many in the Upper Volta, the Mossi showed no initial hesitation in migrating for work or even in being taken as corvée laborers, because their tradition included trading journeys and corvée labor for the chiefs. Subsequent decision on the part of French colonial administrators to use Mossi society as "a reservoir of manpower" did disturb the Mossi people, and many of them left for the neighboring colony of the Gold Coast where they were free from political oppression and able to bargain with their employers for wages. The French later modified labor recruitment in the Upper Volta and finally abolished it altogether, but by that time labor migration had become so institutionalized among the Mossi that they continued to migrate for work. This continued migration is now a source of concern to the African government of the Upper Volta.

The relationship of labor migration to changes in Mossi society is rather complex, as migration is only one of the forces that have affected the society. Furthermore, these forces have tended to support one another. For example, the Mossi needed money to pay taxes, and therefore men were compelled to migrate for work. Because they had to leave at a certain time of the year, however, they cut down on the cultivation of cotton, the one crop desired by the French, because it interfered with their migratory pattern. When the migrants brought back cotton cloth from foreign areas, it became so valued by the people that the need for it became a further incentive to migrate. The demand for foreign cotton cloth in turn led to a corresponding decline in cotton production.

The demand for European cotton cloth was only one change induced by migration. As the young men traveled they brought home new products which aroused the interest of other people and drove them to migrate too. A similar process of change may be observed among other Mossi institutions. When labor migration undermined the structural basis of the Mossi marriage system, the lineage elders endeavored to retain the system nevertheless. They were prevented from doing so because (1) they no longer had exclusive control over the wealth of the society; (2) the traditional sanctions against runaway wives had lost their validity; and (3), of major importance, the French government supported by law the desire of a number of young people to choose spouses for themselves.

Similarly, the political institutions of the Mossi people were affected by a combination of factors such as labor migration, the policies of the French, and the work of the missionaries. Many Mossi families resented the role of chiefs as labor recruiters for the French administration, even while looking to these chiefs to secure and maintain relations with Mossi chiefs in foreign areas who helped the voluntary labor migrants. Yet when educated Mossi who were not migrants attacked the position of the traditional Mossi chiefs, the latter found that they got no support from the expatriate chiefs whose power, too, had been shorn by commoner nationalists in Ghana.

Finally, defeat by the French left Mossi society relatively open to inroads from both Christianity and Islam—forces the Mossi had resisted for centuries because they would have undermined the religion that supported their political organization. Both Christians and Muslims made attempts to convert the Mossi people, but Islam has made relatively more progress than Christianity, especially among former migrants, because the latter see in Islam a religious ideology which unites them with vast numbers of persons among whom they have traveled and worked. In contrast, the image of the Catholic is such that Catholic migrants very often hide their identity, and few migrants return with the idea that it is desirable to be a Christian.

By way of conclusion, it may be stated that while the Mossi were initially forced to migrate for work to earn wages to pay taxes, they now migrate voluntarily because only by so doing can they satisfy many of the new needs they have acquired over the past sixty years. And unless the Upper Volta makes great economic strides in the near future, Mossi young men will continue to leave their homes in order to earn money. Seen in this way, migration does provide the means whereby the Mossi people have adjusted to some aspects of their changing society. On the other hand, migration by no means helps them to adjust to all the institutional changes that are taking place. For the most part these changes were stimulated by Europeans, but were supported in turn by conditions in Mossi country brought about by migration. The cumulative effect of all these changes is that Mossi society is changing at an unprecedented rate. It is possible that in time economic development may permit the Mossi to remain at home and not migrate; however, the changes that accompanied migration will probably continue and contribute to the rapid urbanization of the Upper Volta.

6.

OSHOGBO–AN URBAN COMMUNITY?

by William B. Schwab

Introduction

It is my aim in this paper to discuss some of the conceptual and practical problems of urbanization in Africa as they have appeared in one community, Oshogbo, a precolonial Yoruba town in Nigeria.*

The towns of Africa are very diverse. At one extreme are those typified by the Copperbelt towns of Northern Rhodesia or the commercial centers of Southern Rhodesia which have been created in the last half century solely by Europeans, and have grown mainly in response to the needs of a European market economy. Their African populations are tribally heterogeneous, migrant, and frequently transient. In almost all these towns the social and economic separations that exist between color groups provide a pervasive and predominant theme underlying social relationships. The social matrix of these towns is an industrialized wage-earning system that defines and delimits the social fields in which an African can act.[1] The transition from the rural economy to full-scale urban industrialism is abrupt and discontinuous. The moment an African enters town he must behave as a townsman, at least in some situations. He may also carry with him into town tribal customs and beliefs, but he must utilize them within the context defined by the industrialized system itself.

At the other extreme are towns that were established before systematic contact with the West. The Yoruba towns of Nigeria are a prime example. They are characterized by an indigenous population core which is substantially homogeneous. Migrations play little or no part in their development. The effects of Western industrial civilization have been less direct and more diluted than in towns created and maintained by Europeans. There are no permanent European settlers, and no alienation of land to outsiders has taken place. The economy has expanded but subsistence agriculture remains as its base. Yet changes have occurred. There

---

* I am indebted to the British Social Research Council for their generous financial and other support of the study of Oshogbo.

[1] For notes to chapter 6, see page 191.

have been shifts to a market system which had wide implications for the structuring of relationships throughout the social system. Western values and associations have also been introduced through formal education and the teachings of Christian missionaries. Western modes of behavior and thought have been carried by radio, newspaper, and cinema, and by those who have traveled into the wider world. In most instances the traditional framework has not been able to contain the new sets of interests and values. But the changes that have occurred are substantially within the traditional social system, and there have been no radical departures from traditional social behavior, no violent upheavals in institutions.

Notwithstanding the clear differences between these polar types of African towns, it is equally apparent that they exhibit important similarities. Both have a high population density and increasing social and economic specialization. The underlying factors causing social change—colonial rule, industrialization, or commerce—are basically similar. Moreover, their social systems are characterized by fluidity in social norms and values and by shifting alliances and conflicting loyalties which so often result from the interaction of different and sometimes competing sets of interest.

The striking similarities and equally patent differences among African towns pose critical problems for interpretations of African urbanization. Do we in fact conform to social reality when we group all the densely populated centers under a single heading of urban Africa? Does urbanism inevitably subvert and destroy traditional social forms and impose a uniform and characteristic conformation of its own? To put it another way, do the demands of urbanism itself reinforce certain modes of behavior and kinds of relationships and exclude others? If so, we are within legitimate bounds if we tend to see urbanization in Africa as a relatively uniform social process. We must also ask, however, if what we have labeled in general as African urbanization may not, in fact, involve quite different and distinct processes. It may be that, because we stress the common elements in African towns, many of the inner processes have eluded us. The peoples of Africa have widely varied socioeconomic and political heritages. The rate and the intensity of urbanization have not been uniform for each geographic area. We also cannot ignore the probability that certain areas of social life have much more tenacity or are much more resilient than others, depending on factors that we may not yet fully understand, and that this aspect too may vary from one social system to another. We may therefore expect a very wide range of variations both in the amount and the kind of disruption and in the adaptability of different social systems to the influences of urbanization. What might appear then to be an inevitable concomitant of urbanization in one part of Africa might not be so in another area where traditional principles of social organization and social forms differ.

There is need for a better understanding of the term "urban." What is at issue here is whether we have already isolated or will be able to isolate conceptually a specifically urban social system exhibiting characteristics that mark it as a distinctive form of human group life. Which factors, including the demographic and the ecological, are critical for urbanism? Can we realistically distinguish an urban way of life from the industrial economic mode? Can social characteristics typically associated with densely populated communities arise in quite different ecological and demographic conditions? Finally, is this urban concept scientifically useful in the sense that it can lead us to a better understanding of the social processes involved in the development of African towns? There are many questions and not enough answers. In the following pages I examine some of the processes at work in the changing social relationships as they appeared in one Yoruba town, Oshogbo, and appraise the underlying factors in these relationships. In particular, I want to evaluate these changing patterns in relationship to the emergence of characteristics that have been commonly regarded as specifically urban elsewhere in the world.

Ecology of Oshogbo

There are today about 5 million Yoruba living in the southwestern part of Nigeria.[2] They are divided into various subgroups, geographically separated and distinguished by slight nuances in cultural usage and dialect.[3] Yet, although the Yoruba are aware of their differences and occasionally exploit them for political or other ends, they are united by a substantially homogeneous culture.

In one sense the Yoruba towns are a unique phenomenon in Africa south of the Sahara. The high proportion of town dwellers to the total population is probably unequaled in tropical Africa. If the term "town" is defined statistically and applied to compact centers of more than 10,000 persons, then more than 35 per cent of the Yoruba population is town-dwelling,[4] and in some of the more densely populated areas there is an even higher proportion of town dwellers.[5] Some of the existing towns are very old. Portuguese travelers of the early sixteenth century mention the towns of Ife and Ijebu-Ode. Most of the existing towns, however, were probably founded in the eighteenth and nineteenth centuries. The early history of the Yoruba is obscure. Yoruba myths tell of their descent from Heaven to the present site of Ife, and their proliferation from Ife into a great kingdom. Historians [6] surmise, however, that the ancestors of the present-day Yoruba made their way southward from an unknown site to their present abode in one or more waves. An elaborate political and military organization linking the Yoruba community developed, and several great kingdoms evolved. The eighteenth and nineteenth centuries were marked by periods of internal strife. Wars with Dahomey, and the Fulani invasion of the nineteenth century, coupled with civil strife, resulted in the disintegration of the powerful ancient kingdoms and the formation of smaller, more independent chiefdoms. Many of the existing Yoruba towns were founded by refugee populations during these tribal wars. The newer towns also were by no means isolated sovereign states; they were linked by political and military alliances and economic and kinship bonds. Nevertheless, the Yoruba tended to see their communities as permanent, self-contained economic and social entities. Most activities were carried out within the framework of community life, and a man was expected to grow up, marry, rear his children, and die in his natal community, except when disasters forced him to migrate.

Oshogbo was one of the main termini for refugees fleeing southward from the Fulani. It had been founded about 1800 by a dissident Ijesha chief and a small band of his followers. During the Fulani wars its population was swelled by refugees who were predominantly Oyo Yoruba. Oshogbo today is regarded as an Oyo Yoruba town, and has a population exceeding 120,000 persons.[7] It was built up in a low-lying range of hills in an area transitional from the tropical rain-forest belt to the south and the orchard bush country to the north. Its present site is about a mile from the banks of the Oshun River, which had been the main source of water supply to the community[8] and is, in addition, the home of Oshun, goddess of fertility and patroness of the Oshogbo people. Oshogbo, now a political and economic center for surrounding communities, lies on the main Lagos-to-Kano road through Nigeria, and was for many years the northern terminus of the railroad that now extends from Lagos to Kano. It is also a nodal point for a system of local roads extending to surrounding towns, and is the seat for the administrative officers for Oshun, Ife, and Ilesha divisions.

The land claimed by Oshogbo is divided into town land proper and farmland. Town land comprises an area 2 to 3 miles in radius. Oshogbo people say that this area was formerly enclosed by a mud wall. There is today a small mound at the edge of town which supports this claim. Oshogbo farmland extends for as little as 2 miles to as much as 10 miles on all sides of the town. The majority of Oshogbo men even today are farmers, living in town and farming these peripheral lands. Some make a daily journey to and fro, but where the farms are distant men may spend several days at a time in shelters on their farms. The boundaries between Oshogbo farmland and the farmland of other towns are not clearly defined, and over the years have been an almost constant source of friction and litigation.

Although it would be an exaggeration to say that the spatial configuration of Oshogbo is a physical representation of the existing social structure, much of the social life of the community is reflected in its design. The palace of the paramount chief *(oba)*—Oshogbo's political and spiritual core—is centrally located at the junction of the town's two major thoroughfares. Directly opposite, epitomizing modern government, are the court and treasury buildings. Nearby is the Oshun Temple which enshrines the spirits of the traditional protective deities of Oshogbo. The central mosque and the market of the oba, the largest market in Oshogbo and the primary locus of community interaction, are also located at this crossroad.

There are four distinct settlement zones in Oshogbo. The indigenous core of Oshogbo—the Native Quarter—extends on all sides of the oba's palace. It comprises more than three-fourths of the town area, and in it live more than 90 per cent of the Oshogbo people. The initial impression here is one of formlessness, of the absence of any dominating features. The Native Quarter appears as a labyrinth of red lateritic mud buildings, unpaved roads and footpaths, small stalls and markets. But this appearance is deceiving. The Native Quarter itself is divided into smaller territorial units—quarters or wards. Each quarter, representing the extent of the administrative jurisdiction of a senior town chief, consists of a varying number of compounds, the Yoruba residential units. The traditional compound is usually composed of one or more one-story, sun-dried clay buildings. The buildings within a compound are usually adjacent and frequently built about one or more courtyards. The boundaries are sometimes marked by a blank mud wall; frequently there are no obvious boundaries between one compound and another, but they are invariably known to the inhabitants. In addition to living quarters a compound may include bathrooms, storage huts, work sheds for craftsmen, trading stalls, and shelters devoted to the worship of a traditional god, or a small mosque. Members of segments of one or more agnatic lineages, along with their wives and children, live in a compound. There are 570 compounds in the Native Quarter of Oshogbo, and the size of the compound population may vary greatly. The smallest compound in our sample[9] was composed of 15 persons; there were 450 persons in the largest.

Despite the overwhelming preponderance of the traditional type of Yoruba compound in the Native Quarter, there is also visible evidence of social change. Public mosques, churches, and schools are distributed throughout the area. There is a government hospital with reasonably modern facilities. Modern multiple-story houses have been built on compound land. Near the main arteries of commerce and routes of travel, the compounds are somewhat more congested and densely populated than those on the outskirts of the town.[10] This differential population distribution is at least partly attributable to the preferential economic location near the center of town.[11]

Yet, in overall appearance, the internal structure of the Native Quarter of Oshogbo seems to have been little modified in the last half century. There is, however, ample evidence of commercialization and economic growth on the main Lagos-to-Kano road which almost bisects Oshogbo. Lining both sides of this road—known as Station Road—are nearly 250 small trading stores. Most are owned by Yoruba who have recently migrated to Oshogbo because of its commercial potential. European trading concerns, various government offices, a library, the railway station, the police station, and a bus and lorry depot are established along Station Road.

Near Station Road and on the outskirts of town is an area composed almost entirely of modern multiple-story houses and known as the Foreign Quarter. Government clerks, teachers, shop owners, employees of European concerns, and transient laborers have made their homes here. Almost none are natives of Oshogbo, although most are Yoruba; almost all are better educated and more affluent than the average Oshogbo man. In another area, far from the center of town, is a Hausa settlement inhabited solely by Hausa traders and cattle dealers. Thus there are today in Oshogbo, as in most cities, segregated residential areas depending upon ethnic and economic or educational criteria.[12] Differential value is attached to location, and there is competition for economically advantageous sites. Yet these separate and special areas seem to have been grafted onto the indigenous community, whose central core remains relatively homogeneous and unmarked by extensive differentiation and separation on the basis of economic, educational, or ethnic criteria.

The Traditional Oshogbo Social System

There are, I think, several levels of relationship to be considered in the analysis of the traditional Oshogbo social system. There are, first, the forces for local aggregation and cohesion on the community level, which include notions of community solidarity and loyalty, the position of the chiefs, and the administrative and jural processes which succeed in welding a large aggregate into a coherent social entity. Second, there are the ties of descent and the associated corporate groups. Descent was traced in the agnatic line and the most important unit was the corporate exogamous patrilineage. Finally, there are the bonds created by common residence.

The Oshogbo traditional political structure was based upon a centralized administrative and jural apparatus, pyramidally organized, which defined the channels of responsibility and authority. Final authority and responsibility were vested in a paramount chief (oba) in Oshogbo entitled *atoaja*. He was the ultimate judicial, military, and administrative authority; he was also a sacred king and the supreme ritual leader. Subordinate to the oba were a series of ranked lines of chiefs, some of whose titles carried specific military, administrative, or ritual and religious duties. Others apparently had no clearly specified functions. The senior chiefs formed the Inner Council, which advised the oba on matters of community interest. The minor chiefs were grouped into the Outer Council, which performed many of the administrative functions. The major chiefs also administered the somewhat amorphous groups of compounds which tended to cluster in the vicinity of a chief's compound. The subdivision of Oshogbo into wards, introduced by the British in the early part of the twentieth century, may be seen as the modern counterpart of this older, less formal system of local grouping.

Most of the chieftaincy titles—and all the senior ones—were hereditary within one or more agnatic lineages.[18] These titles were held corporately by the lineage groups, with every male member of the lineage equally eligible, in principle, for office. The members of lineages with rights to political office were accorded superior social position because of the belief that the office was not conferred on an individual, but was vested in a patrilineage of which an incumbent chief was the representative. The members of these lineages also had the right to benefit from a chief's economic prerogatives, which might be considerable. Political power, social position, and economic privilege were thus joined and, in Oshogbo, were determined by birth and concentrated in the hands of a relatively few lineage groups.

Chief and commoner were bound by rigidly prescribed obligations and rights. Each member of the community acknowledged the final, jural, and economic authority of the paramount chief, and owed him total loyalty, taxes, tribute, and military support. In turn, the paramount chief was expected to protect the community from the threat of external injury, and was responsible for its spiritual, economic, and political wellbeing. The atoaja's power was upheld by more than merely the sanction of force. He was also the supreme head of all religious organizations and cults in the community, and symbolized in his person the unity and exclusiveness of Oshogbo. Much of his political power was derived from his spiritual and ritual roles, and these also served to prevent abuses of power and ensured the performance of political obligations. Consequently the stability and solidarity of the community resided in the position of the paramount chief.

The most important single principle of organization in traditional

Oshogbo was kinship. Every facet of life, institutional and individual, was regulated and coördinated, to a greater or lesser extent, by the comprehensive body of legal and moral norms that constituted the Yoruba kinship system. Apart from the usual differentials of sex and age, kinship affiliation was the primary determinant of a person's jural, economic, political, and ritual status. This does not mean that governmental processes were carried out only by kin units, or that religious or economic relationships and residential associations were completely inseparable from those of kinship. Over a wide range of social behavior, however, kinship relationships and political, economic, and religious relationships were, in fact, inseparable; the Yoruba kinship system was the primary articulating factor in community life.

The Oshogbo kinship system was based on segmentary lineages.[14] The most important unit was the exogamous, corporate patrilineage *(idile)* defined by reference to its remotest acknowledged male ancestor and embracing all the agnatic descendants of its founder.[15] The lineage structure was based on two distinct but closely related principles. The first was the principle of corporateness, based on common agnatic descent, which implied group unity, exclusiveness, continuity, and an authority structure. The second was the principle of internal segmentation. The internal segments were hierarchically articulated and characterized by differentiation in terms of both descent and function. The segments of a lineage had varying degrees of internal autonomy, and the rights, duties, and privileges vested in it were limited and prescribed by the wider segments of which it was a component, and by its lesser segments.

Residence was patrilocal and virilocal, and each lineage, or segment, shared a common residence or compound. Rights to town land were granted by the oba to a lineage and held by it in perpetuity. The solidarity of the kin group also implied reciprocal obligations and common interest in marriage, which was ideally polygynous. Each marriage was regarded primarily as a relationship between two mutually exclusive bodies of kin, and only secondarily as a union between a man and a woman. Most marriages were arranged by kin; none could take place without the aid and consent of the lineages of the bride and the groom. Divorce was rare, and, should serious marital difficulties develop, there were strong sanctions available to a lineage to force a husband or a wife into accepted social behavior.

In the spiritual world as well, lineage affiliation played an important role. There were two separate aspects of Yoruba religious beliefs. The first, and more important, was ancestor worship. Yoruba believed in the power and influence of ancestors over the lives of their descendants, and in reincarnation whereby ancestors were reborn into their earthly lineages. The notions of lineage cohesion and temporal continuity, which were central to these ideas, provided one of the most important bases for lineage reciprocities. Further, the elaborate rituals associated with ancestor worship, performed at graves in the lineage home,[16] served as both a source and an expression of lineage unity. The most powerful sanctions in Yoruba society were derived from ancestor worship. The most serious punishment conceivable to a Yoruba was the loss of rights to ancestor communion and its protection, for it involved not only danger here on earth but also the threat of eternal misfortune and the loss of the right to reincarnation. This sanction was invoked only for the two most serious crimes in Yoruba society—incest and murder.

In addition to ancestor worship, each lineage served a common deity (*orisha*).[17] What is important to note here is that, although a lineage tended to worship a single orisha, an orisha cult and a patrilineal unit were not coextensive. The cults thus served to link lineages that might otherwise have no common interests or relationships, and were the only other significant associational units outside kin and residence[18] in Oshogbo. The head of a cult was appointed by the paramount chief and given the rank of a minor chief.

Over a wide sphere of activity, kin and economic relationships were congruent. The occupational structure of the community, the organization of production, and the utilization of resources, as well as motivation for work, were largely regulated by the lineage system. For most males occupation was prescribed by lineage affiliation. Most were subsistence cultivators exchanging whatever surplus they had from domestic consumption and ritual or social obligations for clothing, utensils, ritual objects, or religious or healing services. Oshogbo also had its hunters, skilled artisans, artists and entertainers, doctors and diviners. Lineage affiliation, on the other hand, played little part in the occupations of women. Most of the women helped their husbands on farms. Some followed craft occupations, such as weaving or dyeing, and others were petty traders hawking their husbands' surplus agricultural produce or craft products through the markets.

There was little difference between the farming and other lineages in the organization of productive units and the utilization of resources. Rights to farmland were held corporately by a lineage whose members exercised control over its inheritance. Each member was entitled to an equitable share of farmland—a right passed on from father to sons—and to the economic benefits derived from his labor. Similarly, in other occupations, tools and equipment, skills and knowledge were passed down from generation to generation and guarded from outsiders.

The basic work and consumption unit comprised a father and his sons; but economic relationships in terms of exchange of services and goods extended beyond this unit to the entire group of patrikin. A lineage had collective responsibility for the contribution of goods and services to marriage and funeral ceremonies. It shared in the execution of ancestral and other rituals. It provided for the care of the aged and indigent, and offered its services during peak farming periods for the construction of a house or any other weighty task undertaken by a member.

The jural and ritual head of a lineage was its senior surviving male. He was representative and spokesman of his lineage to the wider society. He was expected to protect the interests of his lineage against those of other lineages, or from abuses by chiefs. It was his duty to speak on behalf of any person or group of persons within his lineage involved in an external dispute or accused of an offense. He bore the responsibility for maintaining internal harmony in the lineage and for arbitrating disputes between individuals or component segments of the lineage. He officiated at ancestral and other rituals. He was also the ultimate authority in the economic organization of his lineage, and had the right to revoke or alter any important decisions made by lineage members concerning marriage, funerals, rituals, or economic activities. An informal council of elders composed of the senior men of a lineage acted as his advisers and aided him in carrying out necessary administrative functions. Various religious, especially ancestral, sanctions, in addition to economic and other secular penalties, supported the authority of a lineage head.

Between the lineage system and the centralized authority there was no real political cleavage. In many affairs, such as accession to political office, as we have seen, marriage, control of resources, or inheritance, lineages discharged manifestly political activities. Insofar as the political activities were consistent with traditional norms, so long as no one made an appeal from a decision of his lineage, the central government did not interfere with or reduce the lineage's autonomy. Nevertheless, the central authority served to minimize the range and type of conflicts between lineages, and, if genuine hostilities emerged between lineages, it exercised its right to adjudicate. The articulation of the formal political authority and the lineage system was, however, most clearly demonstrated in matters of explicit social control. If a man committed a crime against society, the central government apprehended and punished him. As notions of corporate solidarity, however, also imply corporate responsibility, the patrikin group had joint responsibility for guilt. Hence the lineage of an offender was punished as well. In addition, the offender was brought before the lineage head for judgment and received further appropriate punishment. Ancestral and other religious ceremonies were performed to help expiate the crime for the lineage. Legally and morally an individual could not be isolated from his kin group.

Although a patrilineage was the most significant of the units formed on the basis of descent, the web of kinship extended beyond its range. We consider first the ties of clanship. Wherever possible, a lineage lived in a single compound. If the population of a compound increased, however, so that its land resources became inadequate, a segment of the lineage would separate and establish a new compound. If possible, the branch was located close to the parent compound. But bonds that derived from common residence and daily intimacy were not so effective between lineage segments living apart. As time lapsed, the bonds became more attenuated and, in extreme cases, the segments were held together only by vague notions of common agnatic descent and the rule of exogamy which derived exclusively from alleged common ancestry. Yoruba give the name *omolebi* to the genealogical unit formed by these more or less loosely bound lineage segments, the Yoruba clan.

Although the greater part of a person's status was derived from a father and transmitted to sons, a person also maintained ties with his mother's patrilineage. Many of the same rights and obligations that characterized lineage relationships could be granted an individual related through a woman, but remained latent except in times of unusual stress and when the mutual bonds of sentiment were strong.

Although the ties of kinship and the corporate groups based on them were of paramount importance in structuring relationships in traditional Oshogbo, the Yoruba formed other units based on territorial association as well. These two sets of relationships—those of kinship and those of territory—intersected at many points but were not necessarily identical. The residential system was, to a very large extent, based on kinship. The membership of a compound was composed of the adult male members of one or more lineages, of their wives and children, and occasionally of strangers unrelated by blood or marriage. The adult males formed a corporate group known as an *omole*. Where a compound was composed of only one lineage segment, the *de facto* lineage and the omole were identical. In present-day Oshogbo, however, half of the compounds have two or more lineages, and older men insist that multilineage compounds were equally prevalent in the past.

The most important functions of the omole were political. The head of the omole, entitled *bale*, was the senior male. He was advised and assisted by a council of elder men of the resident lineages. The omole allocated compound land for both domestic and working purposes, collected taxes, determined the contribution of goods and services to chiefs, and ascertained and expressed political allegiances. But perhaps its most important function was to reduce and control conflict between its component lineages.

The authority of the omole was based largely on sentiments of unity and common need. A man's daily intercourse was chiefly with members of his omole. It was to them as well as to his kin that he turned when he needed economic help, solace in misfortune, assistance in marriage payments, aid in farm work, or merely guidance in everyday affairs. Frequently one lineage in an omole extended special rights and preferences to another, permitting its members to cultivate their farmlands, participate in important religious rites, or perform major roles in funeral or marriage ceremonies. The extension of lineage sentiments, rights, and obligations to nonlineage omole members was further expressed by the fact that marriage between omole members rarely occurred and was frowned upon, although such a marriage, strictly speaking, was not a breach of customary law. There was thus a bond of fellowship among omole members based on common associations and experiences, reciprocal services, and common loyalties which united this often multilineage unit into a coherent social entity.

This, then, was the Oshogbo traditional social system. Oshogbo was a large, dense, and permanent settlement of people organized around a central political authority which protected its citizens from outside threats and reduced or minimized tensions and conflicts in the community, so that a large population could live in a small area. It had a partly autonomous law. Farming was commercialized to the extent that agricultural surpluses were traded for goods and services. Although there was little ethnic heterogeneity, people were differentiated, at least on the basis of skill, occupation, and political rank. If we were to follow many of the typologies of urbanism, we would be compelled to admit that traditional Oshogbo satisfied most of, if not all, the requisites for an urban community.[19] Yet, if we look beyond these criteria, it is obvious that the patterns of behavior and the social relationships of traditional Oshogbo bore little if any resemblance to those customarily associated with urban communities. Oshogbo had a kin-bound social structure. The rules of kinship regulated and coördinated social behavior in almost all spheres of activity. The corporate lineage was an integrated economic unit and a primary agency of social control. Agnatic descent determined political rank and religious affiliation, and was the basis for residential association. Relationships tended to be conceived in terms of corporate lineage groups rather than in terms of individual interaction.

The notion, then, that patterns of behavior and the form and content of social relationships are inevitably derived from certain ecological and demographic features is clearly contrary to fact in Oshogbo. These features may be requisites for an urban social system or an urban way of life, but they certainly do not determine it.

The Present Oshogbo Social System

In 1900 the first Christian missionaries arrived in Oshogbo, and Oshogbo had its first direct contact with Western ways of life. Shortly thereafter, Muslim proselytizers, penetrating southward from Fulani and Hausa lands, began efforts at conversion which eventually met with considerable success. Today, at least nominally, the vast majority—about 80 per cent—of Oshogbo people consider themselves to be Muslims. Somewhat less than 15 per cent are Christians, although Christianity is the most prestigious religion, and the remainder still adhere exclusively to traditional religious beliefs.[20] It has been possible to become affiliated to Muslim groups without relinquishing certain fundamental traditional beliefs and practices. Thus, for example, Muslim converts may continue to have polygynous marriages, if they can afford it. Perhaps the most serious impediment to the expansion of Christianity in Oshogbo was the insistence of the church leaders that the dead be interred in churchyards instead of in their traditional burial spots in their compounds. Yoruba see this practice as abandoning the spirits of the dead to wander unprotected and unattended in the bush. Moreover, the ancestral spirits would then be unable to exert their protective and beneficent influence over their descendants. The Muslim religion, on the other hand, did not dictate the burial places for the deceased. Yoruba say that this particular difference between the two religions accounts for much of the numerical preponderance of Muslims over Christians. But because the Christians are, in general, better organized and more literate, wealthy, and skilled in ways of the West, they exert an influence in the community which is quite disproportionate to their numbers.

Almost immediately upon their arrival in Oshogbo, the Christian missionaries established schools. Much more recently, government schools have been built. Although the number of children who attend schools is relatively small, formal education has been an important factor for social change. It has provided literacy and new skills for a few. But of more importance is the fact that it introduced an approach to situations quite different from those held in the traditional culture, and therefore provided important conceptual and moral bases for social changes.

By 1905 colonial administration was firmly established in the community. Its introduction had two immediate effects. First, it removed the ultimate power and responsibility for the maintenance of social order from the hands of the chief and vested it in the colonial administration, while maintaining the administrative machinery very nearly intact. As a consequence, the paramount chief was placed at the intersection of two political systems with frequently opposed interests. On the one hand, he was representative of his people against the central government; on the other, he was required to be an agent of the government. His position was equivocal and the relationships between chief and commoners became marked by considerable ambiguity. Second, colonial administration provided various alternative channels of authority, such as formalized courts, which tended to render traditional channels somewhat less effective. Shorn of much of his traditional warranty, the chief could no longer claim complete allegiance or control the various conflicts between lineages based either on old divisions or on new interests. Further, as the society changed, new areas of conflict arose in which there was no precedent for the chief's intervention, and new sources of social control were sought. The central government did not, however, encroach upon the ritual and mystical values attached to the chieftaincy, and the paramount chief has remained the traditional symbol of unity. In 1936 a formal native authority was established in which the rights and obligations of the administrative personnel were defined and delimited. Composed originally of chiefs, only later was it expanded to include appointed and then elected members. It thus opened avenues for political control and for the exercise of power which had hitherto been closed to the wider community. It also permitted the development of political competition which had hitherto been contained by the closed system of political ranking and by the power of the oba.

In 1905 other major events occurred when railway and telegraph lines were extended to Oshogbo from the port of Lagos. Thereafter, for a number of years, Oshogbo was the northern terminus of the railroad. Because of its fortunate economic situation, it very quickly became the center for European commercial houses and for wide-scale trading activities. These events marked the beginning of a widely ramifying change in the economic life of the community. The traditional methods of trading by barter or with cowrie shells were replaced by a more appropriate monetary basis. New avenues of occupation were opened, which were quite independent of lineage affiliation. European firms and governmental agencies needed clerks, buyers, and laborers. Garages, motor-repair shops, and building contractors provided a variety of jobs to be filled. The increased availability and desire for goods and tools encouraged the emergence of small traders, and the marketing of goods involved a complex network of local and foreign middlemen, wholesalers, and retailers. New craft occupations—carpentry, tailoring, and goldsmithing, for example—emerged to help supply the increased wants of the people. Today nearly a third of the adult males in Oshogbo are engaged in occupations that have developed since 1900.[21] Nearly 60 per cent of the adult males are farmers, and the remainder pursue traditional occupations other than farming. The traditional craft occupations seem to have been able to adapt to changing conditions, and the relative numbers of traditional craftsmen do not seem to have diminished considerably.[22] The expanded economic activity of the town attracted some migrants from the surrounding Yoruba towns to Oshogbo to work as laborers, traders, or in other capacities. Cash crops such as cocoa, groundnuts, and cotton were introduced, and agricultural production was characterized by a shifting emphasis from production for consumption to production for sale. Thus there is in Oshogbo today a full-fledged market system, with the wage and contractual ties that it implies, which operates side by side with the traditional ways of earning a living.

These are the main influences that initiated the widely ramified processes of social change in Oshogbo. What is of primary concern here, however, is the form and extent of the changes in the modes of ordering social relationships, and the similarities and differences between these modes and those of towns elsewhere.

Because kinship was the central institution in traditional Oshogbo and provided the predominant structure for ordering relationships, the transformation in kinship relationships which has accompanied Westernization is central to the social system of modern Oshogbo. For many years anthropologists and sociologists asserted that Westernization undermined and destroyed extended kinship systems. More recently, this assertion has been questioned, and there is a growing realization that extended kinship systems may be very resilient even under unusual transitional stress.[23] In Oshogbo there has certainly been a reduction in the scope of kinship rights and obligations. At the same time, kinship claims and loyalties persist and, although modified, the lineage system remains a primary focus of cohesion and source of stability and control. In addition there are new forms of social cohesion and solidarity which sometimes, but not always, express sets of relationships and interests which are antagonistic to traditional ones.

The reduction of solidarity of the kin group and of its authority and control over members is manifested on one level in increased cleavages and conflicts between individuals and between segments in a lineage. In the most extreme instance, a segment comprising a man and his sons may hive off from a lineage and form a separate economic, social, and residential unit. Such units are confined to the few who have achieved complete economic independence from their lineages and have accepted, in part at least, new values and norms so that they are able to tolerate more easily the psychosocial separation from their kin. For most individuals the break from traditional patterns is not so radical. Segments usually continue to live in their lineage compounds and remain within the jurisdiction of the wider group. The conflicts and separations are then expressed in terms of a sharper definition and assertion of individual and group rights within a lineage, and a corresponding decrease in the rights of wider groups. As an illustration, we consider the redistribution of rights over farmland, which remains the principal economic resource. Despite the fact that many men are leaving the farms to work in commerce, farmland has become scarcer because of the expanded value of cash crops and the desire for cash income. The emphasis on cash values has led to a heightened competition for access to lineage land among segments and, within segments, to competition and conflicts among brothers for land. Where the quantity of land is insufficient, relationships between segments or brothers may deteriorate into open conflict. The traditional rules of inheritance which had regulated the transmission of land rights are being ignored or modified to conform more closely to new economic interests. Moreover, although there has been no sale of farmland as yet, a lineage head is no longer able to exercise his final authority in matters of land transfer. In addition, the rights to all fruit-bearing trees on lineage land are being asserted by individuals on whose land the trees grow. This claim is especially pertinent in the case of cocoa and kola nut trees which previously belonged to the lineage and are now an important source of money income. In short, the principles of a market economy and land shortage have brought about cleavages and conflicts that are being resolved at the expense of lineage integrity. It is important to emphasize, however, that separation and competition between segments are intrinsic to any segmentary lineage system. What has happened in Oshogbo is that previously existing fissile tendencies within the lineage system have been exacerbated by modern conditions.

The establishment of alternative economic avenues, in which the significance of kinship is slight, and the concurrent establishment of norms more appropriate to changing economic motives, have had additional repercussions on kinship relationships. The solidarity that obtains when lineage members are joined in the pursuit of common economic goals has lessened. Young men who traditionally would have followed lineage occupations are now attracted to newer and more remunerative ways of earning a living. Many of them have incomes that far surpass those of their elders, and have become financially independent of their lineages for economic status or financial aid. This situation has a number of implications. Wealth, poverty, and social status were, as we have seen, traditionally attributes of a lineage group. Differential income and upwardly mobile elements within a lineage imply a potential, if not actual, status separation of kinsmen on the basis of individually achieved qualities. A new basis of status assignment carries a considerable threat to notions of lineage unity and solidarity.

The sanctions available to a lineage for reinforcing traditional patterns of behavior have also been (in fact, if not formally) curtailed by the diversification of economic roles. If a man is financially independent of his lineage, he places himself outside the range of its economic control; the authority that it derived from the potential withdrawal of economic support diminishes. If a man no longer needs his lineage for economic status or financial aid, he may no longer feel obliged to recognize other reciprocities; he may therefore resent or evade obligations and responsibilities that were previously regarded as imperatives and gave expression to fundamental notions of lineage solidarity and unity.

In the political field, too, kinship has lost some of its relevance. The differential ranking of lineages on the basis of hereditary office has been modified. The powers of the chiefs have been limited and redefined and their control of resources has been restricted; thus, indirectly, the privileges of the chieftaincy lineages have been curtailed. New and effective political groups which are not based on descent have been established, and through them men can achieve status and power which traditionally had not been accessible to them.

On another level of organization, the political function and corporateness of a lineage have been affected. The kin group formerly had corporate responsibility and was the primary agency for social control. Now, legally, the individual is separated from his status as a member of a kin unit. This separation has two important implications. First, the individual is now, according to formal law, responsible for his own actions; should he commit a crime, the guilt is his alone in the eyes of the government. Second, the notion of individual responsibility provides a conceptual and moral basis for individual contractual relationships. A person can now enter into multiple contractual agreements which, on the one hand, are independent of kinship reciprocities and, on the other, may be quite independent of one another.[24]

The increased economic and political diversification has led, as we have seen, to a reduction in the importance of a lineage as a corporate social entity in structuring social relationships. This process is accompanied by a transfer of responsibility and obligation from lineage groups to individuals, and a shift from an emphasis on relationships between persons (which were manifold and endured beyond a specific transaction) to interaction that might be very impersonal and specific. To meet the increased role of specialization and the new sets of economic and social interests, several different modes of organizing social behavior have emerged. Traditional relationships outside the range of lineage, which had hitherto been secondary or latent, have been extended and intensified. For example, in some situations the ties of maternal affiliation have been reinforced. Where there is an opportunity for political or economic gain from association with his mother's kin, a man may form a close bond with one or more of his mother's relatives. He may move to the compound of his mother's lineage or use their farmland and effectively establish himself as a member of that lineage at the expense of his relationship to his own patrilineage. Or, alternatively, he may work with a maternal relative as a trader or mechanic or in any of a variety of new occupations, and share with him certain quite specific economic interests, while living with his patrilineage and maintaining other sets of relationships with them. Hence, whereas traditionally the rights, duties, and obligations that existed between a person and his mother's patrilineage were usually asserted only in times of stress, today there is a marked shift to a more bilateral orientation. In much the same way, relationships with patrikin outside the lineage (*omolebi*) and the residential unit (*omole*) may be intensified, or, alternatively, may become even more attenuated than formerly.

The intensification of kinship relationships outside the range of the lineage has meant that the present-day Yoruba is able to choose his personal network of kinship relationships; he does not have to interact solely within the framework defined by lineage structure. The relevant kin for each individual may now vary, and he is more able to select relationships that are beneficial to his immediate ends and evade others that are less so. In addition, the strengthening of relationships beyond the lineage provides for the extension of behavior that ordinarily is appropriate only to lineage relationships to relatives with whom actual genealogical connection may be quite remote.[25]

Nevertheless, relationships to matrikin and to genealogically distant patrikin are of a different order from those with lineage comembers. Traditional sanctions to authority are absent. The focus of interest and interaction may, but need not, be highly specific, and may not extend into other activities so long as they do not interfere with the immediate goals, which are usually oriented toward a system of market relations in terms of profit making. However modified, though, these relationships still remain within the framework of kinship and, in some measure, are always subject to the claims of kinship and to its stresses and strains.

Another development closely linked to the greater economic and political diversity of Oshogbo is the emergence of associational structures that were not characteristic of traditional life, and stress identity of interest rather than common descent. Some of the groups have as their main binding force the explicit purpose of exerting political pressure and improving the community in terms of Western standards. The largest and most enduring is the Oshogbo Progressive Union, which includes some of the most educated and wealthy members in the community. Other groups are organized around religious or economic interests. There are merchant and craft guilds with purely economic functions. But, although the organizations may affect a large number of people, they are poorly organized and generally ineffectual. Each of the twelve

Christian churches has its own mutual-aid and recreational body. The Muslim youth are organized into a group intended to promote the interests of the Muslim sector of the population. In addition there are numerous social, recreational, and mutual-aid clubs.[26] Frequently these associations are ephemeral, and particular groups disperse or divide after a short period; yet other groups of the same kind spring up to take their place.

The development of these new groups has a deep significance for the Yoruba social system. They express the idea that purposeful, organized social action to promote special interests is appropriate and possible. They cut across traditional ways of grouping and establish radically new and important bases making possible the extension of social relationships. They also provide avenues for increased economic and political status which until now could be attained only within the context of the lineage system. But they do more than provide channels for advancement. Members of the same association tend to see one another as social equals. Moreover, there is prestige attached to many of these associations, which have become symbols of status as well as instruments for achieving it. Finally, the associations serve as a major channel for recruiting outsiders into the social networks of Oshogbo. Clerks, teachers, traders, and others who have immigrated to and settled, permanently or temporarily, in Oshogbo can and frequently do become involved in the social life of the community by joining associations.

I have been discussing relationships that have been more or less defined within the structure of an institution. Kinship relationships, even outside the lineage, are still formalized to an extent by the rights and obligations that characterize the wider kinship system. Voluntary associations also typically have a formal and defined structure. In addition, networks of personal relationships have emerged without the familiar bases of kinship or other institutions. Relationships that develop within the associational framework, for example, often continue to operate in other activities and form a basis for informal personal interaction and friendship. In much the same way, relationships are formed at work or at school which may extend into other spheres and develop into personal friendships of varying degrees of intimacy. Typically, these are expressed in terms of mutual visiting, an informal system of mutual aid, and common participation in leisure activities.

There are also relationships associated with neighborhood and locality. Within the Native Quarter of Oshogbo, kinship or omole ties virtually preclude other ties based merely on physical proximity. But in the Foreign Quarter the ties of neighborhood are a significant source of interaction. The area is characterized by one or more nuclear families living in single modern dwellings. Although almost all the people living in the

Foreign Quarter are Yoruba, few have operative kin ties in Oshogbo to fall back upon for support in the routines and crises of life. Most are better educated, have more skills, and are wealthier than the average person in Oshogbo. The social as well as physical separation of this sector of the Oshogbo population has promoted close and strong neighborhood relationships.

Yet, despite the development of new forms of relationships which express new sets of values and interests, it is important to acknowledge and assess the continuing strength of lineage relationships. Friendship, similar economic status, common work, or associational interests are not yet major alternatives to kinship, and the lineage remains the primary focus of unity and source of stability and security in the society. The vast majority of men remain in their natal compounds. Some of the more wealthy may build European-type houses; others may seek a little more privacy in their living quarters and decorate them more in accordance with Western fashions, but this is done within the limits of their compounds. They thus continue to remain within the jurisdiction of their lineages, physically and otherwise. The reciprocal and mutual services, the bonds of sentiment, and the rituals of kinship which focus on the unity and integrity of the corporate lineage continue to operate. When it seems worthwhile, men may try to evade specific obligations, especially if the kin involved are genealogically remote. But in most circumstances at least a token acknowledgment is made of obligations that exist between lineage members. A Yoruba is well aware that with these obligations there come rights and privileges, and so long as he does not openly controvert the authority of his lineage, he can rely on it for assistance and aid. In times of need, the bonds of friendship or work tend to lapse, and a man turns to his lineage with the realistic expectation that aid will be given him. Even among those who are entirely independent economically of their lineages, few could make a decision that constituted a direct and explicit attack on the solidarity of the lineage.

The solidarity of a lineage remains despite the encroachments that have been made upon it. This was strikingly illustrated by an incident that occurred while I was in Oshogbo in 1951. An Oshogbo man, who had obtained a position as a petty clerk in a government office, was accused of stealing a considerable amount of government money. He was apprehended by the authorities, judged guilty, and sentenced to a term in jail. According to formal law, the case was closed. But it was not closed to the man's lineage. Every member of the guilty man's lineage, including the wealthy and educated, emotionally shared his guilt. Yet, because of modern jurisprudence and the weakening of their own sanctions, they were debarred from expiating their own guilt by punishing him in traditional ways, and expressed frustration at their inability to find any appropriate means to atone for it. Although in the eyes of government corporate responsibility has formally shifted to individual responsibility, in the eyes of the people corporate responsibility and hence corporate solidarity remain underlying principles of social behavior.

It is the most wealthy and educated people who bear the greatest stress and strain in conflicts generated by the competing interests and values of the traditional kin-bound social system and the new sets of interests. But in some measure every individual is affected by, and aware of, the two sets of norms and interests. To some extent the conflicts are borne by individuals selecting and manipulating relationships according to the situation in which they are momentarily involved. In this respect the behavior of the Oshogbo people resembles that of Africans entering the newly created towns of the south and east.[27]

I think that there are, however, two other principal reasons for the absence of major cleavages between individuals and their lineages, or between old and new norms. The more obvious reason is the relative absence of geographical mobility involving a physical separation of kinsmen. There are very few people who have left Oshogbo to find work in other areas. For the handful who have made their way to Lagos or Ibadan the bonds of kinship may have become more attenuated. As education increases, however, and if the rate of economic and social growth in Oshogbo is not rapid enough to provide suitable occupational and other opportunities, some of the more educated and ambitious may migrate to larger centers. If they do, we may anticipate that the bonds of kinship will be considerably weakened.

Another reason for the absence of major divisions between individuals and their lineages lies in the flexibility and adaptability of the lineage system itself. By accommodating the expression of antagonistic claims and by providing a basis to meet changing conditions through the recognition of new authorities and the acknowledgment of new interests and relationships, the lineage system has been able to help channel and contain these conflicts. For example, we find the beginnings of a new administrative system and an altered allocation of authority within a lineage. As the traditional structure of authority and the position of the head of a lineage have weakened, other members of the lineage have achieved positions of influence and control. Members who have succeeded economically, who are well educated, or who have achieved high status through alignments with voluntary associations may exert influence and control over lineage policies or the activities of individual members far in excess of that decreed by their traditional lineage rank. Usually they do not receive formal and explicit recognition as leaders of a lineage, and at times their opinions may differ from those of the traditional authorities; then the conflict may erupt into the open. At other times, however, traditional authorities voluntarily defer to the wider knowledge and skills of these new leaders. As a result there is developing an authority system within lineages which, based on criteria more consistent with the changing social system, gives expression to some of the divergent interests and antagonistic claims in lineage relationships.

Similarly, the lineages have adapted to and have been able to utilize the new associations. In principle the new voluntary groups may be a primary focus of personal conflict for an individual, as membership may involve goals that are incompatible with those of his lineage. If he should choose to support the decisions of his association, he faces a possible breach in lineage relationships. On the other hand, if he should choose to support the interests of his lineage against those of his association, he may be threatened with expulsion from the association and may face the loss of actual or potential gain through it. But frequently the conflicts between associations and lineages are more apparent than real, and a lineage may derive considerable benefits from its linkages with new groups. Formerly a lineage obtained privilege and power through a member who was a chief; today a lineage may gain status and privilege as well through a member who has achieved prominence and influence by his alliance with a new group. Once again, then, status is not entirely an individual attribute but it is seen as transmitted, in part at least, to a lineage group through a member's position. The absence of uniform and widespread conflict between lineage and associational roles is indicative of the changing norms throughout Yoruba social life. In the early part of this century, membership in a Christian church inevitably meant expulsion from a lineage. There is today very little real opposition between lineage and religious affiliations. Most of the lineages in Oshogbo are uniformly Christian or Muslim, apart from the relatively few pagans who are usually elderly men and women scattered among many lineages. The pagans are in general [28] regarded as ineffectual in many areas of community and lineage life, although they may still be seen as holding certain mystical or religious powers, whereas prominent churchmen are among the most effective lineage leaders. Lineage and associational relationships no longer simply express two distinct and opposed sets of values and interests; indeed, there may be considerable compatibility between them.

The changing norms of the Yoruba people are also expressed in other lineage activities. The notions of corporate solidarity and interests are mobilized for entirely new aims. For example, the economic resources of an entire lineage may be tapped in order to send one or two promising young men abroad for a university education. When they complete their education these young men are expected to repay their financial debt to the lineage. In addition, they are expected to make their skills available for the benefit of their lineages and to undertake similar obligations to

educate their younger relatives. Thus there have been generated reciprocal obligations and privileges among lineage members which are oriented
toward new values and goals, but are cast in the traditional matrix of
lineage responsibility and corporateness.

Conclusions

There are several points that I should like to stress in conclusion.
Changes in the modes of ordering social relationships and in the quality
of these relationships in Oshogbo, over the past half century, have given
rise to patterns that in some ways resemble those observed in cities elsewhere. Economic specialization and differentiation have increased, and
there have been changes in the occupational structure necessary for the
establishment of an urban industrial system. The individual has been separated to some extent from his status as a member of a patrilineal group,
and is able to enter into more flexible contractual relationships. Occupational mobility is accompanied by political mobility. The authority and
control of a lineage as a corporate social entity have diminished. Con-
currently, there has been an elaboration of secondary relationships. But
it is not only that the range of relationships has been enlarged; the form
and content have also changed. They reflect a differentiation of interests
and a willingness to interact in sharply limited roles. People are linked
and divided by special-interest associations or networks of relationships.
Men may join together in pursuit of a specific goal, and may be known
to one another only in this limited segment of their lives. Moreover,
secondary controls have begun, in some areas, to supersede the hitherto
powerful primary controls of a lineage.

Changes in the system of social differentiation and status fixing are
another expression of changes in norms and values. It is a traditional
Yoruba belief that rank is not conferred on individuals but is vested in a
lineage. The differential ranking of lineages on the basis of hereditary
office only has been modified by the changes in the political system and
by greater economic role differentiation. Assignment of status is being
made on an individual achievement basis as well as on the basis of
hereditary group ascription. Education, wealth, occupation, and individually achieved political influence have been acknowledged as additional criteria of status evaluation. To a very large extent, the new modes
of status allocation are not independent of one another. Yet, although
there may be considerable consistency among them, these new modes
are incompatible with traditional criteria of social placement. The results
have been status ambiguity in the comparison of persons, and in-
consistency when the modes are applied to the status evaluation of individuals. To some extent the dilemma is being resolved. It is not unusual

in Yorubaland today for a wealthy and educated man to seek and obtain the position of a chief. Similarly, chieftaincy lineages have acknowledged the new criteria of status and are using their resources to educate their young men.

In all these respects, present-day Oshogbo exhibits important similarities to cities of the West and to towns in southern and eastern Africa. But these similarities in the modes of relationships have not been determined by the size, density, or the traditional ways of grouping or dividing in Oshogbo. They have been brought about by the development of a system of market relationships, by increased diversification of economic roles, and by the separation of economic interests from wider kinship relationships. They have also been influenced by changes in the political sphere, in education, and in religious beliefs and customs. Underlying each of these factors is a system of values which stresses individual competition and achievement and judges behavior on impersonal criteria.

Yet these changes must be seen within a wider context. The patrilineal kin group has remained the predominant source and framework of social interaction. The sentiments of common descent, the notions of social continuity, and the corporate solidarity and responsibility which characterize a patrilineage have been weakened, in certain circumstances, by the competing interests and values of new social forms. But they have by no means been destroyed. Where necessary, the principles and structure of a lineage have been modified to accommodate the expression of conflicting interests and to meet changing conditions; they have thus been able to channelize and contain these conflicts. Moreover, Oshogbo has a stable, ethnically homogeneous population sharing a basically uniform system of values. Despite the increased specialization of economic roles, agriculture is still the base of the economy. Apart from the few who have large incomes from trading, and some clerks and teachers, the people of Oshogbo have a substantially uniform economic standard. In addition, although there has been a development of secondary associations, less than 5 per cent of the Oshogbo population are involved in them. Moreover, the secondary relationships, whether associational or more informal, tend to give way to the claims of kinship in most important situations. The flexibility and the continuing strength of the patrilineage, together with the fact that there is still no highly specialized division and organization of labor through a complex system of market relations, have, I think, prevented the fuller development of secondary associations as well as of a greater elaboration of more informal personal relationships.

These factors have also hampered the development of a sharply differentiated social class system in Oshogbo. As we have already seen, the bonds of kinship and the values that support them usually continue to take precedence in virtually every crucial area of social relationships. The greatest stress and strain is placed on the wealthy and educated for whom the lack of compatibility between old and new values is most sharp and painful. In certain circumstances, new status interests can become paramount at the expense of solidarity with kin. But for as long as a man remains within the jurisdiction of his lineage, his commitment to new status and prestige interests must be limited by his equally realistic commitment to lineage obligations and solidarity. The more a man can separate physically, economically, and emotionally from his lineage, the easier it is for him to adopt simultaneous changes in norms and behavior. For example, in Lagos[29] and Ibadan, cities whose populations include many persons who have left their homes and lineages to seek work, there exists a more flexible approach to the adoption of new norms and behavior patterns than in Oshogbo, where persons are still largely compelled to conform to traditional norms and behavior defined primarily by kinship.

Where, then, do the critical differences today lie between Oshogbo and the cities of the West, or even of central and southern Africa? I think some answers may be found in Kolb's argument that only where there is stress on universalism and achievement is it probable that certain demographic and technological features will produce modern urban industrialization.[30] Certainly it is clear that the factors that have produced changes in Oshogbo simultaneously encourage and are based upon a value orientation that emphasizes universalism and achievement. The fact that some important changes have occurred in the Oshogbo social system suggests that, at least on the periphery, norms and behavior are beginning to approximate those more consistent with urban industrialism. But it is equally clear that the kinship system, which is, after all, a system of norms and values and common purposes, and which stresses corporate responsibility and solidarity, ascribed status, and relationships that are intimate and manifold, has thus far prevented and opposed the fuller development of urban social characteristics.[31] It is legitimate to ask how long the traditional values and the kinship system can continue to withstand and adapt to modern pressures without radical changes in institutions and patterns of behavior, and the values that underlie them. If both geographical mobility and intergenerational mobility based on economic differences increase, and if an even stronger emphasis is placed on a market system of relationships, traditional values and principles of behavior may be compelled to give way to those that are more consistent with a Western urban mode of life. Yet, it seems much more likely to me that Oshogbo, missing as it has the full and direct impact of industrialization, will give rise to norms and behavior that are genuinely new, but that the core of orthodox values will remain for the foreseeable future and give their characteristic stamp.

7.

URBAN INFLUENCES ON THE RURAL HAUSA

by Horace M. Miner

The interdependence of urban and rural communities in any society goes far beyond the city's need for agricultural produce. The basic nature of the social order in the one type of community is functionally tied to that in the other. Their destinies are intertwined. In the industrial urbanization of underdeveloped nations, urban development is tied to change in farm culture. It therefore behooves us to consider the rural-urban relationship in societal change.

The preindustrial city[1] was already an ancient feature in West African societies at the time of European contact. Such a city embraced the politico-religious elite of the society, and handicraftsmen organized into craft guilds. It was also the center of commercial contacts with other cities and societies. The small urban elite, through its control of political, military, religious, and economic power, dominated the mass of agricultural peasants who provided the economic surplus and the military manpower which maintained the position of the elite. Aside from this moderate amount of social differentiation and some secularization and impersonalization of market activity, such societies were traditional, strongly kin-oriented, and generally folk in character. They were the expression of the limited complexity of social systems based on hoe agriculture, handicraft technology, and the power of men and animals.

In Africa, the elites of most of these societies shared the same basic culture as the peasants.[2] In contrast, the elites of the world's more complex preindustrial civilizations were the carriers of a distinctive "high culture" or "great tradition," which was found in only a very dilute form among the peasants. Where Islam or Christianity has entered Africa, the elites have become more culturally differentiated from the peasants. Where this occurred under preindustrial conditions, there evolved the type of society that Gideon Sjoberg has called "feudal."[3] Such societies have shown marked resistance to the influences of urban industrial civi-

---

[1] For notes to chapter 7, see page 193.

lizations. The maintenance of the Muslim emirates in Nigeria and the sultanate in Zanzibar, as well as the Coptic state in Ethiopia, all evidence the resilience of such systems.

Even considerable urban development along European lines in other parts of Africa has had strikingly little effect on the peasants. It was in the commercial and administrative centers, which the Europeans either grafted onto preindustrial African centers or created anew, that Africans experienced a more complex urban life. But even the new cities were not the foci of African commercial and industrial societies, but were overseas outposts of European industrial societies. In fact, the organization of the African colonies was in many ways comparable to a feudal order. In both there was an urban elite which maintained its distinctive way of life through control of the peasantry. The latter provided taxes, surplus agricultural (and sometimes mineral) produce, and military manpower for the maintenance of the system. Likewise, the colonial elite was rigidly opposed to industrialization. Even the modes of transportation applied to the vital function of export reflected the noncompetitive tempo of a labor-intensive, rather than an industrial, economy. In general, if rivers were navigable by steamboat, there were no railways, and where the latter were laid, automotive roads were not developed or were not maintained at motorable standards.

Urban and Rural Segments of Economic Development

The two definitive and interrelated characteristics that distinguish industrialized societies from underdeveloped ones are their superior technological control of sources of energy and their marked differentiation into highly specialized and coördinated parts. General literacy, in the language of numbers as well as of words, and the general use of money in mediating economic relationships are functional requisites of so complex a division of labor. Another requirement of the system is that the specialized roles be staffed on the basis of achievement, rather than ascription.[4]

Although the establishment of industries is obviously required for industrial urbanization to proceed, sweeping changes must occur in the rural sector of the society, if for no other reason than that underdeveloped nations are agrarian societies. In economic terms, industrial urban growth can proceed only through the shifting of a large segment of the rural work force into industry, communications, trade, and services. This in itself requires an agrarian revolution capable of preparing and stimulating potential urban migrants to assume their new roles. At the same time, there must be an increase in per capita farm productivity, not only to feed the growing urban population, but also to meet the general rise in population which may be expected. Moreover, agricultural surpluses must help meet the costs of capital outlay in nonagricultural sectors of the economy, and the surpluses must be sufficient to permit the farmers to become consumers of goods from the nation's new industries.[5] Thus the industrial and commercial development of cities can progress only to the degree that the rural economy reaches levels of productivity which require the reorganization of farm life.

In this relationship, the city is the prototype of society toward which the rural areas must change. It is, as well, the center of political and economic power. In these respects the city is the potential source of urbanizing influences, and the seat of power to decide whether or not such influences will be exerted. In the latter regard, it is useful to consider southern Nigeria briefly before turning to the Hausa.

In the south, colonialism weakened the position of the hereditary elites, whose culture was already close to that of the peasants. Although the participation of Africans in the commercial and administrative systems introduced by the Europeans was merely peripheral, the old, conservative preindustrial cities were metamorphosed into mushrooming administrative and trading centers. In them there devoleped a new African elite, which emerged from European-type schools and acquired its power through politics, business, and the professions.[6] It also acquired, under European subjugation, a sense of deep humiliation, which led to reactive nationalism. Even since independence, the drive for socioeconomic development has been heavily motivated by the need to achieve the dignity of modern society.[7] It is this factor that has offset any tendency for the Western-educated elite to assume the role of the colonial elites, as happened in Haiti.

Southern Nigeria provided the political ferment that produced the independence into which the north was reluctantly drawn. The remainder of this paper is concerned with the degree to which the urbanizing influences of colonialism reached the Hausa in the north. The setting of the inquiry is Zaria Province, and its rural population, which I studied in 1957-58,* is of particular interest. We shall be interested in evidence of socioeconomic development beyond that of the precolonial feudal society, and shall be looking for specialization of activity beyond that of ruler, priest-teacher, soldier, handicraftsman, merchant, trader, and farmer. Increasing specificity of function should be linked to increasing use of machines and inanimate sources of energy. The mediating function of money among the more specific functions should be accompanied by the progressive use of the logics of the market. In the allocation of people to functional roles, literacy, skill, and competence should

* The research was made possible by a grant from the Rockefeller Foundation.

have growing importance and should be associated with social mobility. Any such changes in the rural scene should appear through the structural links between city and country. These links are institutionalized in the channels of education, government, commerce, and industry.

The Zaria Hausa

Zaria City, the capital and only major commercial center of a province with 800,000 inhabitants, had a population of 33,000 in 1952, to which may be added another 11,000 in the adjacent "Newcomers' Town" of Sabon Gari. The former city includes the political elite and traditional craftsmen. A quarter of this population is literate in Hausa script (Ajami) and almost a third of the active males are craftsmen, but there are fewer than 500 persons with as much as four years of European-type schooling.[8] Yet Zaria is a focal point in the railway system linking the north to Lagos on the coast. Zaria is a collecting point for agricultural exports, the location of a major cotton gin, a distribution center for manufactured imports, and most recently the site of a cigarette factory.

The extent of commercial activity suggested by these operations requires more than the indigenous skills of the Hausa. The modest degree of industrial urbanization thus far achieved has been possible only because of the influx of some 30,000 Yoruba and Ibo from the south. A third of these immigrants to the province are concentrated in and around Sabon Gari, where a third of the population has at least a fourth-grade education. In terms of development, southern Nigeria trained more literate people than it could absorb in specialized capacities. Many of these people migrated north and provided the skills for development there.

The rural area of the province that primarily concerns us is northern Kubau District, thirty miles east of Zaria City. The first direct effect of the British conquest of Zaria was the establishment of peace in the region. This change was doubtless the most significant step toward development which had occurred, for it was the basis of all others. The first element of modern industrialization to follow was the railroad, reaching Zaria City by 1911, with a narrow-gauge spur through southern Kubau following immediately. A later sign of industrialization, the automobile, did not reach northern Kubau until the mid 1930's, and the inadequacy of the road system has been a continuing hindrance to development. Socioeconomic change in the direction of urbanization is inextricably tied to decreasing isolation. Yet automotive traffic from the coast must still cross the Niger River on a railroad bridge; the road from Zaria to Kubau contended with an unbridged river until 1952, and in

1953 the district headquarters in northern Kubau, Takalafiya, secured a permanent bridge link with the southern Kubau railhead of Dutsin Wai. In 1958 the road from Takalafiya to the latter bridge was made passable during the rainy season. In short, the physical prerequisites of development were but recently established. Our main interest, however, is in the social effects of these prerequisites and, to see change here, we must know something of the original social structure.

Historically the Hausa peasants have long been part of feudal societies, first under the Habe states and then under Fulani overlords. Since the Fulani jihad, or holy war, of 1804-1810, the emirates have set the pattern which even British conquest has not devitalized. The emirs of the various Fulani states owed fealty to the Sultan of Sokoto, the direct descendant of Shehu dan Fodio, who inspired the jihad. The power of the sultan was maintained through the exercise of his traditional right to name all new emirs from among contending members of the ruling lineages in the emirates. Within the emirates, each emir held a similar right to appoint the various fief holders, and even to confirm appointment of the latter's village headmen. The *hakimi*, or lord of the fief, held similar confirmatory control over his village headmen's appointment of heads for the hamlets or wards into which the village areas were divided. The *talakawa*, or peasants, held their rights to village land through their traditional subservience to the chiefs above them. These rights were usually acquired by inheritance or by clearing virgin bush in the village area, with the approval of the chief. Land rights could not be purchased or sold, but its usufruct could be pawned as collateral for a loan. Any talakawa who so desired could move to another fief or village, if he secured the permission of the chiefs of that area and assumed the usual obligations toward them. These obligations involved the payment of taxes to the hakimi, through his village headmen, and the rendering of such labor and military duty as the hakimi might require.

Taxes were collected by the village headmen, who kept a share and passed the bulk of the receipts on to the hakimi. He, in turn, took a larger share for the operation of his own household and court, transmitting the remainder to the emir, who paid therefrom his tribute to the Sultan of Sokoto. While the proportion of the tax money retained by each chief was theoretically fixed, in practice there was wide latitude.

After the British conquest the policy of indirect rule meant a minimum of day-to-day intervention in Hausa affairs, but some effective control had to be established. The basic technique was that of exercising the right to remove emirs who were uncoöperative and the right to confirm or reject their replacements. After the initial replacement of the Sultan of Sokoto and most of the emirs, resistance was broken and removals from office were less frequent. In addition to this implicit threat, the feudal chiefs were made directly dependent upon the central administration by placing them on salaries. The salary of the district headman of Kubau, who is the equivalent of the old fief holder, was about £640 ($1,790) in 1958. This amount is less than 3 per cent of the taxes officially passing through his hands, and is obviously a much smaller share than he would have had in the old days.

The fact that fief holders are now district headmen derives from another fundamental administrative change instituted by the colonial power. The old feudal units were small areas around fortified towns. The fiefs of a lord were scattered. He did not live in any one of them but controlled them through his representatives. These piecemeal holdings were rationalized by the British into a more "modern" system. The emirates became the nuclei of "provinces," each incorporating into "districts" the old fiefs and vassal states, and even some pagan tribal areas. In Zaria Province more than a hundred fiefs were combined into sixteen districts. British control did not, however, alter the fact that provincial government, from top to bottom, remained under the control of the old Fulani elite. Even the manner in which that control was organized experienced little fundamental change.[9]

The Rural Economy

Although extended patrilineal connections are vital to the system of allocation of power within the Fulani elite, the ramifications of kinship have more limited importance for the Hausa peasants. They have no clan or lineage system, kinship being reckoned bilaterally. The really significant kin units are the domestic ones, which may consist solely of a man and his wife, or wives, and their offspring. More often the compound embraces an extended family composed of the elementary families of a number of men, who are usually closely related in the paternal line, through which land rights pass. Both the composition and the organization of such extended family groups vary widely. They commonly hold and operate farmlands jointly, although usually some of the lands are cultivated by individuals for their separate benefit. In other instances there may be several work units within an extended family group sharing a single compound. The principal change resulting from the British conquest was a shift in the agricultural work units. The economy of even extended-family households was formerly based on slave labor. Now it rests on the coöperative efforts of active males in the household.

The farming is done entirely with hoes. Fields located close to towns and villages are cultivated every year, their fertility being maintained by the application of burned refuse from the compounds and such animal manure as is available. More distant fields are cropped in rotation, the length of fallowing varying with soil conditions. The staple crops are guinea corn and bulrush millet.

Despite the fact that food crops are grown essentially for consumption, rather than for sale, the Hausa have been involved in a money economy for centuries. In part, this system provides for their other material needs, but, of more pressing consequence, money has long been used in paying taxes. The growing of a cash crop of cotton has been the traditional method of meeting this obligation, and cotton stands as the third major crop. The other important cash crops are sugar cane and, recently, tobacco. Our knowledge of the household economy of the Hausa peasants rests on M. G. Smith's excellent analysis of a very comparable region in Zaria Province.[10] He found that, although virtually all rural men are farmers, almost 90 per cent of them are also engaged in crafts or trade. These collateral activities account for a third of their total income, including the value of agricultural produce. As for their wives, a few may cultivate plots allocated to them by their husbands but, virtually without exception, they are engaged in commercial activity. Although what the Hausa woman earns is her own, she may lend interest-free money to her husband in times of financial stringency. In all, wives earn almost a fifth of the cash income of the household. Although the commercial activity of the farmers is, to a great extent, carried on in the dry season, women pursue their business activities throughout the year. Spinning and weaving are the major crafts. Next in importance is the preparation of cooked foods for local sale.

The number of men's occupations and crafts runs to at least thirty, exclusive of manual labor and a wide variety of trading enterprises. In addition to administrative positions, there is a professional group of *mallam*'s, or koranic scholars, who function as judges, prayer leaders, and koranic teachers. In recent times the title has been extended to apply to Western-educated men. The latter fill positions as teachers in government schools and as professional specialists in various government departments such as agriculture, veterinary, forestry, and health. With the exception of koranic teachers, government and professional men rarely farm with their own hands, although they may possess and manage farms. Farmers are most likely to be weavers, dyers, tailors, butchers, barbers, builders, thatchers, blacksmiths, drummers, or praise singers. Some of those whose praises are sung may have reached their positions by large-scale trading in local staples and cash crops. The small trader is more apt to retail a few imported items, like kola nuts and salt, or such European products as kerosene and cloth. Garden produce is sold by the grower directly to the consumer. Grain surplus may go to middlemen, who even purchase crop futures during the wet season. Most of the retail trade goes on in the town markets, where male vendors are three times more prevalent than the Hausa girls and old women who may leave the compounds to sell their wares.

Major towns hold weekly markets, on days staggered so that it is possible for the traders of the region to attend them all. Something of the size of these markets can be seen from the fact that 7,000 people were counted in one day at Takalafiya's market. This number was equal to the entire adult male population of Kubau District at the time.

In addition to this regular, local commerce, one man in ten engages in long trading trips (*fautauci*) during the dry season. Hausa traders from Kano arrive in Zaria Province with donkey loads of mats, salt, potash, and dates. From their profits they purchase cane sugar to sell in the north. Zaria men on fautauci take cattle, groundnuts, cotton, and Hausa cloth as far south as the coast, returning with kolas, ginger, Yoruba cloth, and European goods which can be bought advantageously there. Some indication of the extent of this traffic comes from a census of movement on an old Kano trade route running southward, just to the east of Zaria Province. The route does not go through major towns and much of it is not even a motorable track, but the nineteen-day count at the end of February showed a daily average of a hundred men going north or south ·on trading trips. While such fautauci traffic is old, it has been greatly stimulated by British-introduced peace and commercial enterprise, along with truck and rail communications.

Keeping in mind the foregoing sketch of the traditional culture and some of the colonial influences on it, let us consider three avenues of more recent change which have brought Kubau District into somewhat closer contact with Zaria City and the social ferment that lies beyond. How have innovations in education, government, and the economy affected the 50,000 people who make up the district population?

Education

Traditional education in the early emirates consisted of informally organized koranic schools conducted by the mallams, who reached a very limited group. There was also advanced training under *alkali*'s and imams, leading to legal and religious careers. When Sir Frederick Lugard entered Nigeria, he won over the emirs largely through reiterating the promise that the "British government will in no way interfere with the Mohammedan religion. All men are free to worship God as they please. Mosques and prayer places will be treated with respect by us." In later years this promise was interpreted as limiting Christian mission activity to pagans. As the missions were responsible for almost all early education in Africa, Muslim Nigeria has never felt this entering wedge of Western habits of thought and urban skills.

The profound dearth of education in the Northern Region is apparent when we compare school enrollment there with that in the south (Eastern and Western regions). Disregarding koranic students, only 5 per cent of northern children between the ages of seven and fourteen were in school in 1952, compared with 40 per cent in the Eastern Region and 33 per cent in the Western Region. The north had only two approved secondary schools, whereas the other regions together, with about the same population as the north, had thirty-four. That this level of education in the north is of long standing is evident from the data in the accompanying table. The proportion of the provincial population with some nonkoranic education (4 per cent) closely approaches the pro-

EDUCATION AND LITERACY IN ZARIA PROVINCE AND SUBDIVISIONS, 1952
(In percentages of total population)

Area	Some nonkoranic education	Four years of nonkoranic education	Literacy in Ajami script
Zaria Province	4.0	2.1	7.7
Kubau District	1.5	0.8	9.6
Anchau town area[a]	2.6	1.8	7.0

[a]Including Takalafiya.
SOURCE: Census of 1952.

portion of all northern children in school. As low as these figures are, Zaria Province had the highest literacy rate in the whole Northern Region.

Apparent in the table is a concentration of educated Hausa and some "southerners" in Takalafiya, the seat of the district government and a market center. The proportion of the total Kubau population with some formal education (1.5 per cent) is almost the same as the proportion of seven- to fourteen-year-olds from the district who were in school at the time (1.7 per cent).

Another interesting situation revealed by these figures is the greater importance of the koranic schools, indicated by the fact that the proportion of people who have learned to use Ajami script is larger than the proportion of those who have had formal schooling. The truly rural areas are still served almost entirely by these traditional schools. In 1958 the junior primary school in Takalafiya had 67 pupils, and there were 8 local graduates taking fifth-year work in the provincial schools outside Kubau. At the same time there were 86 koranic schools in the district, with 1,106 students.

The Takalafiya junior primary school was established in 1940, and its basic pattern of operation has not altered since then. The ratio of boys to girls in school is two to one. There is a cyclical four-year program: the first and third grades are taught during one year and the second and fourth grades, during the next. Classes are conducted in Hausa, by two male teachers. The subjects taught include arithmetic, geography and history (particularly of Nigeria), the reading and writing of Hausa in Roman script, and a little English. There are also two koranic mallams who give a half hour of instruction daily along traditional lines. In addition, the boys work on a school farm, and all pupils have some craft training. The dropout rate of students during the four-year course has consistently been about 20 per cent for boys and 65 per cent for girls, largely resulting in both instances from failure to pass examinations at the end of the second year. On the average, twenty-one boys complete the fourth grade each biennium, but only two proceed to further training. No girl has ever gone beyond the local school. The wastage is enormous, for even the literacy achieved in four years is unused and quickly lost.

In 1958 this school served almost exclusively the twin towns of Taka-lafiya and Anchau, located a mile apart. The only farm children in the school came from families living in these communities. Even these families had to be coerced into sending their children to school. Farmers' children constituted only 50 per cent of the students, although 92 per cent of the population of the district and 86 per cent of the twin-town population were farmers. The professional, administrative, and trade group from Takalafiya and Dutsin Wai, on the other hand, now want their sons educated. All the boys admitted to post–junior primary schools since 1952 have been from nonfarming families. The occupations of the fathers of these boys are most revealing: district head, judge, three village headmen, two agriculture mallams, forestry mallam, veterinary mallam, sanitary inspector, two cotton buyers, and the domestic servant of a man of this class. It is quite possible that there is truth in the peasants' accusation that these men have used their influence to secure access to higher schools for their sons.

That the Education Department is aware of the problem of adapting education to local needs is evident in the inclusion of koranic instruction, as well as farm and craft training, in the curriculum. It may be argued that these efforts have an integrative effect, making the school seem less strange to the Hausa. On the other hand, it is equally apparent that such training is less adequate than the traditional methods for transmitting the same kind of knowledge. We have seen that the sons of business and professional men are disproportionately well represented in the classes, in comparison with farmers' sons, and that girls figure least of all. This order of representation is a direct reflection of the degree of utility which the people perceive the school as having for these three groups. What is more, their assessment is accurate. The cultural material imparted by the junior primary school is mainly useful to the degree that it leads to further education and occupations outside the local area. Such mobility is already becoming recognized as desirable, and, as the schools improve their ability to meet this need, the farmers' view of primary education will change.

In addition to the primary school, there has been an adult literacy campaign in the district. Through this "War against Ignorance" [11] an average of 1 per cent of the fifteen- to fifty-year-olds became literate annually between 1952 and 1961. This number is twenty times as large as the number graduated from the junior primary school. In the light of the complete failure of an earlier attempt to teach adults through the established schools, the methods of the recent campaign deserve attention. The program makes a fundamental distinction between adult classes and children's classes. The war against ignorance is completely an adult affair, stressing the idea that it is easy for adults to read and write and that they can learn to do so more quickly than children. The latter have "teachers"; the former have "instructors," and the two are never the same individuals. Children go to "school," but the term is studiously avoided in connection with adult education. Even the physical facilities used for the two kinds of education are distinct. There are no desks in the buildings that the adults construct for their classes, and members of the class sit on the floor as they are accustomed to do elsewhere. Illustrating the subtle cultural connection existing between material culture and the social system, it is fascinating to learn that, when some of the adults who have become literate in Hausa undertake the study of English, they consider it necessary to make benches on which to pursue this obviously foreign study.

In summary, the program recognizes the superior status of adults and avoids threatening them with that of children. Such a threat is likely to be felt particularly in developing areas where illiterate adults, despite their age-limited status, actually have less contact than do younger people with the modern world of written communication. Conservatism is a defensive position.

We can now see why the literacy campaign is not a threat, but what need does it fulfill in rural areas where literacy is not used? The answer seems to lie in the fact that the campaign plays on the traditional association of literacy with status. By placing literacy within the grasp of adults in such a way as not to threaten them, the possibility of adult education is created. This possibility becomes a reality with the addition of status symbols (literacy certificates) and the development of group activity focused on their achievement. With a high-status mallam encouraging adults to become literate like himself, and demonstrating that they can do so, the motivation is strong for others to do likewise. Yet, as literacy becomes more general, its status value is debased. On the other hand, its very prevalence establishes it as a norm for adults. This norm is likely to persist only if literacy becomes useful. In short, literacy is a tool and not a goal of development. Unless it can be employed as a tool by the literate, it will not be achieved as a goal by the educators.

We have noted that the highest-status people in Kubau are beginning to appreciate the pragmatic value of education. One of these few is the district headman. A lesson he taught the assembled headmen of his district exemplifies the sort of social change which makes education significant to development. One of the district councilors had proposed that "southerners" be prohibited from acting as cotton-buying agents anywhere in the province. While the proposal was probably made out of personal pique, it played on fundamental Hausa attitudes toward the non-Muslims from southern tribes. Before the British conquest such tribes were valued only as a source of slaves. With conquest and development, these disdained beings became Christian, educated, and rich by local standards. What is more, they took over a large share of the white-collar work in northern commercial houses and government agencies with which the Hausa had to deal. Thus to disdain was added envy. Although fully aware of and sharing this attitude, the district headmen spoke against the proposal as follows:

> What is proposed is understandable. All people prefer to deal with their own kind but, in this case, two things must be remembered. First, a cotton agent must post a bond of £250 to £300 and few of us save enough money to deposit such a bond. Secondly, even if one of us had the money, could he do the work? Few are well enough educated. We must pay more attention to education, which is even more important than saving. We want to fill these positions but, until we have enough education, we must go slowly. The best action is to improve education.

Government

After World War II the British began in Nigeria a series of government changes ultimately leading to the country's independence in 1960. The protectorate and regional governments were those primarily affected, but even the peasants felt some effect. They saw the creation of a representative district council, and had their first experience with voting. In the elections of 1951 the male taxpayers chose town area representatives who, in turn, selected four district electors to join the provincial electoral college. The latter then named the four Zaria members of the Northern House of Assembly.

The individuals chosen as electors from the two neighboring districts of Kubau and Ikara are of interest. The following lists include all the candidates in descending order of the number of votes received:

Kubau	Ikara
1. District head *(sarkin fada*)*	1. District head
2. Chief scribe	2. Chief scribe
3. Judge	3. Primary school teacher
4. *Madaki** (Ministry of Agriculture)	4. Mallam
	5. Mallam
5. Village headman	6. Village headman
6. Village headman	7. Primary school teacher
7. Chief of works *(sarkin ayyuka†)*	8. *Wazirin anchau†* (retired)
8. Educated, rich merchant	
9. *Galadiman damau‡*	

*Emirate title   †District title   ‡Village area title

The fact that the district headman and his chief scribe headed the list in both districts is worthy of note. The introduction of elections in previously stable, nondemocratic societies never produces new leadership immediately. People vote for the only leaders they know—the traditional ones. Reading on down the lists, however, we find that the two districts differ markedly in the other people they selected. In Kubau six of the remaining seven were also officials of one kind or another. Judging from general emphases in the north, Ikara District seems to have been unusual in that half of its chosen spokesmen were either koranic or primary school teachers.

The tendency to elect government officials to the House of Assembly was common to the Northern Region in this election. Eighty-nine per cent of the assemblymen were either district or local officials, 15 per cent being district headmen. Members of the Assembly with educational occupations amounted to only 5 per cent. These figures are in sharp contrast with those from the Western Region, where only 7 per cent of the House of Assembly were government officials and 29 per cent had educational occupations. The political ferment leading to independence came from the south; the relation of education to the rise of nationalism is clear.

With the promulgation of the new constitution, the previously submerged non-Muslim elements of the population of the Northern Region began to feel their power in areas where they were numerically dominant. In Zagon Katab District, which is almost 90 per cent non-Muslim, riots broke out and the Emir of Zaria felt compelled to withdraw his brother to safety from the district headship.[12]

The British also created district councils of elected representatives from all the village areas. In Kubau District each village is represented by its village head, and usually the village scribe. The district headman is the presiding officer, and his chief scribe acts as secretary. Meetings are held three or four times a year, depending upon the number of proposals submitted by the village headmen. Opportunity is then provided for government officials to make announcements and for outsiders to raise problems they have come to present. After these people have withdrawn, the council gets down to its agenda, which has been circulated in typewritten Hausa for the benefit of those councilors who are literate. The items are freely discussed until the district headman expresses what he considers to be the opinion of the group and asks for a general expression of assent. Decision is usually unanimous, a show of hands very rarely being required.

Most of the council business concerns the expenditure of the district fund, which amounted to £1,300 ($3,640) in 1957. A striking feature of the council's allocation of resources is the degree to which the two most progressive village areas—Anchau and Dutsin Wai—secure the majority of the benefits. Together they receive about four times their proportionate share of the funds.

The dominance of the Anchau village area results from the location of the district headquarters, Takalafiya, in that area. A quarter of the total budget is spent on district requirements, much of it in Takalafiya. The newly constructed district council house is an example. The town area also receives a third of the remaining funds for strictly local purposes. The old cotton market and railroad town of Dutsin Wai is simply enterprising. This spirit is evident in its newly elected councilor, a young trader with a primary school education. He expresses himself easily and well, in contrast with the hesitance and the retiring attitude of most of the council members. His facility led to almost immediate selection as one of the District Council's four representatives to the emir's advisory Outer Council. His understanding of practical politics is remarkable. During one of the district meetings he offered no opposition to any of the first ten proposals from other councilors, although the district headman spoke against two of these. One was a recommendation to increase the salary of village heads, all of whom are members of the District Council. The Dutsin Wai representative spoke to the issue by saying that the Outer Council was currently considering the matter, an indirect allusion to his role in the ultimate settlement. When he came to the presentation of the Dutsin Wai proposals, the first was for the construction of a house in Dutsin Wai for the district headman, to be used during that official's annual round of visits through the district. Deliberation on this measure, presided over by the district headman himself, quickly reached the obvious decision. There then followed a request for money to repair the Dutsin Wai rest house and a renewal of an earlier petition for the establishment of a dispensary. Favorable action on the construction items resulted in Dutsin Wai receiving 40 per cent of the funds allocated during this session of the council. Clearly, this young man has a political future.

Only a quarter of the items put before the council required the expenditure of provincial funds or decisions involving governmental units outside the district, but *all* council actions require the emir's approval. Although the emir's action was required, he almost never interfered in strictly local matters. The necessity of securing his sanction for these, however, kept him informed, and also kept his authority continually visible.

Policy matters are involved in no more than a small part of the council's deliberations, there having been only a dozen such issues in two years. Most noteworthy about the policy proposals is the fact that none was approved. Disapproval came equally from the emir and the council itself, with these rejections constituting almost half of all such actions. The general lack of policy questions is understandable in light of the fact that village headmen have never determined local policy, in the sense of issuing legislative orders. Their council behavior simply emphasizes the traditionalism of the society. In addition, the lack of fundamental social change over the past decades is reflected in the absence of structural strains requiring consideration of policy. Eighty-five per cent of such issues stemmed from recent innovations. Five concerned forest reserves and village layouts imposed by the British. Three involved regulation of the use of bicycles. The other issues were about sugar mill permits and the southern cotton buyers. The only problems of traditional policy concerned the opening of new lands and a proposal to tax craftsmen temporarily establishing themselves in Kubau during the dry season. This last move was defeated because imposition of the tax would raise the price of the craft products.

In all, the council refused 14 per cent of the proposals presented. In most of these instances, the presiding district headman, using his authority and his facility for humorous ridicule, had the measure withdrawn. The process was constructively educational. Half of the defeated propositions reflected lack of township responsibility, the concept of which is widening. The comments of the district headman taught the village headmen that they were responsible for the maintenance of intervillage tracks, the regulation of the use of bicycles in the villages, the protection of slaughter slabs from abuse, and the killing of crop-destroying animals. They also learned that, in order to secure a school, they would have to prove that they could keep it filled with pupils. When the district headman opposed a measure to increase the salaries of village headmen, he made use of the opportunity to point out that if they increased the thoroughness of their tax collection, they would receive salary increments. The illustrative figures he employed amounted to an increase of one-third. The comment also served to indicate that the headmen were already augmenting their salaries by tax manipulation.

Finally, the most significant aspect of the council is the fact that it provides an alternative to the traditional method through which the district headman keeps himself informed about district needs. Such information formerly was gained through retainers and personal contacts. The increasing complexity of district affairs, simple as they may seem, makes the use of a council helpful to the district headman, as it has always been to the emir. Although the council has no independent authority, it alters the form of the decision-making process, bringing together the district headman, the village headmen, and their aides. In their joint decisions the former loses his veto power, except as he can persuade the emir to exercise it for him. The effect is to involve the villages more directly in decisions about district affairs. Most importantly, the system, once established, makes further changes inevitable. It is merely a matter of time until the more backward villages make their desires felt.

Much of the success of the council is owing to the qualities of the district headman of Kubau, despite the fact that he is a member of the traditional Fulani ruling class. His use of democratic procedure, albeit with the safeguard of open voting, is not merely a form. Confirmation comes from his willingness to forward the District Council's desire to request a salary increase for the village headmen, despite his criticism of the proposal. And when a youthful trader, like the councilman from Dutsin Wai, joins the councils of the emir, something significant is happening.

Economy

The cotton traditionally grown by the Hausa as a cash crop was employed in the making of native cloth, particularly by the weavers of Kano. Before the establishment of colonial cotton markets, the crop was sold to Hausa middlemen or was processed in the home. As such practice still continues, there is no way of knowing what proportion of the crop reaches buyers for the European trading houses. As late as 1950 it was estimated that at least half of the crop was still absorbed into the native economy.[18] Hand-weaving has, in fact, remained a thriving craft, even in the face of rapidly growing cloth imports from overseas.

Under colonial stimulation the amount of cotton production for export has been increasing. European-owned corporations set up ginning and marketing facilities, the Department of Agriculture provided improved seed and technical assistance to the farmers, and, since 1948, the Cotton Marketing Board has fixed market prices from year to year, removing much of the farmer's risk in expanding production.

One of the first two cotton gins in the north was established at Dutsin Wai about 1925. By 1933 the market there was buying a thousand long tons of raw cotton a year. Within the next twenty years the gin was transferred to Zaria City, but two more markets were opened in Kubau District. The annual average amount purchased in 1955-1958 was 1,800 tons. The income from cotton was roughly £72,000 ($201,600) a year, more than three times the total taxes paid by the district population. The latter fact is relevant when we recall that cotton was traditionally grown and sold primarily to cover taxes.

While part of the expansion of cotton production has resulted from population growth, the amount of land that households put into this crop has also increased. Communal land is still available for development in Kubau. Under these circumstances the problems of landownership, blocking the growth of cash crops in many underdeveloped areas, have not arisen. The expansion of cotton production has not brought any sharp reduction in the production of food crops, but cotton acreages of whole villages may equal or exceed the acreage devoted to foodstuffs. There is even evidence that some villages in the area are no longer self-sufficient in basic foods. We see here a gradual shift toward crop specialization and dependence upon commercial markets.

One type of land, now in limited supply, is the water-logged *fadama* which can be cultivated during the dry season. The utilization of this land began with the cultivation of sugar cane, introduced from Kano. At first used only for chewing, sugar cane came into its own when simple, horse-powered mills were brought in to extract the juice. With government loans, the number of mills in the district increased from one to forty-four between World War I and 1958. Each mill is capable of producing 500 gallons of juice a day. The juice is boiled down to brown sugar in crude vats which are kept fired beside the mill. Working with two horses and a crew of four or five men, such a setup produces 1,800 pounds of sugar a day, worth more than $150. The value of the estimated sugar produced in Kubau during the 1951-52 season was $170,000, distributed among growers, sugarworkers, laborers, and middlemen.

Customary land law experienced a significant change with regard to fadama land. Land rental was contrary to the whole indigenous pattern of land use. When Kano farmers first came south looking for fadama in which to grow cane during the dry season, they were allowed to farm the unused fadama for a fee.[14] The fact that the Kano farmers were external to the local system and could be expected to leave the land and return home doubtless facilitated the new practice of renting land. Once the Zaria farmers adopted the crop, the shortage of fadama made its rental to local farmers both profitable and logical.

In addition to this form of land renting, there is a second type, used particularly in connection with another sort of field in limited supply. These are the farms in close proximity to the village—lands that are manured and farmed continuously. Outlying farmland, harder to reach, may be had for the clearing. Some rich farmers acquire the use of village perimeter lands by lending money to the hereditary tillers of these farms. The farms are held as collateral and farmed by the creditor until the loan is repaid.

Competing increasingly for fadama land is the dry-season tobacco crop. The Nigerian Tobacco Company, with the coöperation of the Department of Agriculture, initiated the cultivation of Virginia Hybrid in 1934. As this crop, unlike cotton, was entirely new, the details of its introduction are particularly interesting.[15] Starting with three farmers with whom agricultural extension agents had already worked, 134 pounds of leaf were produced in the first year. Expansion thereafter was so rapid that by 1951 Zaria produced half a million pounds. This figure is the amount appearing at the tobacco company markets but, as with cotton, an unknown amount of tobacco is absorbed by the native economy for the native manufacture of cigarettes. The first tobacco market in Kubau opened in Dutsin Wai in 1943. By the 1946-47 season, another market was opened in Takalafiya and the total amount purchased at the two was 18,000 pounds. Ten years later the amount had almost quadrupled, adding another $8,000 annually to the economy.

Despite the apparent ease of this expansion, the Hausa have to be persuaded to grow the new crop. The company employs an agent to stimulate and oversee production. He is assisted by the district agricultural mallam who provides continuing technical assistance. The company agent operates through the feudal hierarchy, persuading the district headman to bring the village headmen together and encourage their coöperation. On the major feast day of the year, each headman is given enough sateen for a robe, and the district headman receives enough cloth for two robes. This general procedure, it should be added, is the traditional way to secure any desired favor from chiefs. The village headmen are asked to coöperate by planting the first tobacco in their areas. Seed and careful supervision are provided by the company, the headmen contributing land and labor. The first crop is essentially a status-linked demonstration plot. In the next year the headman is asked to name a local promoter to encourage the peasants to grow the crop. The promoter is paid a modest amount, on a graduated scale, for each acre of tobacco he oversees. The procedure induces farmers to try the crop, but they will continue it only when they are satisfied with the buyer's crop grading and the prices he pays. In short, the peasant is a shrewd farmer. He is willing to try something he has seen to be successful for someone else, and judges his own success in market terms.

Just how rational a farmer he is may be seen in the fact that it was the Hausa themselves who evolved the procedure for growing tobacco in fadama land.[16] The crop was originally planted on higher land during the wet season—and this practice is still general—but it was found that it could also be planted in fadama. This land dries out gradually during the dry season, and, by planting the seedlings progressively inward from the edge of the marshy land as the water level falls, a dry-season crop can be secured. Keen judgment is required in planting so as not to have the soil too moist initially, yet so as to assure a sufficiently long moist period for the plants to mature.

Something should be said regarding the relation of the cash crops to the communication system. The narrow-gauge railway through Dutsin Wai was built to connect the rail junction at Zaria City with the tin mines farther east. That it was the railway that made the expansion of cotton and tobacco production possible is attested to by the role of the railhead of Dutsin Wai. The ultimate closing of the railway in 1958 because of the establishment of a more direct route south for the tin ore forced the development of the automobile road to Zaria. The protests of the tobacco company, which could not reach northern Kubau during the crucial wet season, contributed to the final construction of a car-rending but passable all-season road from Dutsin Wai to Takalafiya.

With regard to cash crops, it is not just the increment to the farmers' incomes which is significant from a development point of view. By growing the crops the farmers contribute to the urban expansion, which feeds back further urbanizing influences such as roads, schools, communication services, technical assistance, and manufactured goods. Kubau's contribution to the half-million pounds of tobacco grown in Zaria was small, yet on the basis of such totals a new cigarette factory came to Zaria City.

In Takalafiya, inanimate energy sources still play only a small local role. The district headman has an automobile, seven government and company employees have motorcycles, and a passenger-carrying truck comes through each day. There are two gasoline-driven mills for grinding peanuts for domestic consumption. Kerosene is generally used in native-made lamps. And that completes the list. It is the mechanical technology of the industrial world which is important at this point. The importance of the sugar mills has been noted, but more significant is the bicycle. By 1958 one out of every seven Kubau males between the ages of fifteen and fifty had a bicycle. Younger men, particularly, use bicycles in place of donkeys for carrying loads. Cycles make more distant markets available, and around the bicycle an entirely new craft, that of repairman, has developed. It is not surprising that the center of this trade is in Dutsin Wai, from whence the repairmen make the round of markets in the region.

Conclusion

If, as the economists would have it, increasing per capita production is the measure of development, the rural Hausa are certainly involved in development, although the only significant change in the sources of energy they employ has been in the area of transportation. The social concomitants of development, which we have viewed as the essential elements of industrial urbanization, are an increase in the differentiation and specificity of roles, their assignment on the basis of achievement, and the development of literacy. What evidence do the Hausa show of change in these directions?

Increasing functional specificity is evident in the new roles created by the government and the corporations, such as dispensary attendants, agricultural advisers, tobacco production agents, and cash-crop buyers. The expansion of cotton production has moved the farmers in the direction of specialization, but the really urbanized situation in this regard will be reached only when cash crops supplant subsistence crops. There is little indication that this shift is taking place. The increased productivity of the Hausa has resulted largely from their becoming more efficient farmers.

Yet even peasants can participate in urbanization through the contribution of personnel to the increasing number of specialized nonfarming roles in the countryside and particularly in the cities. The increase can come about through local social invention, as evident in the appearance of bicycle repairmen. Or it can come about through migration, but here again the Zaria Hausa incorporate seasonal movement into the diffuse functions of peasant life itself. In areas like Sokoto, where land pressure has developed, peasant society is more apt to provide personnel for urban growth. But without literacy or skills, such migrants also fall short of providing the prerequisites for urban development.

In education, the heavy hand of feudal insistence on religion-oriented instruction has been obvious. Despite this, one should not pass too lightly over the fact that urban-oriented education is not only present, but has come to have value for the local elite. This change is probably the clearest example of traditional values having given way to the perception of the importance of new means to desirable ends.

In the political sphere the system is still fundamentally feudal, and the allocation of major power roles is still limited by ascription. The initiation of democratic processes has introduced a new method of allocating political roles on the basis of achievement, and has laid the groundwork for power shifts which the emirs vaguely feared when they resisted British proposals for Nigerian independence. So far, even the achieved roles tend to be filled by members of the elite but, when the social type represented by the councilman from Dutsin Wai becomes the rule rather than the exception, the urbanized political basis for development will have been achieved.

8.
SOCIAL ALIGNMENT AND IDENTITY IN A WEST AFRICAN CITY
by Michael Banton

A distinctive characteristic of sociological thought is its concern with the question of how people come to constitute a society and how this society is maintained. Much of it is summed up in the notion of "consensus," which is frequently used, though we are still far from an adequate understanding of its implications or from developing good measures of so intangible a quality. But, without some degree of consensus, what we know as social action is impossible. People cannot combine with one another unless they share certain goals and agree as to what is admissible or inadmissible to the relationship in which they are to operate. Large numbers of migrants may be brought together in a single settlement without necessarily creating a society.

It would seem to me that American experience in the growth of urban communities is more relevant to African examples than European experience has been. American cities have grown with great rapidity by the inflow of ethnic groups, which, like African tribes, have been vertically divided from one another instead of being split horizontally on a class basis. When the inflow is small, the immigrants can be assimilated to the culture and institutional ways of the host group, but in many American and African cities there has been no host group; ethnic communities have competed with one another for political power, and such consensus as has been achieved has been an amalgamation of competing traditions. The justification for characterizing African urbanization in this way will be better appreciated if it is seen that not only have immigrant communities struggled with the locally dominant tribe, but that the imperial power has functioned as an ethnic group in attempting to impose its conception of the sort of urban society that should develop.

In attempting to conceptualize the interaction of the forces at work in a changing society, a vintage theory which is useful as a starting point is that propounded by Sir Henry Maine more than a hundred years ago.[1] If progress is to be effected, then, according to Maine, law and public opinion must be in balance; law, which represents the bonds that hold society together, has to be slightly more conservative than current opinion. The argument implies that consensus and change necessarily stand in an inverse relation; the faster a society changes, the more maladjustment, reflected in conflict, crime, and mental stress, may be expected until the society is threatened with disintegration. If this view is correct, then the more heterogeneous the elements brought together in one urban center, and the more rapidly internal relations are changing, the more difficult it will be to build a society.

One weakness in this view is its unitary implication that consensus has to be founded on a central core of common values. It takes no account of the social value of an individual's integration into lesser groups within the society, and the positive value of opposition between such groups. On this question the writings of social anthropologists about African societies have much to teach us. Evans-Pritchard's well-known analysis of the political system of the Nuer showed that order could be maintained among a people lacking constituted government by the balancing of opposed loyalties.[2] A man was supported by his close kinsfolk in a dispute with a member of a neighboring community, by the whole district in a dispute with someone from a different district, and by an even larger social unit if his antagonist belonged to a corresponding group. Solidarity, in other words, is not simply a matter of shared values, but of stimulus operating within a patterned social structure. In the same way, consensus exists only on particular issues. People draw together most easily in response to what they perceive as pressure from an outsider, and a poorly integrated society which would break up if left to itself may function relatively well when it is threatened from outside or when its members can be persuaded that they are so threatened. We may note that many early African leaders learned their nationalism abroad when they found how little respect was accorded their countries internationally. They and their followers are still trying to vindicate Africa in the eyes of the world, and this preoccupation has helped bolster some regimes that, internally, have not been very securely based.

In this paper I wish to examine the kinds of social alignment that emerged among tribal immigrants in Freetown, Sierra Leone, during the first half of the present century, to see if the experience there helps illuminate the processes by which immigrants are absorbed into the urban system. I shall try to show that it is useful to rephrase the problem of urban consensus in terms of structural opposition. To consider only the pattern of group alignment would be to take a purely structural ap-

[1] For notes to chapter 8, see page 194.

proach; if we wish to take account also of some of the psychological issues of immigrant adjustment and motivation within the framework of group alignments, it is useful to examine the parallel question of group identities, which has interested observers of American cities. The immigrant comes into a social system in which only a limited number of identities are open to him. Professor Everett C. Hughes told me that when, as a student, he went to work in Chicago during a university vacation, his fellow workers asked, "What are you?" He replied that he was an American, like his parents and grandparents before him; but this answer was not acceptable. "American" was not an ethnic identity, and everyone had to fit into some ethnic category. Eventually they decided that he was an Englishman. This incident raises in one's mind many questions about African urbanization. What kinds of identities are available to the immigrant—ethnic ones, class ones, or identities dependent upon length of settlement? How well do the available identities fit the immigrant's self-conception? Is he able to modify the set of choices and forge an identity more acceptable to himself? If he does so, the pattern of group alignments will be affected. It is possible—let us put it no more strongly than this—that a review of the data on African urbanization in these terms may reveal connections between related phenomena which have not previously been apparent.

Rural-Urban Continuity

The only writers who, in the analysis of African urban society, have consistently applied the model of structural opposition, first stated by Evans-Pritchard, have been Max Gluckman, J. Clyde Mitchell, and A. L. Epstein in their work for the Rhodes-Livingstone Institute. They have argued that under the conditions prevailing on the Rhodesian Copperbelt, Africans unite in opposition to Europeans; only when relations with Europeans are not involved do differences between Africans, like those of tribe and class, become relevant to conduct. The West African urban studies, however, do not show so distinct a pattern of group alignment, and it is necessary first of all to try to account for this. It might be argued that the structural oppositions appear sharper in the Central African studies because the writers have chosen to focus on them as a research procedure. Even so, there are many reasons for thinking that the oppositions are in reality much sharper there than on the West Coast. On the Copperbelt most of the Africans are employed in the mines where there has been a clear-cut racial division of labor; the Africans have moved there relatively recently and live in mine compounds or urban locations. The gulf between Europeans and Africans is apparent and relevant in many spheres of action. On the West Coast, however, there have been relatively few Europeans, and a variety of intermediary groups stand between the immigrants and the colonialists. Settlement has been gradual over a long period, and most of the housing has been owned by Africans. Tensions between immigrants and the locally dominant ethnic groups are much more immediate than those centering upon Europeans.

Another important factor has not been accorded in these studies the attention it merits. I refer to differences between the way of life in the town and the way of life in the districts from which the immigrants come. Max Gluckman argues that the "starting point for analysis of urbanization must be an urban system of relations, in which the tribal origins of the population may even be regarded as of secondary interest. The comparative background for these analyses is urban sociology in general." [3] Earlier he suggests that a radical distinction has to be made between the context of African behavior in the tribal districts and in the cities. An African townsman is a townsman. An African miner is a miner, and as such needs not a chief, but a trade union; not the social relationships his parents knew, but those appropriate to his new situation. Gluckman emphasizes the discontinuity between rural and urban life by claiming that "the moment an African crosses his tribal boundary to go to the town, he is 'detribalized,' out of the political control of his tribe." [4] The rural-urban differences have been smaller in West Africa. The migrant travels a shorter distance and goes to a community less different from the one he has left. On the Copperbelt the sharp group alignment derives not only from the factors already mentioned, but in part from the way rural-urban differences serve to isolate the urban community, bringing migrants of different tribes together on the basis of specifically urban alignment and weakening rural ties which would involve the migrants in other systems of social relations. The Copperbelt miner is above all else an African as opposed to the Europeans, and an urban industrial worker as opposed to a rural farmer. But in West African cities neither of these identities has been so important as in Central Africa.

Confirmation of this thesis can be found in a study of urbanization in North Sumatra. Edward M. Bruner has expressed dissatisfaction with the theories of Maine, Tönnies, Wirth, and Redfield (all of which assume a unitary view of consensus) for explaining the retention of rural customs by Batak migrants to a coastal city in Sumatra. He contrasts his observations there with the position of North American Indians—an example that is very close to Gluckman's, for the Indian can lead a tribal life on the reservation or an urban life in the city, and the two societies are fundamentally different. The Batak, however, preserve their ethnic identity in the urban environment and attach heightened significance to the customs that differentiate them from other groups. There is close communication between the city and their villages of origin, and only the elite, who have more extensive contacts with non-Batak, have to work out social patterns for responding to the new conditions. Because there is no national Indonesian identity, the Batak cannot easily mingle with the other groups in relations of solidarity.[5] This situation resembles the West African one in that there are no racial oppositions on the Rhodesian pattern, and the differences between the rural and urban ways of life are less clear-cut. The sense of ethnic identity is correspondingly stronger.

Urban sociologists have long experienced difficulty in defining their field of study. There has been a general tendency to characterize phenomena as "urban" according to the degree to which they departed from rural patterns, but this distinction means only that by such definitions some towns and sections of towns are more "urban" than others. A series of recent papers has emphasized that much that was previously regarded as characteristic of a specifically urban way of life is to be explained as the outcome of competition and the conflict of interests in the economic order.[6] We must not assume that two urban settlements, because they are comparable in size or because they are both in Africa, are therefore similar in other respects; studies of African urbanization need to be set against a broad comparative background.

The Growth of Freetown

Freetown is, in some respects, a rather special case.[7] In most parts of West Africa, migration to the city has meant movement into a settlement controlled by the local tribe. But in Freetown the established group has been the Creoles, descendants of early Negro settlers and of Africans liberated from the slave ships in the nineteenth century. The Creoles had no common culture, and in the small peninsula on which they were resettled only English law and local ordinances prevailed; there was no "native law and custom" in the colony area. In addition, the intensive missionary effort taught the Creoles to be God-fearing, education-conscious Victorians and to see themselves (with considerable justification) as an outpost of civilization on an inhospitable shore. Freetown therefore developed as the most European of West African cities; the tribal migrants who came there had to work out an orientation to a way of life that not only was urban, but also incorporated different conceptions of civic virtue.

In 1891 the population of Freetown was 30,000, of whom somewhat more than half were Creoles. The remainder were chiefly from tribes in the immediate hinterland (Temne, Mende, Limba), from groups associated with trade to the more distant interior (Mandinka, Fulani), and from the local community of seafaring Kru whose original home was Liberia. But, though the Creoles had only a bare majority statistically, they were the dominant influence in almost every respect. The non-Creoles were split into many sections, and the largest group, the Temne, numbered less than 3,000. The tribal groups often saw one another as being every bit as alien as the Creoles, whereas the latter showed a united front to immigrants. Bishop Ingham, writing in 1894, touched upon relations between the Creoles and the migrants from the hinterland, saying, "The latter form a class for the most part below them. They are their servants. Illicit connection there may be, but not intermarriage." This use of the word "class" had some justification, for many leading Creoles believed they had an obligation to elevate the native peoples and worked to this end, but, like any dominant class, they preferred to restrict social relations to people who observed their own conventions. This situation must often have been paralleled in nineteenth-century New England, as the flood of Irish immigration lapped around the established Anglo-American communities. It introduces, too, one of our problems: the interplay of ethnic and class differentiation.

In studying how the tribal immigrants were incorporated into urban society, we must perforce rely largely upon the evidence implicit in institutional developments. We look first at the governmental practice, dating from the 1880's, of recognizing the leaders of immigrant tribal communities as persons possessing customary authority and as being the proper medium of communication between these groups and officialdom. We must recognize a distinction, however, between the trading tribes of the interior and the people of the immediate hinterland who came to Freetown in search of unskilled employment as laborers and servants. Among the latter, one of the most important services tribesmen demanded of their headman was that he help them in obtaining employment as porters and laborers; legislation enacted in 1908 gave headmen power to investigate any complaint made by one of their men against an employer, and in this way to play an industrial role similar to that designed for the tribal elders in the Northern Rhodesia mines in the 1930's. But the law seems not to have been utilized. At this stage the immigrant had no stake in the new order, and could not have identified himself with the city. He was a tribesman, not a townsman.

It would appear that up to World War I the life of ordinary Temne, Mende, and Limba in Freetown depended upon many of the same institutions as tribal life in the country. The tribal headman acted much like a minor chief, holding court, administering punishments, and accepting fees which could only with difficulty be distinguished from bribes. The norms of relationship between kinsfolk had not changed. The major threat to the maintenance of tradition had been the steadily increasing flow of educated youngsters from the mission schools; many of these had lived as wards in Creole households in the city. After finishing school and obtaining work, an educated tribal youngster found himself awkwardly placed. There was no role open to him in the tribal sections of the city which acknowledged his educational attainment; but, equally, there was no role among the educated Creoles which acknowledged his tribal connections. For many years the Creoles tolerated a tribal man in clerical employment only if he "turned Creole," adopting a Creole name and cutting himself off from associations with tribal people. The only identity open to the educated young tribesman was that of "Creole." Because members of the modern elite were siphoned off in this way, the impact of the new order upon tribal communities in the city was delayed.

After 1918 the population balance swung decisively against the Creoles; of the 44,000 inhabitants of the city, less than 16,000 were Creoles, but they remained the largest single group and by far the most powerful. The shift in political power in Freetown was not really demonstrated until 1957, when the first man of tribal background was sent to the House of Representatives by a Freetown constituency. Well before this time, people with tribal connections, formerly identified with the Creoles, had chosen to emphasize their tribal ties and to use tribal names. The tribal leaders were men who had never compromised in this way, but they had been deeply wounded by Creole attitudes toward them. Their followers were often openly anti-Creole; any Creole who sympathized with the Sierra Leone People's Party found that his expression of a divergent opinion was immediately attributed to his Creole origins, and that proper argument was impossible. There was no place for the Creole in the new political order; now it was he who was faced with an identity problem. Some Creole leaders argued for an autonomous Creole region, others thought they should go "home" to Britain. The missionary and educational work of the preceding century had been so effective that many Creoles really felt closer to the Englishman than to the tribal African.[8]

American writers once liked to point out that by 1890 Chicago was the third-largest German city, the third-largest Swedish city, and the third-largest Norwegian city. Similarly, from the time of World War I, Freetown was the largest Temne city, the largest Mende city, and the largest Limba city. How close is the similarity? The Freetown migrants were in closer touch with their fellow tribesmen in their districts of origin than were the new Chicagoans, despite the immigrant press, for the Freetonians could and did revisit their natal villages and were received there with honor as men from the big city—the source of power and of all sorts of desirable commodities. It might be expected that in such circumstances ethnic ties would be stronger than in America, but, never-theless, such tribal exclusiveness as has resulted hitherto is not very striking compared with the continuing strength of ethnic ties in some American cities.

The tribal immigrants have not settled in separate districts, and the dispersion of incomers is comparable to that which one might find in a Western industrial city. Apart from the Kru Reservation and two out-lying all-Mende communities, there is no neighborhood identified with a particular tribe. Nor, since the early days, has there been any marked concentration of people from the same tribe in a particular occupation (the only really noticeable exception is the traditional affinity of the Kru and the Bassa for seagoing employment). As sensitive an indicator as any is that of tribal intermarriage. From an examination of the birth registers for 1951 and 1952, I found that of 888 births for which one parent was a Temne, in 81 it was the father only, in 234 the mother only, while in the remaining 573 both parents were Temne. Correspond-ing figures for the Mende were 290: 72, 54, 164; and, for the Limba, 653: 67, 63, 523. The high outmarriage rate of the Temne women is doubtless due to the present predominance of Temne in and around Freetown, so that the immigrant male from more distant parts meets marriageable Temne girls more frequently than he meets girls from his own tribe. There are some limitations to these figures, but they do sub-stantiate the impression that tribal origin counts for little in many kinds of situations.

One factor responsible for the comparative harmony of intergroup relations in Freetown has been its slow rate of growth compared with other West African capitals. The population of Freetown was 34,000 in 1901, 55,000 in 1931, 85,000 in 1953, and at least 100,000 in 1961. By contrast, Abidjan, starting from almost nothing, had 18,000 in 1936, 87,000 in 1951, and about 200,000 in 1961. Until recently, the big politi-cal and social splits dividing the African population of Freetown have all coincided with the Creole-tribal distinction; thus the division has been largely a matter of sentiment, very rarely having any base in en-during economic interests. Tribal differences, similarly, are chiefly of relevance in leisure-time contacts between tribal people. In America, ethnic politics have been in large measure a politics of assimilation, de-pending upon the desire of recent arrivals for acceptance and equality. In the Northeast, ethnic labels have been used for identifying people and for classifying jobs because of their salience. The immigrant groups arrived in sequence so that at any given period the established popula-tion would be aware of the particular group coming in, their appearance, speech, customs, and so forth. Ethnic identities became important in such a situation and were cultivated by politicians because they were a more stable basis for providing a following than were prestige classes, with their fluid composition. This policy helped preserve ethnic differentiation. In Freetown, by contrast, there has been a wider variety of tribal groups (twelve have official headmen) which have expanded simultaneously. Europeans and Creoles attached little significance to tribal affiliation in their dealings with natives, and were not very sensitive to differences in appearance, speech, and custom, which, in any event, were often not very evident. Consequently, ethnic differences did not get built into the economic structure.

The Progress of Islam

The two most striking institutional changes among the tribal communities in Freetown prior to the establishment of full-fledged political parties were the steady conversion of the Temne and other tribes to the Islamic faith, and the spread of new forms of voluntary associations. Both developments seem to have been significant for the creation of new identities, and therefore for drawing the immigrants more fully into the urban system.

Interpretations of the spread of Islam will doubtless differ. Some might observe that all the regions to the north of Freetown were Muslim, and go on to argue that, as pagan practice was ill-adapted to city life, and in any event was viewed as mere superstition by Christians and Muslims alike, the tribal immigrants would gradually feel obliged to identify themselves with one of the major faiths; at their current level of education they might be expected to find Islam the more comprehensible and congenial. In my opinion, we need, however, to consider also the way in which religious observance was identified with membership in social groups of varying prestige.

Let us put the matter at its simplest. Bring a number of different tribal groups together in a city and some common denominator must be found whereby qualitative differences among the groups can be expressed as quantitative ones. Tribal practice is exclusive; a man is either one of the group or an alien, and there is little or nothing to choose among different kinds of aliens. In the city such groups are thrown together with aliens as neighbors, fellow workers, and potential relatives by marriage, so they cannot regard them all as being equally foreign. As might be expected, they prefer the company of people from tribes coming from the same region as themselves, speaking a similar language, and having similar laws and customs. Thus, neighboring peoples who are rivals and enemies in rural districts become friends in the city, for they compare well with the incomprehensible people from other regions. But it is not just a question of cultural similarities. Some immigrant groups are more successful because of temperament, schooling, or circumstantial advantage, and they become the pacesetters, envied and respected by the others. Gradually a hierarchy develops, establishing the prestige of the different tribal communities, so that when an immigrant thinks of another group he recognizes it not only in terms of cultural affinity with his own, but also as being socially superior or inferior. I submit that some such process is an inevitable consequence of urbanization in many parts of Africa, though local and industrial conditions will affect the level of group consciousness.

On the Rhodesian Copperbelt, Africans rank tribal groups according to several factors, among the most important being the degree to which a group approximates the urban ideal of a "civilized" or "European" way of life and its traditional reputation in warfare.[9] In Freetown, however, the opposition between European and African culture has been modified by the social significance attached to Islam. The distinction, mentioned earlier, between the tribal immigrants from Freetown's immediate hinterland who were pagans from small-scale forest societies, and those from the interior who were Muslims from relatively large-scale herding and trading societies, is particularly relevant here. It would seem that the prestige that the Muslims themselves attached to correct religious observance soon communicated itself to other groups which viewed the Fulani and the Mandinka with considerable respect. The Europeans agreed in this valuation. Bishop Ingham, in the passage quoted previously, goes on to speak of "superior-looking natives . . . from the interior countries" and their exclusiveness. Another factor contributing to the prestige of Islam was the existence of a community called "Aku" whose members were in many respects similar to the Creoles. The Aku were likewise descendants of captives taken from the slave vessels, but they had retained the Yoruba language and the Muslim faith from the period before their enslavement. The Aku had standards of living and education comparable to those of the Christian Creoles, which proved to the newcomers that progress and Christianity were not inseparably associated.

Politically, there was considerable tension between the Creoles and the tribespeople of the provinces. The Creoles viewed themselves as a successor elite who, because they were more civilized, could lead and govern the country; but, being in a minority of one in fifty, they also felt very much on the defensive. The tribal peoples, and their chiefs, rejected Creole pretensions and resented their attitudes of superiority. Thus the major split within the African population—both nationally and in Freetown—was that between Creoles and tribesmen. One of the distinctive characteristics of the Creoles had become their profession of Christianity. (Twice in 1952-53 I inadvertently asked a Creole to which tribe he belonged, and received instead the answer, "I am a Christian.")

For tribal people, to become Christian was therefore to identify to some degree with an opposed group; to remain pagan was to accept an identity totally lacking in prestige; to become a Muslim was to profess a faith different from that of the Creoles, without being inferior. The assumption that tribal people were Muslims and that Muslims were tribal people was soon accepted by Creoles and immigrants alike.

But Islam did more than provide a cultural foundation for intertribal grouping. Islamic religious practice, in addition to differentiating tribal people from Creoles, provided the common denominator in terms of which differences in the prestige of tribes could be expressed. The better a tribe's reputation for Islamic orthodoxy, the higher its prestige.

Unless one acknowledges the social significance of religious practice in the Freetown situation, it is difficult to account for the steady spread of Islam, not only among the Temne and the Limba, but also among the Mende who have many Christian missions and schools in their home country, and in 1952 had twelve congregations in the city. When I was in Freetown, all the tribal headmen and all the subordinate tribal officials and the more important officers of voluntary association whom I met, whether men or women, professed themselves Muslims. The one exception is itself revealing. Among the Kru and the Bassa no religion other than Christianity is practiced, but the tribal headmen of these two groups supported independent Christian churches, instead of ones with missionary associations. The leaders of the different tribal communities felt ashamed unless they had a mosque of their own which would compare favorably with those of the orthodox tribes, and, as a recent study has shown,[10] this feeling gave rise to a burst of competitive mosque building. In its social aspect, Islam enabled the tribal people collectively to demonstrate their solidarity against outsiders, but separately to symbolize their tribal pride and exclusiveness.

Young Men's Companies

A second line of institutional change which operated in a similar context was the voluntary associations. The tribal communities started to form bereavement benefit clubs on the Creole model before World War I, but it was not until the 1930's that this development took a strong hold. The Temne who came to Freetown had a disagreeable surprise when they found the dignified Fulani and Mandinka looking down upon them for being pagans and "bushmen." The insult was the more galling because the Temne consider that Freetown is situated in Temne territory. In the elaboration of new associations, as in the adoption of Islam, it was this scorn that was the spur to action.

Before the 1920's bereavement clubs and entertainment societies had been separate, but then the Mandinka started two new voluntary associations that served both functions. Each society had its own characteristic dance rhythm, its songs, and a limited number of members who were required to attend regularly and contribute money to help any other member who had been bereaved. These societies became very popular among the youth of many tribes, and numerous branches sprang up in different parts of the city. The Temne at this time ranked well below the Mandinka in prestige. Many of the brighter young Temne joined Mandinka societies, learned to speak a little of the language, and started to pass themselves off as Mandinka instead of Temne. If such a tendency was to continue, Temne pride would suffer a grievous blow. So some of the younger Temne leaders (two teachers in particular) sought to found a distinctively Temne association on similar lines which might counter the drawing power of the others. In doing so they had to risk their own reputation by getting involved with the younger and rougher elements.

The new Temne "company" (or *compin*, to use the local expression) met with instant acclaim; similar Temne societies were formed throughout Freetown, and spread to Temne youth in the hinterland. I have discussed their success and the reasons for it in some detail in my book, and wish here only to recall some of their more important features. A company provided a member who was bereaved with a contribution toward his expenses, and its members were obliged to attend the wake if the burial was held in the city. In the tribal village the lineage would have been there to help at the most important event; in the city a migrant may be on his own. Consequently the wake, and honoring the member's dead kinsman, may be even more important than the material support. Another benefit deriving from company membership was the opportunity to join with other young men and girls for dancing and entertainment in relatively exclusive groups which protected themselves against attacks from the troublemakers who thrive in the new urban centers.

The companies tended to act, unconsciously and consciously, as pressure groups representing the modernist elements among the Temne youth. Their members shared common values appropriate to a semi-industrial society and partly opposed to the traditional order, though they were ready to build on the latter whenever they had the opportunity. They believed in "civilization," meaning thereby the adoption of many European and Creole practices, and it is interesting to note that men who were employed as domestic servants in European households would sometimes show their fellows how to cut cocktail sandwiches for a society gathering. The companies improved standards of dress and demeanor among their members. They sang praise songs in honor of tribal leaders whom they respected, and criticized others in the same way; they brought in outsiders as patrons and distributed honorific titles among themselves; these actions may be seen as an attempt on the part of the young men to confer prestige where it was merited by their standards, and to institutionalize new norms. They were a reformist element trying to improve the Temne identity and to raise tribal prestige.

Some four years after the establishment of the first company, the Temne tribal headman died. The young men, determined to present their own candidate for election to the office, pressed the cause of the schoolteacher Kande Bureh, who had taken the leading part in creating the company. His opponents were much older men, tribal conservatives who were not literate in English. Thanks to the effective organizing work of the companies, Kande Bureh carried the day. He used his new office to continue the process of tribal reorientation which the companies had begun. Soon there were Mandinka who applied to join Temne companies. Though a headman's powers are negligible on paper, the Temne leader soon became one of the most controversial and respected figures in tribal quarters. Temne pride was healed. In 1957 Kandeh Bureh entered the House of Representatives and immediately received a ministerial portfolio.

The companies played a part in Temne society similar to that of Islam in the wider tribal grouping in that they had a powerful effect in drawing the group together and in giving it a new sense of unity, even though only a minority were involved in the new developments. But at the same time—and here again there is a parallel with the religious change—they provided a means of expressing differences within the group. For the companies, I believe, mark the beginning of social stratification among the tribal proletariat. Previously the tribal workers had been an economically and socially undifferentiated mass; a man's obligation to his kinsfolk, and his dependence upon them, remained such that he could never establish himself as belonging in any superior social category except by turning Creole and denying tribal obligations. The companies, however, were made up of the more ambitious younger element who established higher standards of conduct for their members than prevailed outside these associations.[11] Voluntary associations here, as in other African towns, have served as resocializing agencies in which aspiring young people taught themselves the principles of conduct in an achievement-oriented society. The multiplicity of offices, which is characteristic of the independent churches as well as of the voluntary associations, cannot be explained solely as deriving from the desire to confer prestige; the variety of offices permits a high proportion of members to learn how to run an organization and to become familiar with the requirements of leadership. Thus these organizations create new groups within the tribal population.

The incipient stratification is apparent in the differential prestige attached to membership in the various companies. The better companies—those with higher standards—are careful about whom they admit, and make inquiries into an applicant's background; they have a membership of better-behaved young people who observe traditional norms of honoring kinsfolk, but accept European conceptions of education and economic progress while acknowledging the Islamic faith. I suspect that for a Temne to be an officeholder in one of the better companies meant that he was regarded by his neighbors in much the same way as a small shopkeeper in a homogeneous working-class district in a British city; he was recognized as being a little above the ordinary run of people. Being a member of a company or a savings club would also assure a man that he could claim financial support as of right without humbling himself before his kinsfolk; this right, too, has implications for the emergence of economically based social strata.

Social Class

The general view among sociologists has been that, although African townsmen recognize differences in the prestige of the roles held by their fellows, it would be premature to speak of the existence of social classes. One reason for this hesitation is that an acknowledged difference of occupational prestige does not have the significance in other social contexts which the Westerner would expect. People of different "classes" associate in a way that would not occur in an industrial society. As Kenneth Little writes, "Although spending most of his leisure time in the company of other wealthy and well-educated Africans, a member of the elite is quite likely to have one or more illiterate relatives living permanently in his household." [12] It is not simply a matter of providing house room for an aged grandmother, but of an equal association that ignores the prestige differences. It is apparent even in marriage, which identifies the parties more closely than any other relationship. Relatively few wives are educated to the same standard as their husbands. Indeed, according to Little, husbands may prefer it this way, as there is less likelihood of marital discord when the wife is quite illiterate. She is less expensive to maintain than her sister who has had a few years at school and has acquired new aspirations. The illiterate wife makes few demands on her husband's attention, and is less likely to object to the introduction of additional women into the household.[13]

Writing of East Africa, J. E. Goldthorpe expresses the opinion that the Ganda would see nothing strange if a doctor had a brother working as a clerk or a sister married to a carpenter,[14] and he quotes a similar observation about Nigeria: "The Minister has a 'sister' selling cassava in the market; the successful doctor has a 'brother' working as a Public Works Department labourer." [15] Goldthorpe goes on to observe, as others have done, that one of the chief personal problems of educated Africans is that of defending themselves against the avalanche of poor relations who descend as soon as they get their first salaried job. Kinship ties take priority over the embryonic forces making for stratification.

The African household may bring together persons occupying roles far apart in prestige terms because other identifications are more important. In the preindependence situation in West Africa, at least, it was more important for an African to identify himself as an African in opposition to Europeans and Lebanese than to underline distinctions that set him apart from other Africans. Again there were many situations in which an African who stood high in class terms sought the approval of illiterate and semi-illiterate members of his tribe in order to win their political support. In the struggle for power, tribal sentiment was sometimes stirred up for personal ends. In some areas, such as southwestern Nigeria, descent groups seem even to have increased their importance because of their ownership of land and their control over elections.[16] An ambitious man might well cultivate relationships with kinsfolk rather than with men of similar class position.

It would, therefore, be dangerous to assume that urbanization necessarily leads to the weakening of tribal ties and to the substitution of ties of social class. The immigrant to Freetown is involved in a series of oppositions, African versus European, tribesman versus Creole, Temne versus, say, Mende. The identity he adopts at any moment depends upon how he defines the situation in which he is involved.[17] Once clanship played a part in this scheme, so that an immigrant member of the Bangura clan might seek out a fellow clansman to request accommodation, or even someone of a different tribe who observed the same clan taboos. Now, this hardly ever happens.

Class identities seem to develop in three ways. In the first place, class distinctions can be recognized within tribes. Just as the Nuer social structure divides first into tribes and then into primary and secondary sections, so it is possible to see the social structure of Freetown as dividing first on the European-African, then on the Creole-tribal distinctions, while the tribal category then splits into Temne, Mende, Limba, and other groups. The three categories—African, tribesman, Temne—are in a straight hierarchy, and each one can be socially relevant only when the higher-order oppositions do not enter. In the same way Temne might recognize class distinctions among themselves, but deny them when they felt themselves in opposition to a Mende group. Second, tribal membership itself acquires a class value in intertribal relations. A man who is a Fulani gains respect because of the Islamic piety associated with his tribe regardless of his own piety or lack of it; any Loko suffers similarly from the identification of his group with employment as night-soil men. Third, class alignment may form on a basis of individual social evaluations running across the lines of tribal solidarity. The latter is likely to take place first in situations that do not conflict with tribal expectations—like personal friendship—and to the degree that higher-order oppositions are weakened. The weakness of class alignment was probably one of the reasons for the absence, in the early 1950's, of differentiation of urban neighborhoods by functions or quality of housing; new concrete houses stood side by side with rickety shacks, and Africans saw nothing incongruous about such juxtaposition.[18] More recently, a clearer land-use pattern has been emerging, and housing has been built for Africans of higher income in more outlying neighborhoods. This association of class differentiation in housing and the weakening of political opposition along racial lines cannot be purely fortuitous.

Now that the political power of the Creoles has been broken, it is easier for opposition to arise between and within tribes. It is interesting to note, moreover, that so far as political appeal is concerned, tribal affiliation remains much more important than class alignment.[19] Attempts to create a political following by appealing to the class interests of labor have failed, but tribal loyalties have been a sure basis for political maneuvering. In the immediate future, the resemblance to the situation in cities of the northeastern coast of the United States may well become closer.

Conclusion

The tribal immigrant to Freetown is incorporated into the urban society by a dual process of personal adjustment and group alignment. He finds city life attractive because of the freedom it provides and the possibilities of personal advance which it opens up. Like other rural immigrants in cities all over the world, he prefers urban squalor to the more humdrum life of the village, where material conditions are often worse. The change-over in conditions of work and residence does not seem to create serious problems of personal adjustment, partly because the institutional context of urban life is not so very different. But the immigrant finds that, within both the urban and the intertribal systems, he is given an identity at variance with his self-conception. The desire to improve other people's conceptions of his group has led to a whole series of tribal self-improvement campaigns, to an assault on Creole political pretensions, and to a strong and widespread desire to convey a favorable image overseas.

These changes cannot be explained without taking account of the pattern of group alignment, both as it is perceived by the immigrant and as it is affected by the structure of the larger politico-economic system. In this paper I have concentrated upon factors of the former kind. I have held (1) that the immigrant is absorbed into the urban system, not by a process of individual change in line with the melting-pot conception of assimilation, but through his membership in a local group of people drawn from his own tribe; (2) that the definition of these groups and the things that symbolize them are determined by a pattern of structural opposition; (3) that the relative sharpness or diffuseness of these oppositions varies from place to place, and is affected by a number of factors, including the relative discontinuity between the rural and urban environments; and (4) that membership in any particular tribal group often acquires prestige value so that migrants may express concern about the image of their group held by others, and seek to improve it.

The nature of the larger politico-economic system often influences the character of the groups within it. For example, many people have noticed how difficult it has been for the Creoles to unite on any issue. The employment of so many of them in administrative positions, it is said, gives them a "civil service mentality" instead of making them politically conscious; their business interests may have been competitive rather than collaborative; their strongest efforts were directed, not toward resisting tribal claims, but toward achieving English norms which subsequent events have rendered less relevant. Their position in the colonial system was such that very few incidents of any kind could stimulate Creole solidarity, whereas many more could precipitate collective action on the part of tribal groups or of the impatient young men. If we use the model of structural opposition adopted here, we must also look for the kinds of incidents that stimulate group alignment, and determine how these incidents are generated. These considerations are less immediately relevant to the study of immigrant incorporation, but they should not be overlooked.

9.

MIGRATION IN WEST AFRICA: THE POLITICAL PERSPECTIVE

by Immanuel Wallerstein

The migration of people, if they are numerous or if they come from key strata of the population, tends to affect the structure and distribution of power both in the societies from which they come and in those into which they move. Sometimes, indeed, this process of change is cumulative, when the migration of some, by affecting the attitudes and the structural position of the others, contributes to still more migration.

There has been considerable movement of peoples in West Africa for a long time. Furthermore, these movements have generally been recognized to have political significance, and as such have attracted the notice of persons in authority. They have, to be sure, taken many different forms, but there is no reason arbitrarily to exclude from consideration any kind of movement on the grounds that somehow it is not within the terms of reference.[1] In this paper I consider the kinds of movements that have occurred in the precolonial, colonial, and postcolonial eras, and the effects of these movements upon the distribution of power and the spread of political ideas. The incidence of such migratory movements is hard to determine, as present statistics are quite inadequate. Further research might indeed force us to qualify certain conclusions based on assumptions about incidence.

Precolonial Migration

Migration was widespread before the modern colonial era. Men migrated to conquer, and the western Sudan knew a succession of conquering groups. When political structures were weak or frontiers were ill-defined, there were more peaceful movements of peasants in search of better land opportunities. In the course of time this process would transform the political structures of the areas affected. Movements of major

---

[1] For notes to chapter 9, see page 195.

trading communities also had direct political effects. For example, the role of the Dioula in the political development of the kingdom of Kong in the pre-European era was to "settle all over without taking part either in politics or war. One might say that the Dioula were peaceful conquerors who contributed as much as the chiefs of Kong to the creation of the unity of a very heterogeneous region." [2] Finally, within the hierarchical states that grew up in West Africa, much displacement of people was motivated by political considerations.[3] As Lombard notes, "The majority of traditional migrations, whether internal or 'intertribal,' were political in nature." [4]

Although "the movements which have taken place in the twentieth century, great as they have been, are not such breaks with the past as has been suggested," [5] the impact of colonial order on the nature of the movements has been significant. Colonial administration has meant the removal of some restraints, and above all, the creation of new pressures to move. There were a number of restraints on movement in precolonial Africa. In fact, movement was legitimate in few large-scale political units. Linguistic differences formed a barrier, and roads were not free of obstruction and extortion. Indeed, the removal of these restrictions was one of the boasts of the colonial administrations.

Perhaps the most severe restraint on individual migration in precolonial Africa was the relative rarity of political structures to which those who had the wealth, vigor, and initiative to leave their own society (for whatever motive) could move, and in which they could secure a status as good as or better than the one they had held in the society from which they came. Although individuals could and did move about, they normally were assigned politically subordinate places in the community where they finally settled. As it is probable[6] that "emigrants" were recruited from among the higher strata of the traditional community, the subordinate place in the receiving community would mark a lowering of social status and of political power for the prospective migrant. Under such conditions, the natural inertia of loyalty to one's own birth community would largely outweigh the various pressures to leave.

Migration during the Colonial Era

The gradual emergence in West Africa of a modern economy within the framework of colonial administrative structures changed this situation. Deviants had a place to go—the city, the city that makes men free. In West Africa, the colonial administrative city typically was not under the authority of a traditional tribal hierarchy. The political structure was based primarily on nonethnic considerations, as was to a larger extent the system of stratification. The norm that a man might make his own way on the basis of ability became increasingly prevalent. The attractiveness of this kind of social structure to a migrant is evident. Furthermore, the improved methods of transportation created to meet the needs of the modern economy and administration facilitated such migration. These considerations not merely increased the rate of migration; they also affected the use of social sanctions in the traditional, rural communities, as those in authority had to concede more to the deviants if they wished to forestall the possibility of emigration. Here, as in other ways, the constraints of the colonial system tended to dissolve, or at least to alter, the bases of traditional authority.

Although colonial order enhanced the possibility of migration, it also tended to limit it, or to channel it in certain ways. Most obviously, it terminated movements occasioned by warfare and conquest. As West Africa had experienced a substantial amount of such movement in the nineteenth century, the incidence of migration was significantly affected. Furthermore, the introduction of bureaucratic administration and law, and, in particular, the beginning of the use of written records in such matters as land tenure, tended to militate against movement. As Colson reminds us, "The Colonial era was marked by an attempt to tie people to given areas of land as their permanent homes and thus to perpetuate the population distribution that existed when the European powers took over. Permanent migration was discouraged by administrative regulations and by a freezing of the rules under which land was held." [7] Finally, the new colonial boundaries had a reality that it would be a mistake to underestimate. The map of West Africa between 1900 and 1960 took the form of a continuous French area, with the four colonies of British West Africa, Portuguese Guinea, and the independent state of Liberia forming largely noncontiguous enclaves. It is true that many important movements took place across international frontiers, the most notable being the movement of the Mossi, and of Hausa traders across French areas, to the Gold Coast.

Probably there would have been much more migration in West Africa had the entire area been under a single colonial administration. Certainly, during crisis situations, frontiers were tightened. For example, the "military breach between the British Gambia and Vichy French Senegal had, of course, important political consequences; for political and security reasons seasonal migration from Senegal . . . was discouraged by the doubling of the legal tax the stranger farmers had to pay." [8]

Such crises were relatively rare. A more important consideration is that the creation of certain facilitating channels for the migrant encouraged staying within the particular colonial framework. Three main points are relevant. First, each colonial power developed lines of communication and transportation entirely within its own framework, omitting any consideration of integrating the economy of West Africa as a whole. Road networks, telegraph lines, and, above all, railroads, show a peculiar pattern of discontinuity which undoubtedly affected migratory movements. Second, the existence of two principal separate currency systems in West Africa made it easier in many ways for migrants to remain within a single colonial system, for otherwise the transfer of funds brought complications with which they could normally cope only at great expense of time and money. Third, customs fees, both licit and abusive, intimidated potential migrants who might otherwise have crossed frontiers:

For French subjects returning [from the Gold Coast] to French territories, the three successive taxations [of the Gold Coast, Togo, and Dahomey] are considered persecutions. Furthermore, the exorbitant sums demanded (and often without receipt) mean that the homeward trip of a Zabrama [native of Niger] via Lome and Cotonou is considered a dangerous affair. . . . All these abuses have a considerable impact on migration and particularly on the Mossi. The latter constantly asserted to us that their stay in the Gold Coast was so long because of their fear of passing customs into Upper Volta.[9]

Customs thus had the double effect of lessening migration across international frontiers and increasing the length of stay of those who had made the crossing.

In addition to removing some traditional restraints to migration and imposing new ones, colonial administration created new pressures in favor of migration, both direct and indirect. One that is often overlooked was the educational system which, at the postprimary level, concentrated students in a few central institutions in West Africa and, at the university level, in Europe. For the prospective urban elite this "migration" was very often longer in duration than that of a laborer, and more psychologically uprooting. Its political consequences were probably much more significant and more immediate. One of the notable consequences of the rise to power of nationalist movements was the attempt to reduce the proportions of this migratory pattern by establishing secondary schools, and even institutions of higher education, nearer to home, as well as by investing funds in bringing students home for vacation periods.[10]

The effect of taxes on migration was more widespread than that of schools, as indeed it was meant to be. The use of head taxes as a method of inducing people to migrate to work centers was, of course, fundamental to colonial administration. The numbers were, however, often larger than planned by the administration. Although some men migrated in order to pay taxes, others migrated in order to *avoid* paying taxes, or otherwise escape burdens imposed by the colonial administration. Skinner, citing Harrison Church's explanation that the search for "simpler administration" was a cause of migration, suggests that people really "were fleeing from forced labor or punishment for inability to pay taxes." [11] The two major explanations of migration have been given as economic pressures and "the desire to place oneself outside the direct authority of chiefs and elders," and "also of administrative action: recruitment of laborers, etc." [12] Such migration for the purpose of escape met opposition from the colonial governments (and perhaps today from the independent governments), whose functionaries saw in this individual evasion a political threat. In the north of Dahomey the "important migrations of unskilled labor to the Gold Coast were quite evidently not organized by the Administration, who on the contrary viewed them with disfavor, without having, however, the means to stop them." The administration disliked migrations because they "render more difficult the control of the population, collection of taxes, and recruitment of labor." [13] There was also an administrative bias against high rates of movement: "It has become established practice in most territories to report annually upon the percentage of able-bodied men absent from a district and assumed to be at work; high rates have been considered cause for alarm, even though those dependent upon the flow of labor might be demanding more manpower." [14]

Migration, then, probably increased in volume throughout the colonial era, despite the basic cessation of rural movement caused by the imposition of a rational administrative order. In order to assess the political consequences of this increasing movement, it would be well to identify the various types of migration which took place. The most common distinction is drawn between temporary and permanent migration, and, although it is difficult to draw the line, a common-sense distinction based largely on the attitude of the migrant is fairly simple and useful. There were three main categories of temporary migrants. First, the peasant-laborer came either to a town or to a cash-crop area for a limited period and then returned home. Second, the educated, sometimes urban, African migrated first as a student, and later as an official working either for the government or for a private bureaucracy (commercial house, mission, school). In the latter group were the following politically important movements, some of which no longer occur or have diminished in recent years: southerners to the northern regions of Nigeria, Dahomey, Togo, Ghana; Dahomans, Togolese, and Senegalese to other areas of French West Africa; Sierra Leoneans to the Gold Coast, Nigeria, and the Gambia; Creoles to the interior of Sierra Leone (and parallel movements in the Gambia); Gold Coasters to the Ivory Coast. We might attach to this movement of elites the movement of certain commercial trading groups (Hausa, Dioula, Wolof) which, because of the increasing access to educational facilities during the colonial era, have come to play social roles closer and closer to that of the migratory elite.[15] Third, there was the temporary migration of non-African elites, who fall into two main groups: European officials (administrative, commercial, and religious-educational) and Indian merchants in British West Africa.

Permanent migration was less complex. New permanent urban populations which were normally above the level of unskilled labor have emerged. Permanent urban dwellers were often second-generation immigrants. But, as elsewhere in the world, they were able, in an expanding economy, to advance themselves. Some of the children of the migrant unskilled workers became, in the towns, school leavers with clerical occupations, and, in the cash-crop areas, farmers or merchants. Although historically these groups might have settled in any urban area that seemed convenient, with the coming of independence there has been a reshuffling, so that these urban dwellers tend increasingly to reside in cities of the same country as their rural village of origin (or ancestry). Second, there was a new permanent rural middle-class element in cash-crop areas whose ancestors did not reside in the same rural area. Third, Syrian-Lebanese merchants who had migrated to West Africa had begun to intermarry with the local population. Finally, we might add a fourth group, the West Indians. They, however, are disappearing, as they merge into the African urban elite. In the meantime they suffered from certain political disabilities. There was no permanent European-settler class in West Africa, although this possibility has been considered from time to time, most recently in 1953.[16] The rejection of this possibility, rumored to be owing to the "mosquito," has been of major political importance.

The network of migratory movements developed during the colonial era[17] performed the elementary function of widening the political perspective of increasingly large numbers of people. Much migration was short-term and involved a large proportion of the population, giving them wider perspectives on the world and bringing them into contact with new ideas, ideas that were to be subversive of the colonial political order. Moreover, new geographical units of reference, the territory-nation, became known and relevant to many people. Viable alternative status systems also became known and available, thus giving individuals political leverage they did not possess before. Finally, modern social skills, including that of organizing social movements, became widespread.

It was not only perspectives that changed. It was ecology and, with ecology, power. People moved physically away from traditional rulers; they moved into other areas and settled there. The existing local political systems could not remain unchanged in the face of such movements and of the changes in economic structure these movements represented.

Migration affected the rural political structure by altering the age-sex balance, and in this way it often affected the social tasks attributed to various groups, or the ability of certain age-groups to play their traditional role in their society. It often altered the willingness of returned migrants to render authority all its traditional due. But a rural society had not only to contend with individual migrations to work centers. Under economic and administrative pressures, many tribal groups expanded (migrated) to colonize "vacant land," in what Mercier has called "local migration." In his study of northern Dahomey, he cites some of his findings:

a) Dwelling tends to spread out, in a region where it had been grouped. . . . The agricultural encampment in a zone of "colonization" may immediately acquire a large autonomy . . . even if it is not accepted by the traditional chief, or recognized by the administration, which sought for a while to fight against a dispersion that complicated its task.

b) . . . The district chiefs [*chefs de canton*] see the dispersion of those under their authority. The proportion of inhabitants who theoretically live in a village, but who in fact reside elsewhere, may reach 90 per cent. . . .

c) Not only do territorial units break up to give birth to smaller ones, but the new ones are much less stable. . . .

d) . . . The occupation of vacant lands is made without reference to an established authority (although in some instances the head of the family first installed in a given zone tries to take on the attribute of "chief of the land"). Conflicts have broken out lately which are submitted to nontraditional arbitrations.[18]

Over the long run, the pattern of emigration changed. The response was no longer to immediate pressures for cash (to pay head taxes). The rural economy, albeit still basically a subsistence economy, became dependent on the national economy in the sense that the money sent or brought back to the rural areas by the migrants affected the socially defined subsistence level. This change combined with improved health conditions to create new pressures for emigration, as the land can support only a certain number of persons at a given level. The underemployed can be pressed to go to urban areas, if there is even a remote possibility of employment or of living off employed relatives. Colson argues that at some point "the number of people who remain on the land will tend to remain stationary . . . Labor migration then becomes a means of coping with a surplus population that cannot be supported within the region rather than a source of cash supplementing subsistence." [19] As the situation became one in which the rural area wished to divest itself of people rather than to retain them, the local privileged group came to have less moral hold on the young, even on those who remained in the rural area.

The political problem of the returnee was not limited to his disturbing impact on his rural place of birth. Migration and return, with consequent disaffection for traditional ways, led also to the development of what may be called "local urbanism." This pattern exists among the Mossi:

There are several young men in the two districts where I have studied who have never cultivated a stalk of millet since they returned from Ghana. A few of them use their meager capital to buy some stocks of merchandise which they hawk in the markets; and others make short and frequent trips to northern Ghana with livestock and other commodities. Those men who did not like trading, or who failed in their efforts, went off to Ouagadougou to join an ever-increasing urban Mossi population.[20]

Although migration affected in these various ways the power structure of rural areas from which the migrant moved, the consequences were limited in many areas by the fact that the emigrants were of course not present, and direct confrontations with those in authority were minimal. Returnees came back individually, seldom collectively. Numbers and influence remained substantially on the side of the old order.

This was far less true at the other end, the area into which the emigrant moved. There are, of course, two such areas. First, there is the urban center which attracts immigrants because of its administrative, commercial, and sometimes industrial activity. For purposes of this discussion on West Africa, we may include the mining centers as well. Second, there are the cash-crop rural areas into which migrant labor comes and often settles.

The immigrants did not simply spread out along the occupational horizon. They tended to concentrate in certain types of jobs and became identified as belonging to certain strata. Consequently, class and ethnic group became related characteristics, at least for a certain span of time. [21] Some of the causes of this job classification have been identified:

In principle the stranger who has come to the Lower [Ivory] Coast to make money is less fussy about the type of work he does; liberated from his traditional structures, he accepts jobs that doubtless he would never have taken at home. This frame of mind has allowed migrants to approach all sectors of economic life, particularly the commercial sector, with a forceful dynamism which comes to be reinforced by a deep group solidarity. In Kumasi, for example, the Central Market presents a typical illustration of the evolution of the stranger. The latter, pressed by necessity, has invaded domains traditionally reserved for Ashanti women; whole areas of trade have been monopolized. Sexual rivalries have been added to ethnic rivalries.[22]

The immigrants thus have often become highly visible in an economically competitive situation. For their protection and advancement, they became "supertribalized," forming "ethno-professional communities." [23]

This ethno-professional identification became significant not only for the migrant, but for the employer as well. Migrant labor enabled older resident groups to acquire a relatively higher social status, again created and made visible by the phenomenon of migration. This phenomenon was illustrated in Senegal in the relations of cash-crop farmers to migrant labor:

It is quite certain that it is the local farmers who must make the greater concessions . . . because they . . . need [the migrants] and, for multiple reasons, would not know how to get along without them. . . .
Economic reasons, first of all. . . . [There is a] second reason, a social reason, which is all the more effective: There is not a single farmer in certain regions of the Senegal peanut country who would fail to use migrant labor [navétanes] in any plot, for the employment of seasonal labor is a sign of social advancement, of familial and budgetary independence. It is even a goal in itself, and it costs too much later to give it up.[24]

The commercial and job competition in the towns and the competition for land in the rural areas, as migrant labor sought to obtain ownership rights, formed the basis for the local political quarrels that came to the surface in the wake of nationalism in the late colonial era and after independence. Unfortunately, not enough attention has been given to the description of such local politics in West Africa,[25] but the theme of "native" versus "stranger" is a recurrent one and explains much of what, at a national level, often seem minor local disturbances.

Migration thus promoted an "ethno-professional" or "class" consciousness. Such a development, however, is not to be seen as totally divisive in its consequences for the territory as a whole. For this awareness is "modern," and had meaning more in the emerging national framework than in the traditional tribal framework. For one thing, the new ethnic groups often had wider boundaries than traditional tribal groupings, and thus served as a first step toward the creation of new loyalties.[26]

The ethnic associations of the migrants were breeding grounds of modern political organizing ability, and the returning migrants carried back with them the new nationalist ideas they acquired in the urban areas:

In contact with trade-union and political reality, little by little the mass of migrants acquired a clearer perception of their vital interests, and experimented with a certain number of techniques appropriate to defend those interests. Returned to his home, the migrant could not suddenly forget his experience; the new image he had of himself could not fail to provoke profound changes in his home milieu. This transformation, coinciding with the evolution of the former French Union, was one of the numerous factors that accelerated the process by which the former territories took over complete control of their own destinies.[27]

The colonial authorities were always conscious of the function of migrants in spreading political values. In 1956, at the time of the Suez crisis, the French administration tried to make sure that migrants returning from the (presumably too-liberal) British Gold Coast did not bring back "pro-Nasser propaganda from the Moslem political parties in northern Ghana." [28] And in the early days of nationalism, some British administrators blamed it all on migration. In Nigeria, for example,

Migration beyond the capacity of the towns to absorb the newcomers has led in many cases to unemployment, destitution and crime, and these in turn have been a breeding-ground for political agitation. It is among such elements that the extreme nationalist movements find their most vociferous support, and their main branches are in the towns. The relationship between newcomers and the old inhabitants often leads also to problems of local government.[29]

Migrants bring new ideas, to be sure. Yet they are also reconditioned to their own environment fairly quickly. Perhaps the really important impact is to be measured through the increasing number of children born in the towns who return later to the villages with their migrant parents: "Under present conditions, the participation of children in the phenomenon of migration can . . . play an important role in the formation and transmission of a national culture presently being created, in the context of new contacts between ethnic groups and between emerging nations." [30] These children become adults for whom socialization to the values of the nation and use of the nation as a reference group is a childhood experience rather than one acquired in adult life. For them, a village frame of reference is the new phenomenon rather than the reverse.

During the colonial era migration made possible the contacts through which horizons were broadened and administrations were subverted. It led to new economic possibilities and arrangements, and these in turn caused traditional systems of authority to be called into question. Migration was, in short, a phenomenon congruent with both modernization and nationalism.

Migration after Independence

In the colonial era West African nationalists had very little to say about migration. There were, of course, grievances connected with it, and nationalists capitalized on them. But the fact that many people moved about was not in itself a matter of political concern to nationalists. The coming of independence and the need to reinforce a national consciousness tended to change this nonchalant attitude.

Frontiers began to seem very important after independence. It was not that disputes over boundaries loomed large. In the main, the existing boundaries were not seriously questioned, despite the fact that so many were poorly defined. It was rather movement across these frontiers which provoked anxiety. First, the large, continuous French area was broken up into separate states, and increasingly into separate currency units. There were more frontier posts, and more papers were required to cross the boundaries. Although frontiers may still be far from tight, they are in many respects tighter than they were before independence. Frontiers, of course, symbolize a political entity, and are a handy mechanism in the attempt to make citizens aware of their nationality. Furthermore, the building of a political entity requires increasing economic integration. Customs and currency control are ways in which economies can be reconstructed. Indeed, the economic factor may make movement across national frontiers increasingly difficult for the next twenty years.

New states must have nationality laws. Decisions are thereby forced upon many migrants. Before independence, British or French nationality was enough to establish respective political rights. Nigerians voted in the Gold Coast, and Senegalese ran for office in the Ivory Coast. Indeed, on innumerable occasions even the French-British distinction was eliminated for Africans. In the race for control of the party structures that dominate West Africa today, however, migrants feel the squeeze in that their "nationality" is held against them by their "ethno-professional" competitors. Ghana, the first newly independent state, faced this problem immediately after independence, and in many ways set the pattern. There the migrants

... who remain in Ghana for long periods, do take part in Ghanaian politics and create many problems for local authorities. One of the main problems is that some of the local politicians do not want the Mossi to vote because they do not consider them permanent residents of Ghana—and in fact many of them plan eventually to return to their homeland. The second problem is that the many Mossi residents in Ghana are encouraged by their chiefs to support the Moslem Association Party and the Northern People's Party which stand for strong traditional chieftainships rather than the Convention People's Party which favors representative government. The political behavior of these Mossi chiefs explains why many of them were among the persons deported from Ghana for subversive activities after the 1956 election.[31]

At a higher level, the years 1958-1960 saw a large-scale movement of top politicians in French West Africa from their territories of residence to their territories of birth, a decision that was not often voluntary. In any event, strangers had no effective political base. A large number of opposition leaders in trade unions and other voluntary associations have been deported whenever the nationality laws made such action possible.

Even when political participation was not at issue, the fact that strangers, not merely of a different ethnic group but now of a different nationality, held good jobs led to pressures for their repatriation. The most dramatic example was the 1959 riots in the Ivory Coast which caused the mass withdrawal of Dahomans and Togolese. A similar event, for a nonbureaucratic occupational group, was the expulsion of Guinean diamond seekers from Sierra Leone in 1959. Less dramatic instances have been common. Even within the frontiers of one country the same tendency has appeared, as when the Northern Regional government of Nigeria sought to "northernize" the civil service. All these efforts are aimed at the migration of elites in the spirit of combating what one Ivory Coast intellectual has called "black subcolonization." [32]

If independence has led to pressures that cut down migration of elite elements across national frontiers, it has expanded the international migratory patterns between Africa and the rest of the world. Specifically, this expansion takes two important forms. At the university student level, more Africans go to non-African countries other than the former metropole. (But, conversely, there are fewer Ghanaians studying in Sierra Leone and fewer Ivory Coasters studying in Senegal.) Second, recruitment of non-African administrative, commercial, and educational personnel is being broadened, the now-familiar consequence of a foreign policy of neutralism.

Finally, frontier controls have been used as a weapon of foreign policy. Specifically, one of the pressures the Ivory Coast used in 1959 to force the withdrawal of Upper Volta from the Federation of Mali was the threat to expel Mossi migrants from the Ivory Coast. What pushed Upper Volta into seeking close links with Ghana in 1961 was partly the presence of so many Mossi migrants in Ghana. Although the costs of tampering with the migratory pattern might be very high for these countries, the possibility is there, and it now affects political decisions.

These tendencies to limit migration of Africans within West Africa, at least at the elite level, because of the exigencies of nationalism will probably continue, and will probably become stronger in the next few years. Such limitation of migration will be particularly likely if the number of unemployed in general, and of unemployed school leavers in particular, continues to increase. Free movement of Africans fits in with the ideology of Pan-Africanism. But governments struggling with severe economic problems tend to be restrictionist in their reactions, and, under popular pressure, to be even more so. In time of crisis, migration, or rather its limitation, could become a major political issue.

10.

THE ECONOMICS OF THE MIGRANT LABOR SYSTEM

by Elliot J. Berg

The characteristic feature of labor markets in West Africa, as in Africa generally, has been the predominance in the labor force of migrant workers, men temporarily in paid employment who shuttle between home villages and employment sites. Most observers have not taken a kindly view of the migrant labor system. Migration is often pictured as a major factor contributing to high labor turnover in paid employment, the low level of African skills, the low general level of wages, and the backwardness of African agriculture. On the side of social costs, an even grimmer picture emerges from much writing on the subject. Migration is said to lead to the destruction of tribal social stability, to "immorality" and the distortion of traditional marriage arrangements (owing to the absence of men from the villages), to the spread of disease (particularly venereal disease, because migrants associate with prostitutes in towns), and to the decline of birth rates. The following is a typical statement:

> The system of migratory labour is sometimes defended on the ground that it eases the transition from a subsistence to an exchange economy. But workers who are neither peasants nor full-time wage earners to a large extent get the worst of both worlds, and the system imposes costs on employers, and on the economy as a whole, that keep African wages down. The employer bears all the adverse consequences of high labour turnover and the particularly heavy expense of recruiting when the sources of labour are so far distant. The economic loss to the community as a whole includes the adverse effect on tribal agriculture and land, loss of productivity and possibilities of acquiring skill and experience resulting from high labour turnover, the great wastage of manpower involved in the constant trekking back and forth between tribe and town, and the economic consequences of the social disruption caused by the system.[1]

It is no surprise that migration has few defenders, and that demands for

[1] For notes to chapter 10, see page 197.

its abolition and for stabilization of the labor force are so commonly expressed.[2] The main group friendly to it has been the proponents of apartheid in South Africa, who favor it for political and ideological reasons. This support, of course, has further discredited labor migration in the minds of other people.

In this paper I focus on some of the economic aspects of labor migration; its social effects are not considered. I attempt to show that the migrant labor system represents an "efficient" adaptation to the economic environment in West Africa. Historically, it permitted West Africa to enjoy more rapid economic growth than would otherwise have been possible. It continues to benefit both the labor-exporting villages and the recipient areas. Because migrant labor permits a better allocation of resources than would be possible under any other form of labor utilization, it is not likely to disappear until fundamental changes occur in West African economies.

The Migrant Labor Market

As the general pattern of the West African migrations is well known, only certain features need be mentioned here. Several main migratory flows can be distinguished. One is the movement from north to south, from the Sudanese belt countries of Mali, the Volta and Niger republics, and the northern parts of coastal countries to the coastal areas. The second is the east-to-west movement, from Mali, the western parts of Senegal, and the northwestern parts of Guinea to Senegal and the Gambia. There are in addition significant lateral movements along the coastal regions, from Togo, Dahomey, and eastern Nigeria to neighboring countries. The numbers involved in these movements are known only roughly. The eastward migrations involve perhaps 75,000 men annually, most of them *navétanes*, or peanut sharecroppers, in Senegal and Gambia, the rest wage earners in Dakar and other Senegalese urban centers. The southern and lateral movements may number in the neighborhood of a million men a year, about half of them in Ghana and the Ivory Coast.

The migrations thus involve large numbers of men, and provide much of the labor force in the money sector of the economy. The total labor force in paid employment in West Africa is about 2 million, including those employed as sharecroppers on African farms. It is difficult to estimate the proportion of migrants in this number, partly because of conceptual difficulties inherent in defining a "migrant,"[3] partly because of the lack of information. But almost all those in paid agricultural employment, and perhaps half of those in nonagricultural employment, are temporary migrants; overall, it is probable that more than half of those who work for remuneration are migrants.

The migrations cover vast geographical areas, cutting across climatic zones and political boundaries. In a certain measure much of West Africa forms a single market for migrant labor, an interrelated whole where changes in wage rates or job opportunities, or changes in the prices of crops commonly cultivated under sharecropping arrangements, affect the size and the direction of labor flows. Thus changes in the price of peanuts in Senegal (and hence the remuneration of peanut sharecroppers from Mali and Guinea) have some effect on the supply of labor to the Ivory Coast, as Mali migrants have customarily gone to both places. And changes in wages or job opportunities in Ghana influence the flow of Voltaics to the Ivory Coast, for Ghana and the Ivory Coast are alternative destinations for migrants from the Volta Republic. The intensity of these connections—in technical terms, the cross elasticity of supply—varies from place to place and over time; nowhere are these relationships the predominant influence on wage levels, but they are significant factors, particularly in the Ivory Coast and Ghana.[4]

Labor markets in West Africa not only are large in geographical scope, but tend also to be highly flexible and sensitive, close approximations to "perfect markets" in the economic sense. There are many buyers and sellers in these markets. The migrant labor force is homogeneously unskilled and transferable between employments. Physical and occupational mobility is a notable feature. Knowledge of job opportunities and of conditions of employment circulates widely, and individual migrants are sensitive to differentials between employers, industries, and even countries.[5]

With respect to international mobility, certain inconveniences, notably customs control on the return journey, are always involved in crossing frontiers. In the past these were rarely of sufficient importance to obstruct the flow of labor from one country to another. Since 1957, with the emergence of independent states, the frontiers have become more significant barriers, but there is little evidence so far that international movement of unskilled laborers has been appreciably affected. Because of the predominance of migratory labor, there occurs what amounts to a periodic recontracting of employment terms, which magnifies the degree of mobility in the market.

Most of the migrants are young; few are over thirty-five. They are mostly bachelors; if married, they usually leave their wives and children in the villages. While the "typical" length of stay in employment varies widely, from several months to several years, two general categories may be defined: the seasonal migrant who is away for less than a year, usually eight or nine months or even less; and the short-term migrant, who may stay in paid employment anywhere from one to three years, and occasionally longer.[6]

Migrant Labor and Economic Change

The process of economic development in Africa brings structural change, that is, the shift of land and labor resources from subsistence to market-oriented production. How did the development of the migrant labor system affect this process of widening the scope of the market economy?

There can be no question that migration stimulated the growth of money economy. It did so by creating easier labor-supply conditions, by making entry into paid employment more attractive to villagers. If African villagers had been presented only with the choice between permanent entry and no entry into paid employment, there would have been very few volunteers for West Africa's emerging labor force. The quantity of effort available for income earning would have been reduced, and the rate of growth of marketed output would have been smaller than it was.

Although the demand for wage labor by European employers and by colonial governments was less in West Africa than in other parts of the continent, from early in the century African farmers were relatively heavy users of hired labor. Labor scarcities persisted in various parts of the region until the late 1920's, and in some instances until later. The development of a work force presented special difficulties in West Africa. Because population was sparse in most of the region, labor was a relatively scarce factor, and land resources were relatively abundant. Overpopulation and rural misery could therefore not be counted on to "push" Africans out of their villages into employment. Nor could the "pull" of demand for higher income operate very effectively in the early decades of modern development. The villages were largely self-sufficient, their members touched little by the desire for new goods. Population concentrations were in the interior savanna regions, far from mines, towns, and cash-crop farms (located usually along the coast and in coastal forest areas); therefore, long-distance movements of men were required. These usually meant risky journeys and unhealthful changes in climate. The social system was intimately tied in most instances to land-tenure arrangements, and few men were prepared to abandon their place in traditional society and their rights over land. Given these conditions, the possibility of working for a short period outside the village was probably the most effective single stimulus to the release of a voluntary labor supply.

Several features of the West African economic environment made temporary migration a particularly suitable instrument for the growth of the African agricultural export sector, which is the foundation of these economies. In the savanna zones, the relatively densely populated areas, men are underemployed during the dry season. In the forest and coastal zones, where conditions are favorable to the growth of export crops, suitable land is abundant and people are relatively scarce. At the same time, climatic zones in West Africa are so ordered that the slack season in the savanna zones is the busy season along the southern coast. Thus there is a seasonal dovetailing; the period of inactivity in the savanna regions corresponds to the time of peak agricultural demands in the cocoa and coffee regions of the forest zone. Short-term movement from savanna to forest was thus a natural adaptation, particularly because the kinds of work required in the cocoa and coffee regions, harvest labor and the clearing of new plantations, lent themselves to seasonal or casual performance. Without the inflow of migrants, inelasticities of labor supply would unquestionably have restrained the expansion of the export sector.

Migration thus facilitated the development of African agricultural exports at the slightest possible real cost in terms of sacrificed production of traditional crops. It made labor available to African farmers in the most productive regions; it spurred export-crop production directly by encouraging a gradual transfer of people semipermanently to more productive regions. In Ghana and the Ivory Coast particularly, export-crop production owes some of its development to migrant laborers who took rights over cocoa and coffee land as a form of payment from local growers, and created their own plantations.[7]

The Impact of Migration on the Village Economy

To analyze the economic effects of migration it is necessary to distinguish the area where migrants work from the area where they originate. We will call the former the "outside" economy, the economy where the migrant is employed as wage earner, sharecropper, or casual laborer. The villages of origin we will call the "village economy." This distinction is more convenient than the usual separation into "subsistence" and "market" or "exchange" economies, because activity in most West African villages is in fact divided between subsistence and market purposes; analysis of the economic effects of migration must proceed by the consideration of the possible consequences to both outside and village economies, and to the various types of activity within the village economy.

Migration increases the supply of labor available in the outside economy by providing villagers with the alternative of temporary employment; it therefore benefits the outside economy by permitting a higher level of output there and accelerating the enlargement of the exchange economy. Not all groups in the outside economy necessarily benefit. Because of migration, the general level of wages of unskilled labor tends to be lower than it would otherwise be; whether the aggregate wage bill of those originating in the outside economy will be more or less depends on the elasticity of demand for labor there. In any event, it is certain that the labor-importing economy enjoys a net advantage from the migrations.

The effects of migration on the village economy are more relevant to the present discussion. They also are complex. On the one hand, it may be presumed that migration occurs because villagers cannot earn at home the money income they need, or can earn it at home only with more intense effort. The result of movement from the village into the outside economy, therefore, is a higher income per unit of effort of each migrant, and a higher level of income per migrant. The incomes of some members of the village economy are thus increased by an amount equal to their net earnings in paid employment.

There are, on the other hand, certain costs involved in the migrations. The general economic advantage or disadvantage to the village economy can be determined, at least in the short run, by balancing benefits thus obtained against the costs suffered by the village economy as a result of the absence of men. The necessary data for drawing up such a balance sheet in quantitative terms do not exist. But some qualitative appreciation of the probable weights to be assigned to the various costs and benefit items can be arrived at analytically.

Let us first suppose that all migrants are seasonal migrants. Let us further suppose that they arrange to be away from the village during the dry season, and that they take into account the seasonal fluctuations of village labor requirements, leaving after the harvest is completed and returning home in time for the following season's planting. A very large group of migrants in West Africa follows approximately this pattern; they migrate for a period somewhat less than a year, a period usually determined by harvesting and planting requirements in their villages of origin.

The unpublished results of a study I completed in 1959 revealed a very high proportion of seasonal migrants in the north-south movement from the French-speaking areas to the Ivory Coast and Ghana. Of 195 men returning north from employment in the Ivory Coast, about 45 per cent claimed to have been in employment six months or less, and slightly under 40 per cent, between six months and a year; only about 7 per cent said they had been in employment for more than two years. Of the 317 migrants descending to the Ivory Coast with previous work experience,

20 per cent had worked less than six months on their last trip, and 50 per cent, less than a year. Of the 102 Voltaic migrants questioned on their return from Ghana employment, exactly half claimed to have been in Ghana six months or less, and another quarter, between six months and a year. Of the 107 Voltaics questioned as they descended into Ghana for employment, 84 said they planned to stay six months or less, and the rest, under one year. These findings, which involve many Mossi laborers, are not confirmed by Skinner, who says that "Mossi migrants, more so than men of other groups, tend to remain in Ghana from two to three years before returning home."

In seasonal migrations the benefits far outweigh the costs. This imbalance is true for the individual migrants; their net gains are equal to their earnings in paid employment minus transport costs, their cost of subsistence while in paid employment, and their foregone production in the village economy, which is likely to be negligible. At the same time, the income (or real consumption) per head of those who remain at home is also likely to be higher with migration than without it. For the harvest, completed by the migrants before their departure, may be regarded as the village's stock of goods to be gradually consumed over the course of the year. The absence of the migrants diminishes the number of stomachs to be filled, and hence allows each remaining villager a larger share. It is revealing that throughout northern Nigeria seasonal migrants are apparently referred to in the local language as "men who while [eat?] away the dry season," and R. C. Abraham's *Dictionary of the Hausa Language* gives a definition of "migrant" as follows: "In order to eke his corn out, he has gone to spend the hot season elsewhere in exercise of his trade." [8]

The absence of men, even seasonally, may reduce the stock of goods and services over which villagers have command in any or all of four ways. (1) If the cost of transport exceeds the migrant's share of the harvest, there will be an actual reduction in the per capita consumption of those who remain in the village. (2) Village capital formation will be neglected in such matters as well digging, hut repair and maintenance, path clearing, and road maintenance; the general convenience of life in the village will to this extent be impaired. (3) The village will have available to it fewer tools and consumer durables, to the extent that village craftsmen or handicraftsmen, men who would have produced something during the dry season, have migrated. (4) The village output of agricultural goods will decline (*a*) if the agricultural system is such as to make exacting demands as to timing of planting and preplanting preparatory work, and if men are absent at the precise time they are needed, and (*b*) if, because of migration, men reduce their income-earning efforts in the village economy by cutting back on cash-crop production.

The quantity of "leisure" available in the village will also decline.

Those villagers who migrate are not able to participate in village amusements and repose, in traditional ceremonies and entertainments. Those who remain in the village may enjoy fewer of these activities because of the necessity to work harder in the absence of migrants.

The weight of each of these cost elements varies from area to area, depending on distance from employment sites and average transport costs, on the proportion of men who are seasonally absent and how long they stay away, and on the character of the agricultural system. The transport item is probably unimportant for most migrants, given the relatively low cost of long-distance transport in West Africa, at least since the development of road networks after World War II, and the fact that the migrant finances at least his return journey from his earnings in paid employment. The apparent ease with which West Africans travel long distances for relatively short periods also leads to a presumption that transport costs are not burdensome. Recruiting arrangements in many areas, furthermore, reduce migration transport costs to near zero. Thus the Senegalese peanut sharecroppers receive free transport if they procure a "navétane card," and those workers in the Ivory Coast's agricultural labor force recruited through SIAMO, the recruiting organization, also receive free transport.

Nor is deterioration of the village's stock of public capital likely to be appreciable in the event of seasonal migration, even with the absence of relatively large numbers of young men. The extended family of the migrants can step up their efforts, and coöperative work groups can fill in such manpower gaps as arise.[9]

Similarly, the effect of seasonal migration on subsistence output is probably not significant. It is true, as Miss Haswell's heroically patient study of peanut growing in West Africa and other less intensive studies have shown, that village output does decline if men are absent at precisely the right time for planting.[10] If seeds are put into the ground too late for the first rains, and if weeding is not thorough after the early rains, output suffers. But if the migrants are "perfect seasonals," they would take these conditions into account. And in practice there is good reason to believe that many of them do, for the seasonal migrant knows that the value of a day's labor in the villages at planting time is particularly high; his incentive to return home on time is strong. At the same time powerful social pressures emerge within the village to assure the presence of migrants when they are most needed. All these factors tend to minimize the effect of seasonal migration on food output:

> The Mossi have now built up an ideal pattern of the way in which migration must take place if it is not to upset their socio-cultural system. Of course, not all the migrants accept this system, and many of the elders accept it only because their opposition to migration is fruitless. Ideally, the migrants should not leave for work

in the cities, mines, vegetable and cocoa farms of Ghana until the end of November, when most of the crops have been harvested. They should remain in Ghana for about five months, during which period they should hoard all their money. . . . When the flowering of certain trees . . . shows that the rains are approaching, the migrants should collect their seasonal wages. The next step is to visit the markets of Kumasi in order to buy goods, including presents for wives and parents. And without dallying along the road the migrants are expected to hurry home in time for the planting. Unless this goal is accomplished most Mossi families feel that their cultivation will suffer. The migrants endeavor to follow the schedule because they look forward to a few weeks for the display of their new clothes before settling down to serious cultivation.[11]

It is in the production of cash crops and in the output of village handicraftsmen and weavers that the impact of seasonal migration appears to be strongest. Much of the cash-crop growing is "men's work," and many men have chosen to earn income through migration rather than by growing crops for sale. Also, in the agricultural cycle the cash crops tend to be sown late and harvested late, which conflicts with the seasonal migrant's schedule. Finally, some migrants are weavers and blacksmiths, or traditional craftsmen of other kinds, who continue to produce during the dry season. The village is deprived of their output. But cash crops and village handicrafts are normally a minor part of the total productive activity of the village. And though retrenchment in their production means some decline in the supply of goods and services available to the village when men migrate seasonally, it is not likely to be greater than the decline in the number of claimants on village resources. So long as this is true the villagers who remain at home will be better off, as will those who migrate. That is, in order for the per capita income of the villagers remaining at home to decline, the relative fall in output following migration must exceed the relative decline in the number of people to be fed. If all migrants were pure seasonals, this would be most improbable.

We have thus far considered only the effects of seasonal migration. But not all migrants are seasonal. Many stay away a year or more. The same cost and benefit elements are present in this situation as in seasonal migration. But, because the short-term migrants are absent from the village during the annual agricultural cycle, their absence introduces other elements which must now be considered.

It is first of all clear that public facilities tend to deteriorate more than when migration is seasonal. In seasonal migration, all the men of the village are present during the busy planting and harvesting season, and some proportion—say half or more—are home during the rest of the year. In short-term migration, a third to a half of the village's able-bodied manpower (and possibly more) are away all the time. Those who remain are forced to shift their energies to the most immediate tasks, notably the maintenance of food output.

Second, for the same reasons as in seasonal migration, cash-crop output and handicraft production will fall substantially. Not only does subsistence production claim most of the time and energy of those remaining in the village, but the most urgent demands for money income are being satisfied through migration; there is thus less desire as well as less ability to grow crops for sale.

The decline of village public facilities and the fall in the proportion of village output that is marketed are significant but not crucial effects of short-term migration. What really matters is the effect on food output, the major element in village production. Only if it declines appreciably is there a possibility that the benefits of migration are outweighed by its costs to the village economy as a whole.

To analyze the possible effects of short-term migrations, let us first recall briefly the general nature of work organization in West African traditional agriculture. Although there are considerable variations between groups, a similar pattern of division of labor by sex recurs everywhere. Men do work that requires special strength; they clear land, cut trees, lop branches in preparation for preplanting fires; they "ridge" the ground for seeding, and participate in weeding and harvesting. Men also do much of such cash-crop production as may take place in the village. Women do a large share of the planting, weeding, and harvesting of food crops and of some cash crops, and do all the postharvest processing. Under the system commonly called "shifting agriculture with long fallow periods" (which prevails in most of the region), felling trees and cutting branches, the tasks connected with clearing new land and preparing it for planting, are the man's major and indispensable contributions. Every few years (normally between two and four) he must prepare new plots for cultivation. Although his contributions to the annual tasks of planting, weeding, and harvesting are important, other people— mainly the women—carry much, if not most, of the burden. The women do not assume the task of clearing new plots.[12]

Under these circumstances, per capita food output of those remaining at home will decline only if (1) the amount of new land brought under cultivation declines more than proportionally to the decline in village population resulting from migration; (2) the absence of men leads to a deterioration in agricultural practices, such as insufficient attention to branch cutting, for example, or a forced stretch-out of planting which causes deviations from optimum planting time with respect to rainfall, inadequate weeding in the early stages of crop growth, or slow harvesting.

Several features of traditional agricultural practice and village social arrangements serve to minimize both these effects. The first is the fact that new land must be brought under cultivation periodically—one plot every two to four years in most areas. Suppose, then, the migrant follows an economically "rational" course. He would leave after having completed the harvest and perhaps after having devoted several months of the dry season to the clearing of a new plot of land. He would then seek paid employment in the external economy for just as long as the cleared land can be cultivated by family and friends left in the village, perhaps eighteen or thirty months, and the output of the village would not suffer from lack of cleared land available for cultivation.

A second factor operates to encourage the cultivation of such land as has been cleared despite the absence of migrants: the existence of communal work arrangements. The migrant, first of all, is a member of an extended family, the other members of which can intensify their efforts on the family's fields while he is away. Second, and more important, coöperative work organizations, where they are common, provide a highly effective system of mutual aid and a means of mobilizing village manpower.

The effectiveness of these factors in preventing falls in food-crop output will obviously not be the same in all places and at all times. Three main considerations seem to be basic in determining the extent to which they will be effective.

The first is the proportion of males generally absent from the village. If, over a long period, relatively high proportions of the young and strong men of the village are away on short-term migration, per capita village food output will tend to fall. But what does "relatively high proportions" mean? A generation ago the magic figure was 25 per cent; it was widely believed in many parts of Africa that if more than 25 per cent of the young men of the village were away, the social and economic stability of the village was threatened.[13] But the 25 per cent figure was entirely arbitrary; it was arrived at by a Belgian commission investigating labor conditions in the 1920's, and was put forward as an approximation without any sound basis in fact. Recent studies in various parts of Africa have shown villages apparently thriving, even though 50 per cent or even more men are away in most years.[14]

The technical conditions of production are a second important factor in determining whether per capita food output will be more or less maintained. Where the type of agriculture is such that the physical effort involved in preparing the fields for planting is relatively great (tree cutting, heavy branch cutting, ridging, etc.), women, children, older men, and those younger men remaining in the village may not be able adequately to prepare new ground for planting, even if much of the clearing work has been done. Or, as noted earlier, in seasonal migration, if the agricultural cycle is delicately balanced with respect to rainfall so that yields are very much a function of time of planting, scarcity of labor at planting time may sharply reduce output. Finally, where is is necessary to gather and store the crop quickly to avoid losses from birds, insects, monkeys, and the like, the absence of hands will make a significant difference in "barnyard yields"—the amount of output actually available for use.

The third factor is the nature of the village social structure and kinship arrangements. Where kinship organization, coöperative work societies, and other village institutions play an important role in production, the migrant's family is likely to benefit from mutual aid, and per capita output of staple foods is less likely to fall. Although such coöperative work arrangements appear everywhere in Africa, their vitality and the degree of economic resiliency they provide for the village economy seem to vary with residence patterns more than with any other single factor. In patrilocal (virilocal) societies, where the wife takes up residence with the husband in his village, the absent migrant is connected more tightly through kinship and age-group obligations with other men in his village, which makes coöperation and aid to his family more certain. This hypothesis has been put forward at least with reference to eastern and central Africa.[15]

How do these considerations apply in West Africa? Evidence is sparse and it is hard to know how representative it is. But such information as is available suggests that they have operated to minimize the effects of migration on village output. The proportion of males between eighteen and forty-five absent from West African villages appears to range from 10 to 15 per cent in some villages of the Sudanese belt, and to 40 or 45 per cent in others;[16] no instances of higher rates of migration seem to have been recorded. Technical conditions in West African agriculture apparently do not present serious obstacles to the maintenance of food production, despite a short and exacting agricultural cycle in most areas. And, most important, an extremely varied assortment of mutual-aid arrangements, mainly the existence of coöperative work groups, plays an important role in most West African villages.[17]

One recent study of a Malinke-related village in Mali identified at least five different types of coöperative work associations, which illustrate the variety of these organizations: (1) an association of males, adults and children, which performs a given piece of work on the fields of any of its members; (2) a small association comprising from three to nine young men who cultivate together the fields of the fathers of any of their fiancées, in accordance with the customary obligations of sons-in-law; (3) a highly organized association of young men of the same age who work on the fields of any member of the village in return for payment, in order to purchase meat for their feast days; (4) a group of men of different ages who work on one another's lands in turn, to help the least strong among them; and (5) a group of men of a given quarter in the village who work at the request of anyone in the village who needs help.[18]

Skinner says that in the Mossi villages he studied "communal help is now almost unobtainable because most families have to compensate for absent men," [19] and J. Lombard finds the coöperative work arrangements weakened in some Dahoman villages.[20] These appear to be the only studies for West Africa which do not give the coöperative work group an important place in village economic life.

This analysis suggests that village output should not be much affected by migration in West Africa. Village production of cash crops and handicrafts does decline, and the stock of public facilities in the villages might be smaller than it would be in the absence of migration. (Even these negative effects are diminished, however, if longer-term considerations are taken into account, as the loss in man-hours devoted to public improvements and cash-crop production is at least partly balanced by a secular, migration-induced trend toward new and better techniques. These arise, on the one hand, from the importation of ideas and knowledge, and, on the other, from the use of goods whose purchase has been financed by migrant earnings: cement, better and cheaper axes, buckets, bottles, for example, and bicycles (which are an important form of transport in the village).

But most important, because of the seasonal character of much West African migration, and because even when it is not seasonal there is an increase of effort by migrants' families and by other villagers, the output of subsistence crops, the bulk of village output, should not show a marked decline on a per capita basis, and should actually be greater in many instances than it would otherwise be. The analytic balancing of short-term costs and benefits from migration thus points to a considerable net gain for the village economy, for while output in the village declines only slightly, the aggregate incomes of village residents are swelled by the net earnings of those who migrate.

It might be tempting to interpret this situation as an example of disguised unemployment. But it would be incorrect to do so. Properly defined, disguised unemployment means that men can be removed from agriculture without any decline in output and without significant changes in methods of production; implicitly, at least, the quantity of effort expended remains unchanged. But West African migrations do have some effects on output: aggregate village production of subsistence crops probably falls (though per capita production may not), cash crops may tend to be abandoned, and village handicraft production shrinks.

Further, hut maintenance is neglected and village public facilities decline in number and quality. Finally, subsistence output is maintained not only because of the transfer of energies from these other activities, but because everybody in the village tends to work harder in the absence of migrants. The quantity of effort increases and the community's stock of leisure is reduced. The concept of disguised unemployment is hardly elastic enough to include this case, for not only is there some effect on output, but the general reduction of leisure must be accounted for. If this effect on leisure is admitted into the definition of disguised unemployment, such unemployment exists everywhere and at all times.

Most of the slender evidence available supports this analysis. In their study of the Hsu of the Cameroons, the Ardeners estimate that, despite the absence of more than 40 per cent of the adult males, village output has shown no ill effects: "This is one more example of a situation which occurs in so many West African tribes. . . . The loss of young manpower has not made subsistence farming decline importantly." [21] Prothero, in his study of the migrations from northern Nigeria, notes that although from 33⅓ to 45 per cent of the men are away in paid employment, subsistence output appears unaffected; indeed, he implies that per capita food consumption increases in the villages.[22] Another writer comments on some tribes of northern Ghana:

> It is generally considered in Ghana that the annual exodus of a large number of adult males does not appear to have any unfortunate effects on the social and economic life of the Northern Region, and the main reason for this appears to be that over the years the exodus is almost balanced by the number returning. Since the main southerly migration takes place after the harvest and the main northerly migration before the planting season, agricultural production does not suffer from this particular cause, and the absence of a large number of adult males in the dry season when food is short is undoubtedly beneficial, especially in the crowded north-eastern districts.[23]

Only in Skinner's study of two Mossi villages are doubts expressed about the maintenance of food production, and these are put forward very tentatively.[24]

The Tenacity of the System

The above discussion indicates the depth of the economic roots of the migrant-labor system. On the level of the village economy as a whole, labor migration is the most efficient way to meet money-income needs. It allows village society to maintain itself by providing a way to improve village life within the traditional framework. For the individual villager, migration permits the maximizing of the income of his household as a consuming unit. For permanent employment in the outside economy to become economically attractive, the migrant's anticipated earnings in paid employment must be more than his combined family income from village sources and temporary migration. And, as the large majority of West African villagers prefer life in the villages, the income differential obtainable through permanent commitment to paid outside employment would have to be substantial in order to be effective. The fact that in most instances the differentials do not yet impel stabilization tends to maintain the migration system on the supply side by affecting the willingness to be "stabilized" in the outside economy. This has recently been recognized in many different parts of Africa.[25] What has not been so generally perceived is that also on the side of demand there are strong forces tending to maintain the system. Aside from some manufacturing enterprises, most employers have not been fundamentally averse to the system of migration.

There are three main reasons for this. First, a substantial proportion of total labor requirements in most West African countries was for agricultural enterprises, which are indigenous in Ghana, Nigeria, and Senegal, and indigenous as well as expatriate in the Ivory Coast, Guinea, and the ex-French and British Cameroons. In agriculture, labor requirements vary seasonally, so there is no real need for a permanently fixed work force; only a core group of stabilized workers is required, usually a small group.

Second, neither in agriculture nor in the other main sectors of the modern economy (mining and construction) did employers appear to suffer unduly from the inefficiencies of migratory labor. Work arrangements within these industries could be organized so as to minimize concern with supervision and labor efficiency. The best way to do this was by the wholesale introduction of piecework and subcontracting, wherever it was feasible. The general procedure was to set standard daily tasks: so much land cleared, so many bushels of cocoa pods picked, so many yards of ditch dug (in construction). When the daily task was completed, the laborer could leave work (or continue on for higher earnings if he chose). From the employer's point of view it makes little difference whether the standard task is completed slowly or quickly. Subcontractors in African mining and construction enterprises tended to use piecework systems particularly widely.[26] In this way concern with efficiency was shifted either to the worker himself or to the subcontractor; also, training costs became a secondary factor, where they were considered at all.

Finally, to stabilize work forces under African conditions requires a large expenditure on social services, better housing, and support of workers' families. In many parts of the world these are exclusively the concern of the public authorities; in Africa they were often a direct charge on employers, at least in part. Most employers in the modern sector were until recently reluctant to undertake this kind of effort, particularly as its success was uncertain. By adjustments of their internal work organization, they have been able to live not too uncomfortably with a highly unstable labor force.

From this analysis it is clear that the migration phenomenon will persist until certain basic changes occur in the general economic environment:

1) Conditions in the village must become either much worse or much better. Men will be willing to leave the village more or less permanently only when the net economic and other advantages of permanent paid employment become clearly superior to the option of combining village life with periodic migration. This could occur if life in the villages were to become intolerable or impossible, because of land shortages following population increase, for example. It could also occur if wage rates for permanent wage earners were to rise to the point where returns from permanent wage earning alone exceeded the returns from migration and family income from village sources. The migrancy system could also lose its vigor if income-earning possibilities increase in the villages so that (rising) money-income needs can be met without migration.

2) Conditions in the outside economy must evolve so that stabilization becomes advantageous for employers. This occurs under any or all of three circumstances: (a) the difficulties or costs of continually recruiting fresh workers becomes so burdensome to employers that they are led to make the investment required to stabilize the work force; (b) secondary industry becomes significant so that needs for operatives and other semiskilled workers grow, and training costs become a larger element in total costs; and (c) wage rates rise faster than either the cost of loanable funds or capital equipment. Employers will then be stimulated to economize generally on unskilled labor and to substitute more capital-intensive methods of production for unskilled labor-intensive methods.

In most parts of Africa where one or another of these changes has occurred, there have emerged strong tendencies toward stabilization and the withering of the migrant labor system. This is notably true of South Africa, where the deterioration of village conditions, combined with the demands of secondary industry, has overridden ideology and politics. Here some 27 per cent of the African population, or 2 to 3 million people, lived in urban areas in the mid-fifties, and of these at least 1.5 million were permanent town dwellers.[27] These people are more or less permanently committed to paid employment in that country, and the figure would undoubtedly be much higher in the absence of the restraints set down by apartheid policies. In the Congo, and particularly in Katanga, it was the cost and trouble of recruiting the workers in the late 1920's, combined with massive expenditures on social overheads, which led to successful stabilization of the labor force. West Africa, with different conditions of labor supply, and with a different structure of production, has experienced few of these pressures toward stabilization. As wage rates have risen in the past decade, however, and as secondary industry becomes more significant, employer desires to stabilize work forces have grown, and the proportion of permanently fixed workers in the total labor force has tended to increase. But this situation has as yet developed in relatively small sectors of West African economies.

Migrancy and Economic Growth: Long-Term Considerations

We have argued above that the migrant labor system was historically a stimulus to economic growth, and that it represents an optimum allocation of resources under existing conditions. There has nonetheless been a general reluctance on the part of students of these matters to give full endorsement to continued labor migration as a system of labor utilization. To some extent this reluctance is based on the social evils commonly said to be associated with the migrations: disrupted family life, falling birth rates, spread of disease, shattered traditional ties, and others. A growing body of evidence suggests that these supposed social consequences of migration have been much exaggerated.[28] But, in any event, the heart of the criticism of the migrant labor system is usually economic. Sometimes the charge is vaguely made that migration is somehow economically irrational. Thus one French writer grants the strength of the underlying economic impulses to migration, but urges measures to slow it down, including "a campaign of popular education which will teach him [the villager] to handle his goods, to calculate his self-interest, to buy, sell, economize, and, above all, to show him the uselessness, even the danger, to the group as well as to the individual, of thoughtless movements of labor and systematic departures to cities."[29] The basis for this kind of rejection of labor migration is essentially visceral; little need be said about it except to note that it is precisely the villager's insight into the economic calculus that leads him to periodic migrations.

A more serious criticism is that the benefits of migration to the village economy are short-run; in the longer run, migration is a retarding factor. This view is widespread, not only in West Africa, but everywhere on the continent. It is not systematically or cogently presented in any one study, but is implicit in many. It runs as follows: Granted that under existing conditions temporary migration represents the income-maximizing alternative available to villagers and, hence, the optimum pattern of resource allocation, it is an obstacle to structural change, which is required if there is to be rapid growth in the village economy. The migrant labor system represents a kind of low-level equilibrium trap. So long as it exists, African villagers will remain neither good farmers at home nor good employees in the external economy.

The following statement about an East African situation illustrates the tenor of the argument:

... the very fact that a man can go abroad to work and earn money thereby lessens his desire and efforts at home ... increased efforts do not yet appear to him either worth while or even possible. There is therefore a general depressing effect on the tribal economy and the tribal standard of living. Men are sapped of a certain self-responsibility to work and earn at home. Were they compelled through the lack of the alternative of labor migration to rely on their own efforts in their own fields to maintain their incomes and their standards of living, there would of necessity have to be greater application and persistence of effort and a learning of the idea of being a whole-time farmer.[30]

The underlying notion here seems to be that without tensions, without challenges to which creative agricultural responses can be made, there can be no fundamental transformation of village agriculture. Implicit in it is a kind of Hirschman-like view of the nature of the development process—development by dislocation and response to stress in the existing system.[31]

Put this way, the argument about the long-term depressive effects of migrant labor on village economy suggests a number of observations. The very fact of migration indicates that returns to labor are higher in the outside economy, and hence that the productivity of labor is higher there too. The situation might of course change if increases in village output brought substantial "external economies," that is, general increases in factor productivity, and this is doubtless the economic meaning behind the dour views about the long-term effects of migration. But for the argument to have force it is not enough that "external economies" follow increased village output. For if such economies are anticipated in the labor-exporting village following increases in output, they can equally be anticipated in the economy beyond the village. Indeed, given the generally more favorable economic environment in the outside economy, coupled with the still-low level of development there, greater "external economies" might well be anticipated outside the villages. Therefore, for the argument to have substance, it is necessary that anticipated "external economies" be greater in the labor-exporting village than outside. Although not impossible, this development is unlikely. Second, the argument seems to assume that agricultural revolution in the labor-exporting village economy can be brought about without ancillary changes. If, somehow, men would only dedicate themselves to transforming subsistence agriculture, the revolution would occur. But this is surely not true. The development of agriculture in the relatively poorly endowed areas from which most of the migrants originate entails a wide range of auxiliary investment, from roads to research. Investment resources, however, are scarce in the areas from which migration takes place, and the yield from such investment would probably be far smaller in most instances than the yield obtainable from equivalent agricultural investment in the better-endowed areas, the destinations of the migrants.

There is one possible amendment to this analysis. What we have been saying is that the level of income and the rate of growth of income of the outside and village economies together will be higher with migration than without it. But it does not necessarily follow that the rate of growth of each sector separately will be higher, for there are differences in the nature of some of the benefits obtained by the two sectors. The village economy enjoys a higher level of personal income. Its people are better clothed and transported, and probably better fed. Because of higher income, the village can enlarge and enrich some part of its stock of durable goods; for example, purchases of plows, of rifles for hunting, and of bicycles would be fewer without migration. Even public revenues in the territory of origin derive some benefit; because incomes are higher, customs duties on migrants' imports can be significant revenue items, imports increase indirectly through remittances of migrants to families remaining at home, and, more indirectly, exports probably increase owing to inflows of new tools and ideas.

These are not inconsiderable benefits. But those derived by the outside economy are more substantial. It is the outside economy that enjoys most of the invigorating general changes that accompany greater output. Cities and towns spring up there, not in the villages of emigration. The wheels of commerce hum, and the web of public and private services expands. Tax revenues rise because of increased exports, incomes, and consumption. Transport facilities grow, and transport costs fall because of greater utilization. The general economic environment becomes more conducive to further growth.

Now, none of these results are cause for concern if the outside economy and the village economy are in the same political unit. There is no reason that better-endowed areas in a country should not grow faster than less well-endowed ones, and political instruments, such as tax and investment policies, are available to correct regional disparities in growth if it should be necessary. The possibility for alarm arises when the outside economy and the village economy are in different political units, or different countries; then it might seem that the labor-exporting area is helping transform an economy somewhere else, while its own moves forward slowly.

It is this kind of consideration that underlies the dissatisfaction with the migrations common in the countries of West Africa, which are heavy exporters of labor. Because it is important in this respect, and because stabilization of the work force—that is, the cessation or restriction of migration—is so commonly expressed as a desirable goal of social and economic policy, it is worth considering briefly the probable consequences for the village economy of an imposed restraint on migration.

The effects of cessation or reduction of migration on the village economy would seem to depend on four main factors:

1) It would depend on the availability of land in the villages and the technical and economic possibilities for the production of marketable crops. It is the economic restraint that is most serious, and, in particular, the matter of markets and transport costs. As distances are usually great between points of production and potential markets, and as most of the commodities whose expansion can be envisaged (meat, staple foods, peanuts, cotton, etc.) are heavy in weight, the provision of cheap and efficient transport is fundamental.

2) It would depend on the level and elasticity of demand for the agricultural commodities of the labor-exporting areas. Some increase in output could be absorbed within the village, such as more variation in foods and increase in cotton output and handicrafts. But the major share of any increase in output would have to find a market outside, either in the richer areas along the coast or abroad.

3) It would also depend on the level and shape of the income-effort function of villagers. Whether or not villagers will devote themselves to agricultural production in the villages depends on the extent to which they are prepared to expend effort for income. It cannot be assumed— as is done implicitly in the argument about the "long-term depressant" effects of migration outlined above—that the villager staying at home will devote the same quantity of effort to income earning as he would expend in the external economy as a migrant. For the effort price of income is higher in the village than outside, and at the higher price some reduction of effort can be anticipated.

4) Finally, it would depend on the availability of public investment resources, and particularly on the difference in tax yields on income at home and on income earned abroad. Without a massive effort in the transport area and in agricultural research and education, prospects for agricultural expansion are dim. If public revenues were increased because of greater domestic production (despite the fact that aggregate incomes with migration are lower), then the possibilities of such investment would be increased.

This summary suggests the circumstances under which the labor-exporting area would be better off without—or with less—migration: that the demand of the villager for income is inelastic downward, so that villagers do not reduce by much their income-earning efforts even though the effort price of income has risen; that markets can be found for increased output, at prices that yield significant increases in aggregate agricultural revenues, which is to say that the demand for the new output must be relatively elastic; that resources are available for the requisite parallel investment in transport facilities, research, and agricultural extension services, so that new crops can be introduced and productivity can be increased in the production of existing commodities.

There is no a priori reason to expect any of these conditions to be easily realized. At higher effort prices for income, most villagers would probably reduce their income-earning efforts, as the intensity of demand for income is still slight in some areas. This is particularly likely when we think in real terms, for the migrant is able to buy consumer durables near his place of work, or on the way home, in markets that are larger and more competitive, and at prices that reflect lower transport costs. Indeed, because the differential income return between effort as a migrant in the external economy and effort within the village is often so large, and would probably remain so for at least some time, many migrants might simply abandon most income-earning activity. One of the subsidiary advantages of migration for young men is the freedom from family demands which it offers, a freedom that allows them to accumulate savings for bridal transactions and other relatively large investments. The absence of this alternative would probably further accentuate impulses toward reduction of income-earning effort.

Second, the economic restraints are forbidding. Significant reductions in transport costs require heavy investments, and, to find markets, prices must be competitive with output from more favorably located areas. The most likely markets are in the relatively high-income areas to which migrants now go. But with the reduction of migration (other things unchanged), income and output in these areas would probably be lower, or would be growing more slowly.

Finally, there is no apparent reason to expect tax revenues to increase significantly after curtailment of migration. It is true that although the level of income is lower, more is domestically produced, and this might provide possibilities for increased public levies. But some part of the new local production will not enter the market at all, such as more varied food crops, cotton for village weaving, and so on. Imports will probably be smaller (because of lower income), and price will be so important in marketing exports that there will probably be little room for export duties.

There is thus little to be gained, and much to be lost, by the village economy if migration is restrained. There are, of course, differences in the extent to which different labor-exporting areas are affected by the above arguments. Some places, because of ecological conditions or because of their distance from markets, would be severely hurt by the lack of potential alternatives to migration. And all would find the job of development harder, not easier.

The prevalence and persistence of the migrant labor system, then, do not arise from the perversity or wickedness of men. The system has a secure foundation in the economic environment of West Africa. It cannot be wished away. Nor can it be legislated away, save by the introduction of massive and profound transformations in both rural and urban areas. It is not, as is so frequently claimed, a cause of West Africa's economic ills; it is rather a symptom of a specific set of economic circumstances. It will change when these circumstances change. And until the economy does change, migration continues to make good economic sense, from the point of view both of the individuals concerned and of the economy as a whole.

NOTES

NOTES

1. Introduction

[1] The change in legal relationships, from status to contract, originally formulated by Sir Henry Maine, is contingent on sociopolitical and economic factors. The situations in which status persists, or conflicts with contractual arrangements in newly industrialized societies, depend on their structural and ethical antecedents.

[2] George C. Homans, *English Villagers of the Thirteenth Century* (Cambridge: Harvard University Press, 1941), p. 52.

[3] Peter C. Lloyd, *Yoruba Land Law* (London: Nigerian Institute of Social and Economic Research, 1962), p. 54.

[4] G. E. von Grunebaum, "The Structure of the Muslim Town," in *Islam: Essays in the Nature of a Cultural Tradition*, American Anthropological Association Memoir no. 81 (London: Routledge and Kegan Paul, 1955).

[5] William R. Bascom, "Urbanism as a Traditional African Pattern," *Sociological Review*, VII (July, 1959), 29-44. See also "Les Premiers Fondements historiques de l'urbanisme Yoruba," *Présence Africaine*, n. s., no. 23 (Dec., 1958–Jan., 1959), 22-40.

[6] Gideon Sjoberg, "Folk and Feudal Societies," *American Journal of Sociology*, LVIII, no. 3 (1952), and *The Preindustrial City: Past and Present* (Glencoe: Free Press, 1960).

[7] Lloyd, *op. cit.*, p. 55.

[8] M. G. Smith, Introduction to M. F. Smith, *Baba of Karo* (London: Faber and Faber, 1954), p. 27.

[9] Peter Marris, *Family and Social Change in an African City* (Evanston, Ill.: Northwestern University Press, 1962).

[10] A. R. Radcliffe-Brown, *Method in Social Anthropology* (Chicago: University of Chicago Press, 1954), pp. 39-41; M. G. Smith, "History and Social Anthropology," *Journal of the Royal Anthropological Institute*, XCII, Pt. 1 (1962), 73-85.

[11] H. R. Palmer, "The Kano Chronicle," *Journal of the Royal Anthropological Institute*, XXXVIII (1908), 58-98, and *Sudanese Memoirs* (3 vols.; Lagos, 1928), III, 66-76.

[12] Points disputed include the belief in a "dynastic race," held, for example, by W. B. Emery, *Archaic Egypt* (New York: Penguin Books, 1961). Emphasis on Egypt as responsible for the emergence of state organizations is also evident in A. J. Arkell, *History of the Sudan to 1821* (London, 1955). The other viewpoint is expressed by Basil Davidson, *Old Africa Rediscovered* (London: Gollancz, 1959).

[13] For example, Fustel de Coulanges places his emphasis on religion in *The Ancient City* (New York, 1956). Sir Henry Maine, *Ancient Law* (London: J. Murray, 1861), emphasizes the substitution of territoriality for kinship, separating the individual

from his family and forcing him to contractual as distinct from status relationships. Frederick W. Maitland developed the "garrison theory" in *Township and Borough* (Cambridge: The University Press, 1898). Henri Pirenne explained the city in terms of economic institutions, associating it with the development of the merchant class, in *Medieval Cities* (Princeton: Princeton University Press, 1946).

[14] Stuart Piggott, "The Role of the City in Ancient Civilizations," in *The Metropolis in Modern Life*, ed. Robert Moon Fisher (New York: Doubleday, 1955).

[15] J. R. Firth, *The Tongues of Men* (London, 1937), chap. x. See also Joseph Greenberg, "Concerning Inferences from Linguistic to Non-Linguistic Data," in *Language in Culture*, ed. H. Hoijer (Chicago: University of Chicago Press, 1954), pp. 13-19.

[16] Professor Wolf Leslau argues that in Ethiopia national loyalty might be stronger if Amharic were not enforced and other languages were not denied recognition.

[17] *Urbanization in Asia and the Far East*, proceedings of the Joint UN/UNESCO Seminar, Bangkok, August 8-18, 1956 (Delhi: Research Center on the Social Implications of Industrialization in Southern Asia, 1957). See also the articles in Carl H. Kraeling and Robert H. Adams, *City Invincible: A Symposium on Urbanization and Cultural Development in the Ancient and Near East* (Chicago: University of Chicago Press, 1960).

[18] See Sidney M. Greenfield, "Industrialization and the Family in Sociological Theory," *American Journal of Sociology*, LXVII (Nov., 1961), 312-322; Harry Sharp and Morris Axelrod, "Mutual Aid among Relations in an Urban Population," in *Principles of Sociology*, ed. R. Friedman, A. Hawley, and W. S. Landecker (New York: Holt, 1956); and also *The Reports of the Detroit Area Study* (Ann Arbor: University of Michigan Press, 1952).

[19] Elizabeth Bott, *Family and Social Network* (London: Tavistock Publications, 1957); Raymond W. Firth, ed., *Two Studies of Kinship in London* (London: Athlone Press, 1956).

[20] Robert Redfield, "The Folk Society," *American Journal of Sociology*, LII (Jan., 1947), 294, and *The Folk Culture of Yucatan* (Chicago: University of Chicago Press, 1941). There are, in fact, major theoretical distinctions, often not recognized, between the "masters," more especially Durkheim and Weber on the one hand, and Tönnies, Wirth, and Redfield on the other. The most straightforward simplification of contradistinctive models is expressed by Redfield. The psychological attributes are carefully developed in Georg Simmel, "The Metropolis and Mental Life," in *The Sociology of Georg Simmel*, trans. Kurt Wolff (Glencoe: Free Press, 1950), pp. 409-417.

[21] Horace Miner, *The Primitive City of Timbuctoo* (Princeton: Princeton University Press, 1953). For a concise statement of Miner's approach, see his "The Folk-Urban Continuum," *American Sociological Review*, XVII (Oct., 1952), 529-537.

[22] William R. Bascom, "Urbanization among the Yoruba," *American Journal of Sociology*, LX (March, 1955).

[23] This approach is related to the "social area analysis" as formulated by Eshref Shevky, Wendell Bell, and Marilyn Williams. For its possible applicability as a comparative, cross-cultural tool, see Dennis C. McElrath, "The Social Areas of Rome: A Comparative Analysis," *American Sociological Review*, XXVII (June, 1962), 376-391.

[24] Emile Durkheim, *The Division of Labor in Society* (1893), trans. George Simpson (Glencoe: Free Press, 1947).

[25] Louis Wirth, "Urbanism as a Way of Life," *American Journal of Sociology*, XLIV, no. 1 (1938), 8.

[26] This approach is used by Hoselitz in Bert F. Hoselitz and Wilbert E. Moore, eds., *Industrialization and Society* (Paris: UNESCO and Mouton, 1963).

[27] Ralph L. Beals, "Urbanism, Urbanization and Acculturation," *American Anthropologist*, LIII (Jan.-March, 1951).

[28] The main exponents are Gluckman, Epstein, and Mitchell. The point of view is clearly stated by Max Gluckman, "Anthropological Problems Arising from the African Industrial Revolution," in *Social Change in Modern Africa*, ed. A. Southall (London: Oxford University Press, 1961), pp. 67-82. See also J. Clyde Mitchell, *The Kalela Dance* (Manchester: Manchester University Press, 1956); A. L. Epstein, *Politics in an Urban African Community* (Manchester: Manchester University Press, 1958), and "The Network and Urban Social Organization," *Human Problems in British Central Africa*, Rhodes-Livingstone Publications, no. 29 (1961).

[29] Reinhard Bendix, "Concepts and Generalizations in Comparative Sociological Studies," *American Sociological Review*, XXVIII (Aug., 1963).

[30] For an analysis of American material see Morton White and Lucia White, "The Intellectual versus the City," in *From Thomas Jefferson to Frank Lloyd Wright* (Cambridge: Harvard University Press, 1962). See also Lloyd Rodwin, ed., *The Future Metropolis* (New York: George Braziller, 1961), and, of course, Lewis Mumford, *The City in History* (New York: Harcourt, Brace and World, 1961).

[31] Typical of this outlook is the statement: "That modern industrial society has become the primary model for the world as a whole can scarcely be doubted" (Talcott Parsons, Introduction to Max Weber, *The Sociology of Religion*, trans. Ephraim Fischoff [Boston: Beacon Press, 1963], p. lxi).

[32] Don Martindale, Preface to Max Weber, *The City*, trans. and ed. Don Martindale and Gertrude Neuwirth (London: Heinemann, 1958), p. 62.

2. The Location and Nature of West African Cities

[1] Maps of the monthly patterns of usable roads and waterways are published in my *Transportation and Physical Geography in West Africa* (Washington: National Academy of Sciences, 1960).

[2] For two different methods of defining and mapping these islands of development, see L. P. Green and T. D. J. Fair, *Development in Africa* (Johannesburg: Witwatersrand University Press, 1962), and William A. Hance, V. Kotschar, and J. Peterec, "Source Areas of Export Production in Tropical Africa," *Geographical Review*, LI (1961), 487-499.

3. Some Thoughts on Migration and Urban Settlement

[1] Roland Oliver and J. D. Fage, *A Short History of Ghana* (Harmondsworth, 1962), chap. 9; J. D. Fage, *Ghana: A Historical Interpretation* (Madison: University of Wisconsin Press, 1959), chap. 1.

[2] The fullest examination is in Jan Vansina, *De la tradition orale* (Tervueren, 1961); cf., for West Africa, J. D. Fage, "Africa and Historical Studies," in *The Social Sciences in Africa*, ed. R. A. Lystad (London: Pall Mall Press, 1963).

[3] E. L. R. Meyerowitz, *Akan Traditions of Origin* (London: Faber and Faber, 1952); Ivor Wilks, *The Northern Factor in Ashanti History* (Institute of African Studies, University College of Ghana, 1961); R. E. Bradbury, *The Benin Kingdom* (London: International African Institute, 1957).

[4] Oliver and Fage, *op. cit.*

[5] Roland Portères, "Berceaux Agricoles Primaires sur le Continent Africain," *Journal of African History*, III, no. 2 (1962).

[6] It is not suggested that these are the only major lines along which historical influences were apt to flow during the precolonial period in West African history, or that these lines were necessarily more important than others. Within the area covered by these two axes and their ramifications, for example, one may discern a number of transverse axes. One of these, from west to east and readily discernible historically, runs from Mandeland along the line of the Niger through Songhai to Hausa. There would also appear to be an east-west axis close to the coast, which is much more difficult to assess. It could be no more than a southern branch of the northeast axis which has been turned west by the sea, and, in effect, it is treated rather in this manner in this paper. But it also corresponds to the east-west distribution of the Kwa group of languages, and it may therefore be of remote prehistoric significance. Yet a third lateral axis may lie between these two, being represented today by the line of islands of Mande-speaking groups running westward through the Gur-speaking area, at about latitude 11° N., to the region of Bussa. It also seems likely to be prehistoric in origin.

[7] David Kimble, *A Political History of Ghana, 1850-1928* (London: Oxford University Press, 1963), pp. xv-xviii.

[8] J. S. Trimingham, *A History of Islam in West Africa* (London, 1962), p. 31.

[9] Es-Sadi, *Tarikh es-Soudan* (*c.* 1655), trans. O. Houdas (Paris, 1900).

[10] Meyerowitz, *op. cit.*, pp. 34-35.

[11] Jack Goody, "The Ethnography of the Northern Territories of the Gold Coast West of the White Volta" (mimeographed; London, 1954); D. H. Jones, "Jakpa and the Foundation of Gonja," *Transactions of the Historical Society of Ghana*, VI (1962).

[12] See, for example, Trimingham, *op. cit.*

[13] A mere historian is apt to be intrigued, for instance, by the fact that the Twi word for "state" is *oman* (pl., *aman*), and by the occurrence of this *man* element in other politically significant Akan names: e.g., Asanteman Council (the supreme council of Ashanti), Asantemanso (the mythical place of the origin of the Ashanti nation), Bono-Mansu (the capital of Bono). Charles Monteil, "Les Empires de Mali," *Bulletin du Comité d'Etudes Historiques et Scientifiques de l'AOF*, XII (1929), 297, says that in Soninke, the word *mande* means the "place where the master resides"; hence, it means the seat of royal power and also the country and the people ruled from it. (Mali is the Fulani variant of the same word.) Bono-Mansu could therefore mean "the capital of Bono."

[14] Frank Willett, "Excavations at Old Oyo and Ife," *Man* (1959).

[15] P. de Marees, *Beschrijvinge ende Historische Verhael van het Gout Koninckrijck van Gunea* (1602), ed. S. P. l'Honoré Naber (Linschoten Vereeniging, 1913).

[16] Jacob U. Egharevba, *A Short History of Benin* (3d ed.; Ibadan, 1960).

[17] H. R. Palmer, *Sudanese Memoirs* (3 vols.; Lagos, 1928).

[18] An exception is Kuka (Kukawa) in Bornu. But this foundation is very recent (early nineteenth century), and the opposition here is not between immigrants and locals, but rather between the rulers and their officials on the one hand, and the commoners on the other, in a rather sharply stratified society.

[19] J. Lombard, "Un Système politique traditionnel de type féodal: Les Bariba du Nord-Dahomey," *Bulletin de l'IFAN*, XIX (1957).

[20] J. P. Lebeuf and A. Masson-Détourbet, *La Civilisation du Tchad* (Paris, 1950).

[21] Could these possibly have been Nilotes?

[22] See, e.g., Y. Urvoy, *Histoire de l'Empire du Bornou* (Paris, 1949).

[23] Palmer, *op. cit.*, III, 132 ff.

[24] Samuel Johnson, *The History of the Yorubas* (Lagos: C.M.S. Bookshop, 1937); S. O. Biobaku, *The Lugard Lectures* (Lagos, 1955).

[25] There is reason to believe that this may have been accomplished by the intervention of mounted invaders.

[26] Egharevba, *op. cit.*

[27] See, e.g., A. Mathews, "The Kisra Legend," *African Studies*, IX (1950); Palmer, *op. cit.*, II, 61-63; and Leo Frobenius, *The Voice of Africa* (London, 1913), II, 617-641.

[28] A. J. Arkell, *History of the Sudan to 1821* (London: Athlone Press, 1955); A. D. H. Bivar and P. L. Shinnie, "Old Kanuri Capitals," *Journal of African History*, III (1962); Raymond Mauny, personal communication. (Much of this information is still in the process of publication.)

4. Urbanism, Migration, and Language

[1] For an account of Timbuktu, see Horace Miner, *The Primitive City of Timbuctoo* (Princeton: Princeton University Press, 1953).

[2] See in particular the study by Jean Rouch, "Migrations au Ghana (Gold Coast)," *Journal de la Société des Africanistes*, XXVI, no. 1-2 (1956), 33-196.

[3] For examples of the treatment of sociolinguistic problems by linguists, see C. A. Ferguson and J. J. Gumperz, eds., *Linguistic Diversity in South Asia* (Bloomington: Indiana University Press, 1960).

[4] A. Diop, "Enquête sur la migration Toucouleur à Dakar," *Bulletin de l'IFAN*, XXII, no. 3-4 (1960), 414. Some or all, however, may have known Wolof in their rural habitat.

[5] See A. I. Richards, ed., *Economic Development and Tribal Change: A Study of Immigrant Labour in Buganda* (Cambridge, Eng.: Heffer, 1954), p. 15.

[6] Rouch, *op. cit.*; Elliott P. Skinner, "Labour Migration and Its Relationship to Socio-Cultural Change in Mossi Society," *Africa*, XXX (Oct., 1960), 375-399. Skinner adds (personal communication) that practically all Mossi who learn Ghanaian languages cease to maintain their Mossi tribal allegiance.

[7] Skinner, *op. cit.*, p. 295.

[8] *Ibid.*, p. 391.

[9] Richards, *op. cit.*, p. 176.

[10] Michael Banton, *West African City: A Study of Tribal Life in Freetown* (London: Oxford University Press, 1957), p. 165.

[11] See in particular Kenneth Little, "The Urban Role of Tribal Associations in West Africa," *African Studies*, XXI (1962), 1-9.

[12] Rouch, *op. cit.*, p. 151.

[13] The following statement in the Report of Working Group 4, Third Leverhulme Conference, University College of Ibadan, 1962, p. 1, is apropos: "The problems need to be investigated from all angles: in many which on the surface seem linguistic, there are close ties with other subjects, and conversely the linguistic situation in most countries is such that practically all problems of development have a linguistic aspect."

5. Labor Migration among the Mossi of the Upper Volta

[1] Salfo Albert Balima, "Notes on the Social and Labour Situation in the Republic of Upper Volta," *International Labour Review*, LXXXII (Oct., 1960), 359-360.

[2] "La Haute Volta," *Magazine AOF*, XVII (Nov., 1955), 9.

[3] Elliott P. Skinner, "An Analysis of the Political System of the Mossi," *Transactions of the New York Academy of Sciences* (June, 1957).

[4] Elliott P. Skinner, "The Mossi *Pogsiouré*," *Man*, LX (1960), 4.

[5] Felix Dubois, *Timbouctou la Mystérieuse* (Paris, 1899), p. 300.

[6] Elliott P. Skinner, "Christianity and Islam among the Mossi," *American Anthropologist*, LX, no. 6 (1958), 1103.

[7] Elliott P. Skinner, "The Diffusion of Islam in an African Society," *Annals of the New York Academy of Sciences*, XCVI (Jan. 20, 1962), 661-663.

[8] Dr. Crozat, "Rapport sur une mission au Mossi (1890)," *Journal Officiel de la République Française*, Oct. 5-9, 1891, p. 4848.

[9] Louis Tauxier, *Le Noir du Soudan* (Paris: Emile La Rose, 1912), p. 538.

[10] Eugene P. Mangin, *Les Mossi* (Paris: Augustin Challamel, 1921), p. 61.

[11] A. de Beauminy, "Le Pays de la Boucle du Niger: Etude économique," *Revue Géographique et Commerciale de Bordeaux*, VI (1919), 71-78.

[12] Paul-Louis Ledange, "Une Colonie nouvelle, la Haute Volta," *La Revue Indigène*, XVII (1933), 133-136.

[13] Raymond L. Buell, *The Native Problem in Africa* (2 vols.; New York: Macmillan, 1928), p. 178.

[14] Albert Londres, *Terre d'Ebéne (La Traite des Noirs)* (Paris: Albin Michel, 1929), p. 126.

[15] Robert Delavignette, "Le Dynamisme de l'A.O.F.," *L'Afrique Française*, XLII (1932), 530-531.

[16] Virginia Thompson and Richard Adloff, *French West Africa* (Stanford: Stanford University Press, 1958), p. 174.

[17] Henri Labouret, "L'Afrique Française," *L'Evolution de l'Afrique Française en 1937*, XLVIII (1938), 20. In contrast, the French had extreme difficulty with the *corvée* system among the acephalous and weakly organized Lobi people, who lacked this institution. As a result, while the Mossi were shipping thousands of laborers to administrative and privately owned labor camps, the Lobi were still shooting poisoned arrows at French labor recruiters and tax collectors. Isaac Schapera, *Migrant Labour and Tribal Life* (London: Oxford University Press, 1947), p. 26, found that the Kgatla had structural features in their society which influenced the ease with which they had migrated to the mines, and William Watson, *Tribal Cohesion in a Money Economy* (Manchester: Manchester University Press, 1958), p. 36, found similar conditions among the Mambwe.

[18] Labouret, *loc. cit.*

[19] Buell, *op. cit.*, p. 179. The mortality rates for the men working on the construction of the Ivory Coast Railway were as follows:

Year	Effective	Morbidity percentage	Mortality per 1,000 Per month	Per year
1923	3,491	1.90	3.5	42.0
1924	2,300	2.34	3.7	44.4
1925	2,057	2.82	2.5	30.0

[20] *Ibid.*

[21] *Ibid.*

[22] Delavignette, *op. cit.*, p. 531.

[23] R. B. Davidson, *Migrant Labour in the Gold Coast* (Achimota: University College of the Gold Coast, 1954), pp. 31-37; Jean Rouch, "Migrations au Ghana (Gold Coast)," *Journal de la Société des Africanistes*, XXVI, no. 1-2 (1956), 93; and

Elliott P. Skinner, "Labour Migration and Its Relationship to Socio-Cultural Change in Mossi Society," *Africa*, XXX (Oct., 1960), 386.

24 Rouch, *op. cit.*, p. 139.

25 Pierre Dufour, "L'Économie de la Haute Volta," *Paris-Dakar*, CLI (April 9, 1956), 3.

26 Schapera, *op. cit.*, p. 191.

27 Londres, *op. cit.*, p. 126.

28 Ivory Coast, Service de la Statistique et de la Mécanographie, "Enquête nutrition-niveau de vie: Subdivision de Bongouanou, 1955-56" (Paris, 1958), p. 129.

29 Dufour, *op. cit.*, p. 3.

30 M. P. Piault reports the existence of "real Mossi or Wangara villages, where one finds—contrary to the other foreign communities in Ghana—a fairly high percentage of women and children." He does not, however, give specific figures for these expatriate Mossi families ("The Migration of Workers in West Africa," *Bulletin of Inter-African Labour Institute* [Feb., 1961], 108).

31 G. Le Moal, "Un Aspect de l'émigration: La Fixation de Voltaiques au Ghana," *Bulletin de l'IFAN*, XXII (July-Oct., 1960), 446.

32 Elliott P. Skinner, "Traditional and Modern Patterns of Succession to Political Office among the Mossi of the Voltaic Republic," *Journal of Human Relations*, VIII, no. 3-4 (1960), 397.

33 Mangin, *op. cit.*, p. 18.

34 Skinner, "An Analysis of the Political System of the Mossi," p. 743.

35 Rouch, *op. cit.*, p. 182n.

36 *Africa Digest*, V (1957), 73.

37 *New York Times*, Feb. 18, 1959, p. 4.

38 "Ghana and Upper Volta Agree To Open Border," *Africa Report*, VI (1961), 10.

39 Skinner, "The Diffusion of Islam in an African Society," pp. 661-663.

40 Skinner, "Christianity and Islam among the Mossi," p. 1102.

41 Delavignette, *op. cit.*, p. 531.

42 Rouch, *op. cit.*, p. 167.

6. Oshogbo—An Urban Community?

1 For excellent analyses of social systems of towns in Northern Rhodesia see Max Gluckman, "Anthropological Problems Arising from the African Industrial Revolution," in *Social Change in Modern Africa*, ed. A. Southall (London: Oxford University Press, 1961); J. Clyde Mitchell, *The Kalela Dance* (Manchester: Manchester University Press, 1956); and A. L. Epstein, *Politics in an Urban African Community* (Manchester: Manchester University Press, 1958).

2 *Population Census of the Western Region of Nigeria, 1952* (Lagos, 1953-1954).

3 The main Yoruba subgroups are Oyo, Ilesha, Ekiti, Ife, Ijebu, Egba, and Ondo.

4 K. M. Buchanan and J. C. Pugh, *Land and People in Nigeria* (London: University of London Press, 1955). Yorubaland has seven cities of more than 50,000 persons.

5 In Ibadan and Oshun divisions, the figure is more than 60 per cent.

6 See, among others, W. M. Hailey, *Native Administration in the British African Territories*, Part III (London: H.M.S.O., 1951); Sir Rex Niven, *A Short History of the Yorubas* (London: Longmans, Green, 1958); J. D. Fage, *An Introduction to the History of West Africa* (London: Cambridge University Press, 1955).

[7] *Population Census of the Western Region of Nigeria, 1952.*

[8] There is today a pipe-borne water supply.

[9] Most of the demographic data of Oshogbo are based on a 10 per cent survey of the residential units (1950). The arithmetic mean of compound populations is 122.9 persons, and approximately a third of the compounds have populations ranging between 80 and 140 persons.

[10] The population density of Oshogbo is roughly 5,000 to 6,000 per square mile. In an area approximately 1.5 miles in radius about the palace, the density is roughly 17,000 to 18,000 per square mile.

[11] It is also true, of course, that formerly all of Oshogbo was clustered close about the atoaja's palace, and these compounds have therefore been settled for a longer period.

[12] The population distribution in Oshogbo is 91 per cent in the Native Quarter, 3.5 per cent in the Foreign Quarter, 4.5 per cent along Station Road, and 1 per cent in the Hausa Quarter.

[13] Access to political office and the rank of a chief were not entirely restricted by birth. Sometimes commoners were appointed to political positions without regard to customary inheritance procedures, because of unusual capabilities or valor.

[14] For a more detailed description of the Yoruba lineage system, see Peter C. Lloyd, "The Yoruba Lineage," *Africa*, XXIII (July, 1955); W. B. Schwab, "Kinship and Lineage among the Yoruba," *Africa*, XXV (1955); "Continuity and Change in the Yoruba Lineage System, *Annals of the New York Academy of Science*, XCVI (1962).

[15] In present-day Oshogbo the number of generations, reckoned from living adults to the apex of a lineage, varies from one lineage to the next. Some lineages can trace only three generations, while others may have a depth of ten generations.

[16] A deceased person was buried in the ground of his room in the compound in which he lived.

[17] Yoruba believe that *orisha* were descended from heaven at the creation of earth. They are often regarded as personifications of natural forces. See William R. Bascom, *The Sociological Role of the Yoruba Cult Group*, American Anthropological Association Memoir no. 63 (1944); E. G. Parrinder, *West African Religion* (London: Epworth Press, 1949).

[18] There were no age-set groups in Oshogbo, as there were in some other parts of Yorubaland. Nor did significant political-religious groups develop as in other Yoruba areas.

[19] See William R. Bascom's discussion of Yoruba urbanization in "Urbanization among the Yoruba," *American Journal of Sociology*, LX (March, 1955), and "Some Aspects of Yoruba Urbanism," *American Anthropologist*, LIV, no. 4 (1962).

[20] See William B. Schwab, "Growth and Conflicts of Religion in a Modern Yoruba Community," *Zaïre*, VI (Oct., 1952).

[21] It is interesting to note that 69 per cent of the Christians, 30.7 per cent of the Muslims, and only 5.8 per cent of the followers of the indigenous cults are engaged in new occupations. These figures suggest that there is more than a casual relationship between religion and occupational mobility. The reasons for the linkage are complex, and include education, psychological adaptability and commitments, and age.

[22] See Peter C. Lloyd, "Craft Organization in Yoruba Towns," *Africa*, XXIII (Jan., 1953), for an analysis of modern Yoruba craft organization.

[23] For an excellent summary of past and current anthropological thought on

changes in extended kinship systems as a result of Westernization, see P. C. W. Gutkind, "African Urban Family Life," *Cahiers d'Etudes Africaines*, no. 10 (1962).

[24] Cf. Sir Henry Maine's argument in *Ancient Law* (15th ed.; London: J. Murray, 1894) that the critical factor in the development of societies is a substitution of contractual relations for those based on kinship.

[25] In these respects, the extension and intensification of extralineage kinship ties in Oshogbo have something in common with the kinship relationships observed in the industrialized towns of central and southern Africa, where each person has to discover and establish his own set of kinship relationships.

[26] Tribal associations, which play so conspicuous a role in central African towns, are entirely absent in Oshogbo. The relatively few non-Yoruba in Oshogbo have not grouped into formal associations.

[27] See also A. L. Epstein, "The Network and Urban Social Organization," *Human Problems in British Central Africa*, no. 29 (1961).

[28] The exceptions are the heads of certain still-powerful traditional religious cults. These men still exercise considerable power and influence in the community.

[29] Peter Marris points out that even in Lagos the ties of kinship survive as a most important basis for social interaction. See his *Family and Social Change in an African City* (Evanston, Ill.: Northwestern University Press, 1962).

[30] W. L. Kolb, "The Social Structure and Function of Cities," *Economic Development and Cultural Change*, III, no. 1 (1954-1955).

[31] In many respects Oshogbo resembles towns of India or China, or other preindustrial communities in which primary-group orientation is very strong. These towns, however, are marked by the existence of powerful caste or class systems which also define and regulate social behavior. Kinship, here, is functionally integrated with social class. There is no such system of social division in Oshogbo, nor does it seem likely that there will be in the near future. See Gideon Sjoberg, *The Preindustrial City: Past and Present* (Glencoe: Free Press, 1960).

7. Urban Influences on the Rural Hausa

[1] The characteristics here enumerated are among those indicated by Gideon Sjoberg in "The Preindustrial City," *American Journal of Sociology*, LX (March, 1955), 438-445, and *The Preindustrial City: Past and Present* (Glencoe: Free Press, 1960).

[2] L. A. Fallers, "Are African Cultivators To Be Called 'Peasants'?" *Current Anthropology*, II (1961), 108-110.

[3] Gideon Sjoberg, "'Folk' and 'Feudal' Societies," *American Journal of Sociology*, LVIII, no. 3 (1952), 231-239.

[4] Marshall Sahlins points out (in *Evolution and Culture* [Ann Arbor: University of Michigan Press, 1960], pp. 21-22) that both biological and cultural evolution involve not only increasing thermodynamic efficiency, but also the extent to which this efficiency is employed in creating and maintaining a level of organization which is more differentiated into specialized and effectively integrated parts. Marion Levy, in considering the significant differences between industrialized and nonindustrialized societies, cites the technological factors, the greater functional specificity of social relationships, and the use of universalistic criteria in role assignment ("Some Sources of the Vulnerability of the Structures of Relatively Non-Industrialized Societies to Those of Highly Industrialized Societies," in *The Progress of Underdeveloped Areas*, ed. Bert Hoselitz [Chicago: University of Chicago Press, 1952]

pp. 115-118). Bert Hoselitz concludes that the Parsonian pattern variables that distinguish economically advanced societies are achievement, universalism, and specificity, and he also includes, with qualification, "collectivity orientation" in contrast with "self-orientation" (*Sociological Aspects of Economic Growth* [Glencoe: Free Press, 1960], pp. 30-42).

5 W. W. Rostow, *The Stages of Economic Growth* (London: Cambridge University Press, 1960), pp. 22-23.

6 Hugh Smythe and Mabel Smythe, *The New Nigerian Elite* (Stanford: Stanford University Press, 1960).

7 Rostow, *op. cit.*, pp. 26-27.

8 *Population Census of the Northern Region of Nigeria, 1952* (Lagos, 1952).

9 This subject is amply documented in M. G. Smith, *Government in Zazzau* (London: Oxford University Press, 1960).

10 M. G. Smith, *The Economy of Hausa Communities of Zaria* (London: Stationery Office for the Colonial Office, 1955), and "Exchange and Marketing among the Hausa," in Paul Bohannan and George Dalton, *Markets in Africa* (Evanston, Ill.: Northwestern University Press, 1962).

11 Warner Vanter, "The War against Ignorance in Northern Nigeria," *Oversea Education*, XXXII (1961), 174-177.

12 M. G. Smith, personal communication.

13 K. M. Buchanan and J. C. Pugh, *Land and People in Nigeria* (London: University of London Press, 1955), p. 146.

14 R. Mansell Prothero, "Land Use, Land Holdings and Land Tenure at Soba, Zaria Province, Northern Nigeria," *Bulletin de l'IFAN*, XIX (1957), 559.

15 R. Mansell Prothero, "Land Use at Soba, Zaria Province, Northern Nigeria," *Economic Geography*, XXXIII (1957), 72-86.

16 *Ibid.*

8. *Social Alignment and Identity in a West African City*

1 Sir Henry Maine, *Ancient Law* (London: J. Murray, 1861), chaps. ii, iv.

2 E. E. Evans-Pritchard, *The Nuer* (Oxford: Clarendon Press, 1940).

3 M. Gluckman, "Anthropological Problems Arising from the African Industrial Revolution," in *Social Change in Modern Africa*, ed. A. Southall (London: Oxford University Press, 1961), pp. 67-82.

4 *Ibid.*, p. 69.

5 Edward M. Bruner, "Urbanization and Ethnic Identity in North Sumatra," *American Anthropologist*, LIII (1961), 508-521.

6 See, among others, William L. Kolb, "The Social Structure and Function of Cities," *Economic Development and Cultural Change*, III, no. 1 (1954-1955), 30-46; Bert F. Hoselitz, *Sociological Aspects of Economic Growth* (Glencoe: Free Press, 1960), chap. 7; Gideon Sjoberg, *The Preindustrial City: Past and Present* (Glencoe: Free Press, 1960); Elwin H. Powell, "The Evolution of the American City and the Emergence of Anomie," *British Journal of Sociology*, XIII (1962), 156-168. Particularly useful is Herbert J. Gans, "Urbanism and Suburbanism as Ways of Life," in *Human Behavior and Social Process*, ed. Arnold M. Rose (Boston: Houghton Mifflin, 1962), pp. 625-648. Gans concludes that "if ways of life do not coincide with settlement types, and if these ways are functions of class and life-cycle stage rather than of the ecological attributes of the settlement, a sociological definition of the city cannot be formulated."

7 A fuller exposition and discussion of the material relating to Freetown will be found in my *West African City* (London: Oxford University Press, 1957).

8 I am indebted to Mr. J. Jonah for interpretations of Creole sentiment expressed in conversation.

9 J. Clyde Mitchell, *The Kalela Dance* (Manchester: Manchester University Press, 1956). This is the pioneering study that opened up many important problems of African urban life for comparative investigation.

10 L. Proudfoot, "Mosque Building and Tribal Separatism in Freetown East," *Africa*, XXIX (1959), 405-415.

11 For a discussion of this point and of the use of status symbols, see my "The Restructuring of Social Relationships," in Southall, *op. cit.*, pp. 13-25.

12 Kenneth Little, Introduction to "Urbanism in West Africa," special issue of *Sociological Review*, VII (July, 1959), 11.

13 Kenneth Little, "Structural Change in the Sierra Leone Protectorate," *Africa*, XXVI (1955), 217-233.

14 Southall, *op. cit.*, p. 151.

15 Sylvia Leith-Ross, "Development of a Middle Class in Tropical and Sub-Tropical Countries," in *Record of the XXIXth Meeting*, International Institute of Differing Civilizations (Brussels, 1956), pp. 181-182.

16 P. C. Lloyd, "The Yoruba Town Today," *Sociological Review*, VII (July, 1959), 45-63.

17 This analysis follows Mitchell's closely. I have developed it somewhat differently in "Role Congruence and Social Differentiation under Urban Conditions," Proceedings of Pan-American Union Seminar on Social Structure, Stratification, and Mobility, 1962.

18 For illustrations, see my *West African City*, pl. II, *a-b*.

19 I. Wallerstein, "Ethnicity and National Integration in West Africa," *Cahiers d'Etudes Africaines*, III (1960), 129-139, discusses functional and dysfunctional aspects of ethnicity in West African towns. By reserving the term "tribe" for the group in the country and "ethnic group" for that in the town, he guards against certain confusions, but it must be remembered that the extent of discontinuity between the two groups is a matter for empirical investigation, and that it varies from place to place.

9. *Migration in West Africa: The Political Perspective*

1 The dangers of arbitrary distinctions and their ideological origins have been pointed out by Elizabeth Colson, "Migration in Africa: Trends and Possibilities," in *Population in Africa*, ed. Frank Lorimer and Mark Karp (Boston: Boston University Press, 1960), p. 61: "It has usually been assumed that labor migration and permanent migration are unrelated phenomena and that they are basically different in their motivations and consequences. The one is held to be motivated by a desire for cash, the other by population pressure. This is probably a carry-over from the early thinking which held that labor migration was alien to Africa and that it served to provide a cash income to be spent on taxes or luxury goods, while land produced a basic subsistence for the family unit. Today labor migration may provide the basic necessities of life, while land may be the source of a cash income."

2 E. Bernus, "Kong et sa région," *Etudes Eburnéennes*, VIII (1960), 255.

3 "In a centralized, absolutist royalty, as in the ancient kingdom of Abomey in Dahomey, the majority of the displacements were the doing of the king, intervening for all the affectations of his governors, dignitaries, and representatives in the prov-

inces, and ordering at his pleasure the installation in one of his cities of a family invested with a well-defined public function, either administrative or commercial" (J. Lombard, "Le Problème des migrations 'locales': Leur rôle dans les changements d'une société en transition (Dahomey)," *Bulletin de l'IFAN*, XXII [July-Oct., 1960], 456).

[4] *Ibid.*

[5] Colson, *op. cit.*, p. 60.

[6] I know of no empirical evidence for this assertion. The statement of probability is a logical deduction, based on the assumption that it was not easy to emigrate. In most traditional societies, a decision to migrate might meet both social opposition and material impediments.

[7] *Op. cit.*, p. 61.

[8] H. R. Jarrett, "Stranger Farmers of the Gambia," *Geographical Review*, XXXIX (Oct., 1949), 652.

[9] J. Rouch, "Migrations au Ghana (Gold Coast)," *Journal de la Société des Africanistes*, XXVI, no. 1-2 (1956), 138-139.

[10] In fact, however, the simultaneous expansion of numbers attending school meant that, although a larger proportion attended schools nearer home, a larger *absolute* number migrated a considerable distance.

[11] Elliott P. Skinner, "Labour Migration and Its Relationship to Socio-Cultural Change in Mossi Society," *Africa*, XXX (Oct., 1960), 388 n. 3.

[12] P. Mercier, "L'Affaiblissement des processus d'intégration dans les sociétés en changement," *Bulletin de l'IFAN*, XVI (Jan.-April, 1954), 152.

[13] *Ibid.*, p. 150.

[14] Colson, *op. cit.*, p. 63. This administrative bias may, however, have been somewhat stronger in East and Central Africa than in West Africa because of the pressue of white settlers. Colson drew heavily upon her own experience in this area in writing her article.

[15] It is well to bear in mind, in considering the migration of the elites, another pattern of movement which could only marginally be termed migration, but which also had important political consequences. Increasing temporary travel for business, sport, and personal affairs, and more recently for politics itself, has been made possible by wealth and better transportation.

[16] Robert Delavignette, "Mouvements migratoires au sein de l'Union Française," *Journal Officiel, République Française—Avis et Rapports, Conseil Economique* (Paris), April 9, 1953, pp. 323-354. The report speculates (p. 331) on the possibility of European migration to the mountainous regions of Black Africa. Two possible areas mentioned are the Fouta-Djallon in Guinea and the mountainous zone of the Cameroun.

[17] In fact, the pattern took shape quite early and remained relatively stable until independence. For example, Rouch, *op. cit.*, p. 52, notes: "Beginning in 1910, the migration movement in the Gold Coast took approximately its present form."

[18] *Op. cit.*, pp. 152-154.

[19] *Op. cit.*, p. 67.

[20] Skinner, *op. cit.*, p. 385.

[21] The political consequences of this overlapping of the characteristics of class and ethnicity are developed in my "Class, Tribe and Party in West African Politics," *Proceedings of the Fifth World Congress of Sociology*, Italy (1964), III, 203-216.

[22] M. P. Piault, "Migration des travailleurs en Afrique de l'ouest," *Bulletin of the Inter-African Labor Institute*, VIII (Feb., 1961), 122-123.

[23] J. Rouch, "Problèmes relatifs à l'étude des migrations traditionnelles et des mi-

grations actuelles en Afrique occidentale," *Bulletin de l'IFAN*, XXII (July-Oct., 1960), 376. I have outlined my view on the concept of "supertribalization" in "Ethnicity and National Integration in West Africa," *Cahiers d'Etudes Africanies*, III (1960), 129-139.

24 P. David, "Fraternité d'hivernage (le contrat de navétanat): Théorie et pratique," *Présence Africaine*, XXXI (1960), 53.

25 But see H. Raulin's discussion of the 1956 electoral fight in Gagnoa, Ivory Coast, where the victorious SFIO candidate, Digna Bailly, won out against the all-powerful RDA by representing local interests against the immigrant Dioula, who were prominently associated with the local section of the RDA ("Problèmes fonciers dans les régions de Gagnoa et Daloa," part 3 of "Mission d'étude des groupements immigrés en Côte d'Ivoire" [mimeographed; Paris, 1957], pp. 88-93). Also see R. L. Sklar, *Nigerian Political Parties* (Princeton: Princeton University Press, 1963), *passim*.

26 I have developed this point at length in my "Ethnicity and National Integration in West Africa." Even in as "controlled" a territory as Portuguese Guinea, this process is occurring: "Once the traditional ethnic frontiers were broken down as a result of the occupation, intense cultural contacts grew up. . . . Certain ethnic groups imposed themselves. . . . This is manifestly the case with the cultural extension of the Islamized Pauls and Mandingos over the Balantes of the region to the north of Bissorra, over the animist populations of Oio and Bijene and even over the Mandjaques of Pelundo and over the Brames of Bula. This phenomenon is already known as 'mandingoization' or 'soudanization'" (A. Carreira and A. Martins de Meireles, "Quelques notes sur les mouvements migratoires des populations de la province portugaise de Guinée," *Bulletin de l'IFAN*, XXII [July-Oct., 1960], 383).

27 Piault, *op. cit.*, p. 116. See also Skinner, *op. cit.*, p. 397: "Since the migrants are not the main carriers of new political ideas, they are not the main catalysts for the growth of nationalism in the Volta Republic. Yet the mission-trained young men, who have never migrated to Ghana for work but who formed the incipient political parties in Mossi country, were undoubtedly stimulated by the events in Ghana, a country of which they were wholly aware, since a large number of their relatives and countrymen work and have found asylum there."

28 Skinner, *op. cit.*, p. 396. Skinner adds in a footnote: "It was the French themselves who first tried to use returning migrants as subversive agents. During the Second World War, the Free French Forces in Ghana gave returning migrants anti-Pétain leaflets to distribute in Mossi country."

29 Ivor Bulmer-Thomas, "The Political Aspect of Migration from Country to Town—Nigeria," in *Record of the XXVIIth Meeting*, International Institute of Differing Civilizations (Brussels, 1952), p. 480.

30 J.-C. Pauvert, "Migrations et éducation," *Bulletin de l'IFAN*, XXII (July-Oct., 1960), 475.

31 Skinner, *op. cit.*, p. 395. Actually the Mossi were not deported until 1957, after independence.

32 M. E. Amos Djoro, "Réflexions sur la vie politique en Côte d'Ivoire: Le problème de la 'sous-colonisation' noire," paper presented at the *Table Ronde* of the Association Française de Science Politique, March, 1959.

10. *The Economics of the Migrant Labor System*

1 "Inter-Racial Wage Structure in Africa," *International Labour Review* (July, 1958), pp. 48-49.

2 Cf. International Confederation of Free Trade Unions, *Report of the African*

Regional Conference, 1960; Inter-African Labour Institute, *The Human Factor in Productivity in Africa* (2d ed.; London, 1960), pp. 93-95; *East African Royal Commission Report, 1953-55* (London, 1955), chap. 15.

[3] J. Clyde Mitchell, "Urbanization, Detribalization and Stabilization in Southern Africa: A Problem of Definition and Measurement," in *Social Implications of Industrialization and Urbanization in Africa South of the Sahara*, prepared under the auspices of UNESCO by the International African Institute, London (1956), pp. 693-711.

[4] Elliot J. Berg, "Backward-sloping Labor Supply Functions in Dual Economies: The Africa Case," *Quarterly Journal of Economics*, LXXV (Aug., 1961); Henri Labouret, "Sur la Main d'œuvre autochtone," *Présence Africaine*, no. 13 (1952), pp. 124-136.

[5] Cf. Labouret, *op. cit.*

[6] Jean Rouch, "Migrations au Ghana (Gold Coast)," *Journal de la Société des Africanistes*, XXVI, no. 1-2 (1956), 33-196; R. B. Davidson, *Migrant Labour in the Gold Coast* (Achimota, 1954); Elliott P. Skinner, "Labour Migration and Its Relationship to Socio-Cultural Change in Mossi Society," *Africa*, XXX (Oct., 1960), 375-399.

[7] Cf. G. Le Moal, "Un Aspect de l'émigration: La Fixation de Voltaiques du Ghana," *Bulletin de l'IFAN*, XXII (July-Oct., 1960), 446-454. See also H. Raulin, "Mission d'étude des groupements immigrés en Côte d'Ivoire," part 3, "Problèmes fonciers dans les régions de Gagnoa et Daloa," Document du Conseil Supérieur des Recherches Sociologiques Outre-Mer (mimeographed; Paris, 1957).

[8] R. Mansell Prothero, "Migratory Labour from North-Western Nigeria," *Africa*, XXVII (July, 1957), 253.

[9] See n. 16 below.

[10] M. R. Haswell, *Economics of Agriculture in a Savannah Village*, Colonial Research Studies no. 8 (1953); Skinner, *op. cit.*, p. 381.

[11] Skinner, *loc. cit.*

[12] Cf. P. Gourou, *Les Pays tropicaux* (Paris, 1948), chap. 4; Henri Labouret, *Paysans d'Afrique Occidentale* (Paris, 1941), pp. 107-181; and Skinner, *op. cit.*, pp. 383-384.

[13] See Elizabeth Colson, "Migration in Africa: Trends and Possibilities," in *Population in Africa*, ed. Frank Lorimer and Mark Karp (Boston: Boston University Press, 1960), p. 63.

[14] William Watson, *Tribal Cohesion in a Money Economy: A Study of the Mambwe People of Northern Rhodesia* (Manchester: Manchester University Press, 1958), pp. 110-111; J. Van Velsen, "Labor Migration as a Positive Factor in the Continuity of Tonga Tribal Society," *Economic Development and Cultural Change*, VIII (April, 1960).

[15] Cf. Margaret Read, "Migrant Labour in Africa and Its Effects on Tribal Life," *International Labour Review*, XLV (June, 1942); Van Velsen, *op. cit.*; Philip H. Gulliver, "Nyakyusa Labour Migration," *Rhodes-Livingstone Journal*, XXI (March, 1957); Watson, *op. cit.*, esp. Introduction by Max Gluckman.

[16] A. Diop, "Enquête sur la migration Toucouleur à Dakar," *Bulletin de l'IFAN*, XXII (July-Oct., 1960), 395; L. V. Thomas, "Esquisse sur les mouvements de populations et les contacts socio-culturels en pays Diola (Basse-Casamance)," *ibid.*, p. 493; Edwin Ardener and Shirley Ardener, "Migration among the Esu," in *Plantation and Village in the Cameroons* (London: Oxford University Press, 1960); Prothero, *op. cit.*, p. 25; G. Brasseur, "Etude de géographie régional: Le Village de Tenentou (Mali)," *Bulletin de l'IFAN*, XXIII, no. 3-4 (1961), 660 ff.

[17] Labouret, *Paysans d'Afrique Occidentale*, pp. 170-181; Haswell, *op. cit.*, pp. 8-11; D. Ames, "Wolof Cooperative Work Groups," in *Continuity and Change in African Cultures*, ed. W. R. Bascom and M. J. Herskovits (Chicago: University of Chicago Press, 1962), pp. 224-237; Meyer Fortes, *The Web of Kinship among the Tallensi* (London: Oxford University Press, 1949), p. 27; Brasseur, *op. cit.*, pp. 641 ff.; H. Raulin, "Changes in the Socio-Economic Structure of Family Groups," unpublished manuscript (Niger Republic).

[18] R. P. D. Malgras, "La Condition sociale du paysan Minyanke dans le Cercle de San," *Bulletin de l'IFAN*, XXII, no. 1-2 (1960), pp. 281 ff.

[19] Skinner, *op. cit.*, p. 381.

[20] "Les Bases traditionnelles, de l'économie rurale bariba et ses fondements nouveaux," *Bulletin de l'IFAN*, XXIII, no. 1-2 (1961), 179-242.

[21] *Op. cit.*

[22] Prothero, *op. cit.*, p. 256.

[23] T. E. Hilton, "Prafra Resettlement and the Population Problem in Zuarungu," *Bulletin de l'IFAN*, XXII (July-Oct., 1960), 432.

[24] Skinner, *op. cit.*, p. 385.

[25] Cf. *East African Royal Commission Report*, chap. vii.

[26] Gold Coast Colony, *Labour Department Report, 1938-1939*, pp. 17, 27 ff.

[27] *Summary of the Report of the Commission for the Socio-Economic Development of the Bantu Areas within the Union of South Africa* (Pretoria, 1956), p. 28.

[28] Colson, *op. cit.*; Watson, *op. cit.*; Van Velsen, *op. cit.*

[29] Thomas, *op. cit.*, pp. 507-508.

[30] Philip H. Gulliver, *Labour Migration in a Rural Economy* (Kampala, Uganda: East African Institute of Social Research, 1955), p. 35.

[31] A. Hirschman, *The Strategy of Economic Development* (New Haven: Yale University Press, 1958).

BIBLIOGRAPHY

BIBLIOGRAPHY

Abraham, Willie E. *The Mind of Africa*. London: Weidenfeld, 1962.

Acqua, J. *Accra Survey*. London: University of London Press, 1958.

Africa Digest, V, no. 2 (1957).

Al-Bakri. *Description de l'Afrique Septentrionale* (1607). Trans. M. G. De Slane. Paris, 1859.

Ames, D. "Wolof Cooperative Work Groups," in *Continuity and Change in African Cultures*. Ed. W. R. Bascom and M. J. Herskovits. Chicago: University of Chicago Press, 1962.

Ardener, Edwin. "Social and Demographic Problems of the Southern Cameroons Plantation Area," in *Social Change in Modern Africa*. Ed. A. Southall. London: Oxford University Press, 1961.

Ardener, Edwin, Shirley Ardener, and W. A. Warmington. *Plantation and Village in the Cameroons: Some Economic and Social Studies*. London: Oxford University Press, 1960.

Arkell, A. J. *History of the Sudan to 1821*. London, 1955.

Aujas, L. "La Région du Sine-Saloum: Le Port de Kaolack," *Bulletin du Comité d'Etudes Historiques et Scientifiques de l'Afrique Occidentale Française*, XII (1929).

Avice, Emmanuel. *La Côte d'Ivoire*. Paris: Société d'Editions Géographiques, Maritimes et Coloniales, 1951.

Balima, Salfo Albert. "Notes on the Social and Labour Situation in the Republic of Upper Volta," *International Labour Review*, LXXXII (Oct., 1960).

Banton, Michael. "The Restructuring of Social Relationships," in *Social Change in Modern Africa*. Ed. A. Southall. Pp. 13-25. London: Oxford University Press, 1961.

———. "Role Congruence and Social Differentiation under Urban Conditions," Proceedings of Pan-American Union Seminar on Social Structure, Stratification, and Mobility, 1962.

———. *West African City: A Study of Tribal Life in Freetown*. London: Oxford University Press, 1957.

Barth, Henry. *Travels and Discoveries in North and Central Africa, 1849-55*. London, 1857-1858. 5 vols.

Bascom, William R. *The Sociological Role of the Yoruba Cult Group*. American Anthropological Association Memoir no. 63. 1944.

———. "Some Aspects of Yoruba Urbanism," *American Anthropologist*, LIV, no. 4 (1962).

————. "Urbanism as a Traditional African Pattern," *Sociological Review*, VII (July, 1959), 29-44.

————. "Urbanization among the Yoruba," *American Journal of Sociology*, LX (March, 1955).

Beals, Ralph L. "Urbanism, Urbanization and Acculturation," *American Anthropologist*, LIII (Jan.-March, 1951).

Bendix, Reinhard. "Concepts and Generalizations in Comparative Sociological Studies," *American Sociological Review*, XXIII (Aug., 1963).

Berg, Elliot J. "Backward-sloping Labor Supply Functions in Dual Economies: The Africa Case," *Quarterly Journal of Economics*, LXXV (Aug., 1961).

————. "French West Africa," in *Labor and Economic Development*. Ed. Walter Galenson. New York: Wiley, 1959.

Bernard, Augustin. *Afrique septentrionale et occidentale: Géographie universelle*. Vol. XI. Paris: Librairie Armand Colin, 1937-1939.

Bernus, E. "Kong et sa région," *Etudes Eburnéenes*, VIII (1960).

Biobaku, S. O. *The Lugard Lectures*. Lagos, 1955.

Bivar, A. D. H., and P. L. Shinnie. "Old Kanuri Capitals," *Journal of African History*, III (1962).

Boateng, E. A. *A Geography of Ghana*. London: Cambridge University Press, 1959.

————. "The Growth and Functions of Accra," *Bulletin of the Ghana Geographical Association*, IV (1959)

Bott, Elizabeth. *Family and Social Network*. London: Tavistock Publications, 1957.

Bradbury, R. E. *The Benin Kingdom*. London, 1957.

Brasseur, G. "Etude de géographie régional: Le Village de Tenentou (Mali)," *Bulletin de l'IFAN*, XXIII, no. 3-4 (1961).

Brasseur-Marion, Paule. "Cotonou, Port du Dahomey," *Les Cahiers d'Outre-Mer*. Bordeaux, 1953.

————. "Porto Novo," in *Porto Novo et sa Palmeraie*. Dakar: IFAN, 1953.

Briey, Pierre de. "Industrialization and Social Problems in Colonial Africa," *International Labour Review*, LXIII (May, 1951).

Brochure Tricentenaire de la fondation de la ville de Saint-Louis. Saint-Louis-du-Sénégal: Chambre de Commerce, 1959.

Bruner, Edward M. "Urbanization and Ethnic Identity in North Sumatra," *American Anthropologist*, LIII (1961), 508-521.

Buchanan, K. M., and J. C. Pugh. *Land and People in Nigeria*. London: University of London Press, 1955.

Buell, Raymond L. *The Native Problem in Africa*. New York: Macmillan, 1928. 2 vols.

Bulmer-Thomas, Ivor. "The Political Aspect of Migration from Country to Town —Nigeria," in *Record of the XXVIIth Meeting*, International Institute of Differing Civilizations. Brussels, 1952. Pp. 476-484.

Carreira, A., and A. Martins de Meireles. "Quelques notes sur les mouvements migratoires des populations de la province portugaise de Guinée," *Bulletin de l'IFAN*, XXII (July-Oct., 1960).

Church, R. J. Harrison. *West Africa: A Study of the Environment and of Man's Use of It*. 2d ed. London: Longmans, Green, 1960.

————. "West African Urbanization: A Geographical View," *Sociological Review*, VII (1959).

Collins, G. R. "Movements of Population from Rural to Urban Areas in Sierra Leone with Special Reference to Economic Aspects, and to the Colony Rural

Areas," in *Record of the XXVIIth Meeting*, International Institute of Differing Civilizations. Brussels, 1952.

Colson, Elizabeth. "Migration in Africa: Trends and Possibilities," in *Population in Africa*. Ed. Frank Lorimer and Mark Karp. Boston: Boston University Press, 1960.

Coursin, Léon. "Dakar: Port Atlantique," in *Les Cahiers d'Outre-Mer*. Bordeaux, 1948.

Crozat, Dr. "Rapport sur une mission au Mossi (1890)," *Journal Officiel de la République Française*, Oct. 5-9, 1891.

David, P. "Fraternité d'hivernage (le contrat de navétanat): Théorie et pratique," *Présence Africaine*, XXXI (1960).

Davidson, Basil. *Old Africa Rediscovered*. London: Gollancz, 1959.

Davidson, R. B. *Migrant Labour in the Gold Coast*. Achimota: University College of the Gold Coast, Department of Economics, 1954.

De Beauminy, A. "Le Pays de la Boucle de Niger: Etude économique," *Revue Géographique et Commerciale de Bordeaux*, VI (1919), 71-78.

De Coulanges, Fustel. *The Ancient City*. New York, 1956.

Delafosse, M. *Haut-Sénégal-Niger*. Paris, 1912. 3 vols.

Delavignette, Robert. "Le Dynamisme de l'A.O.F.," *L'Afrique Française*, XLII (1932).

———. "Mouvements migratoires au sein de l'Union Française," *Journal Officiel, République Française—Avis et Rapports, Conseil Economique* (Paris), April 9, 1953.

De Marees, P. *Beschrijvinge ende Historische Verhael van het Gout Koninckrijck van Gunea* (1602). Ed. S. P. l'Honoré Naber. Linschoten Vereeniging, 1913.

Denis, Jacques. "The Development of Wage-earning Employment in Tropical Africa," *International Labour Review*, LXXIV (Sept., 1956).

Desclercs, R. "The Manpower Problems of the Ivory Coast and Their Solutions," *Bulletin of the Inter-African Labour Institute*, VII (March, 1960).

Diop, A. "Enquête sur la migration Toucouleur à Dakar," *Bulletin de l'IFAN*, XXII (July-Oct., 1960).

Djoro, M. E. Amos. "Réflexions sur la vie politique en Côte d'Ivoire: Le problème de la 'sous-colonisation' noire." Paper presented at the *Table Ronde* of the Association Française de Science Politique, March, 1959.

Dresch, J. "Les Villes d'Afrique Occidentale," *Les Cahiers d'Outre-Mer*. Bordeaux, 1950.

Dubois, Félix. *Timbouctou la Mystérieuse*. Paris, 1899.

Dufour, Pierre. "L'Economie de la Haute Volta," *Paris-Dakar*, April 9, 1956.

Durkheim, Emile. *The Division of Labor in Society* (1893). Trans. George Simpson. Glencoe: Free Press, 1947.

Egharevba, Jacob U. *A Short History of Benin*. 3d ed. Ibadan, 1960.

Elkan, Walter. "Migrant Labor in Africa: An Economist's Approach," *American Labor Review*, XLIX (May, 1959).

———. *Migrants and Proletarians*. London: Oxford University Press, 1960.

Emery, W. B. *Archaic Egypt*. New York: Penguin Books, 1961.

Epstein, A. L. *Politics in an Urban African Community*. Manchester: Manchester University Press, 1958.

———. "The Network and Urban Social Organization," *Human Problems in British Central Africa*, no. 29 (1961).

Es-Sadi. *Tarikh es-Soudan* (c. 1655). Trans. O. Houdas. Paris, 1900.

Evans-Pritchard, E. E. *The Nuer*. Oxford: Clarendon Press, 1940.

Fage, J. D. "Africa and Historical Studies," in *The Social Sciences in Africa*, ed. R. A. Lystad. London: Pall Mall Press, 1965.

———. *An Introduction to the History of West Africa*. London: Cambridge University Press, 1955.

———. *Ghana: A Historical Interpretation*. Madison: University of Wisconsin Press, 1959.

Fallers, L. A. "Are African Cultivators To Be Called 'Peasants'?" *Current Anthropology*, II (1961).

Feilberg, C. G. "Ibadan," *Kulturgeografi*, LIX (1958).

Ferguson, C. A., and J. J. Gumperz, eds. *Linguistic Diversity in South Asia*. Bloomington: University of Indiana Press, 1960.

First, Ruth. "The Gold of Migrant Labour," *Africa South in Exile*, V (April-June, 1961).

Firth, J. R. *The Tongues of Men*. London, 1937.

Firth, Raymond W., ed. *Two Studies of Kinship in London*. London: Athlone Press, 1956.

Forde, Daryll. *The Yoruba-speaking Peoples of South-Western Nigeria*. London: International African Institute, 1951.

Fortes, Meyer. *The Web of Kinship among the Tallensi*. London: Oxford University Press, 1949.

Fortes, Meyer, R. W. Steel, and P. Ady. "Ashanti Survey 1945-46: An Experiment in Social Research," *Geographical Journal* (London), CX (1947).

Frobenius, Leo. *The Voice of Africa*. London, 1913. 2 vols.

Fry, E. Maxwell. "Town Planning in West Africa," *African Affairs* (1946).

Galletti, R., K. D. S. Baldwin, and I. O. Dina. *Nigerian Cocoa Farmers: An Economic Survey of Yoruba Cocoa Farming Families*. London: Oxford University Press, 1956.

Gans, Herbert J. "Urbanism and Suburbanism as Ways of Life," in *Human Behavior and Social Process*. Ed. Arnold Rose. Boston: Houghton Mifflin, 1962.

Gardiner. R. K. "The New Industrial Communities in West Africa," in *H. R. H. Study Conference on the Human Problems of Industrial Communities within Commonwealth and Empire: Oxford 1956*. London, 1958.

Gautier, E. F. *L'Afrique Noire Occidentale: Esquisse des Cadres Géographiques*. Paris: Librairie Larose, 1935.

"Ghana and Upper Volta Agree To Open Border," *Africa Report*, VI, no. 7 (1961).

Gluckman, Max. "Anthropological Problems Arising from the African Industrial Revolution," in *Social Change in Modern Africa*. Ed. A. Southall. London: Oxford University Press, 1961.

Goody, Jack. "The Ethnography of the Northern Territories of the Gold Coast West of the White Volta." Mimeographed. London, 1954.

Gosselin, M. "Bamako, Ville Soudanaise moderne," *L'Afrique et L'Asie* (1953).

Gould, Peter R. *Development of the Transportation Pattern in Ghana*. Evanston: Northwestern University Press, 1960.

Gourou, P. *Les Pays tropicaux*. Paris, 1948.

Green, L. P., and T. J. D. Fair. *Development in Africa*. Johannesburg: Witwatersrand University Press, 1962.

Greenberg, Joseph. "Concerning Inferences from Linguistic to Non-Linguistic Data," in *Language in Culture*. Ed. H. Hoijer. Chicago: University of Chicago Press, 1954.

Greenfield, Sidney M. "Industrialization and the Family in Sociological Theory," *American Journal of Sociology*, LXVII (Nov., 1961), 312-322.

Guide Ouest Africain: L'Afrique Occidentale. Dakar: Agence de Distribution de Presse, 1960.

Gulliver, Philip H. "Incentives in Labor Migration," *Human Organization*, XIX (Fall, 1960).

————. *Labour Migration in a Rural Economy: A Study of the Ngoni and Ndendeuli of Southern Tanganyika.* Kampala, Uganda: East African Institute of Social Research, 1955.

————. "Nyakyusa Labour Migration," *Rhodes-Livingstone Journal*, XXI (March, 1957).

Gutkind, P. C. W. "African Urban Family Life," *Cahiers d'Etudes Africaines*, no. 10 (1962).

Hailey, W. M. *Native Administration in the British African Territories.* Part III. London: H.M.S.O., 1951.

Hall, R. de Z. "Local Migration in Tanganyika," *African Studies* (Johannesburg), IV (June, 1945).

Hammond, Peter B. "Labour Migration and the Continuity of the Mossi Economy." Paper presented at the annual meeting of the American Anthropological Association, Philadelphia, November, 1961.

Hance, William A. *African Economic Development.* New York: Harper, 1958.

————. "The Economic Potentials of Africa: Economic Development in Tropical Africa," *American Economic Review*, XLVI (1956).

————. "West African Industry: An Analysis of Locational Orientation," *Journal of International Affairs*, XV (1961).

Hance, William A., V. Kotschar, and J. Peterec. "Source Areas of Export Production in Tropical Africa," *Geographical Review*, LI (1961), 487-499.

Harley, G. W. "Roads and Trails in Liberia," *Geographical Review*, XXIX (1939).

Haswell, M. R. *Economics of Agriculture in a Savannah Village.* Colonial Research Studies no. 8. London, 1953.

Hawarden, Eleanor. "The Social and Economic Cost of Migrant Labour," *Race Relations Journal*, XII, no. 2 (1945).

Heads, J. "Urbanization and Economic Progress in Nigeria," *South African Journal of Economics*, XXVII (1959).

Heigham, J. B. "Notes on Labour in the Gold Coast." Mimeographed. Accra, 1952.

Hilton, T. E. "Prafra Resettlement and the Population Problem in Zuarungu," *Bulletin de l'IFAN*, XXII (July-Oct., 1960).

————. *Ghana Population Atlas.* Edinburgh, 1960.

Hirschman, A. *The Strategy of Economic Development.* New Haven: Yale University Press, 1958.

Hodder, B. W. "The Growth of Trade at Lagos (Nigeria)," *Tijdschrift voor Economische en Sociale Geografie*, L (1959).

Homans, George C. *English Villagers of the Thirteenth Century.* Cambridge: Harvard University Press, 1941.

Hoselitz, Bert F. *Sociological Aspects of Economic Growth.* Glencoe: Free Press, 1960.

Hoselitz, Bert F., and W. E. Moore, eds. *Industrialization and Society.* Paris: UNESCO and Mouton, 1963.

Houghton, D. Hobart. "Men of Two Worlds: Some Aspects of Migratory Labour," *South African Journal of Economics*, XXVIII (Sept., 1960).

Houis, Maurice. *La Guinée Française.* Paris: Editions Maritimes et Coloniales, 1953.

Institut Français d'Afrique Noire. *L'Agglomération Dakaroise.* Saint-Louis: IFAN, 1954.

————. *La Presqu'île du Cap Vert.* Dakar: IFAN, 1949.

Inter-African Labour Institute. *The Human Factors of Productivity in Africa: A Preliminary Survey.* 2d ed. London, 1960.

International Confederation of Free Trade Unions. *Report of the Africa Regional Conference.* 1960.

International Labour Office. *African Labour Survey.* Geneva, 1958.

"Inter-Racial Wage Structure in Africa," *International Labour Review* (July, 1958).

"Inter-Territorial Migrations of Africans South of the Sahara," *International Labour Review,* LXXVI (Sept., 1957).

Ivory Coast. Service de la Statistique et de la Mécanographie. "Enquête nutrition-niveau de vie: Subdivision de Bongouanou, 1955-56." Paris, 1948.

Jarrett, H. R. "Bathhurst—Port of the Gambia River," *Geography,* XXXVI (1951).

———. *Geography of Sierra Leone and Gambia.* London: Longmans, 1954.

———. "Population and Settlement in the Gambia," *Geographical Review,* XXXVIII (1948).

———. "Some Aspects of the Urban Geography of Freetown, Sierra Leone," *Geographical Review,* XLVI (1956).

———. "Stranger Farmers of the Gambia," *Geographical Review,* XXXIX (Oct., 1949).

———. "The Port and Town of Freetown," *Geography,* XL (1955).

Johnson, Samuel. *The History of the Yorubas.* Lagos: C.M.S. Bookshop, 1937.

Jones, D. H. "Transactions of the Historical Society of Ghana." Forthcoming article on the history of Gonja.

Kimble, David. *A Political History of Ghana, 1850-1928.* London: Oxford University Press, 1963.

Kolb, W. L. "The Social Structure and Function of Cities," *Economic Development and Cultural Change,* III, no. 1 (1954-1955), 30-46.

Kraeling, Carl H., and Robert M. Adams. *City Invincible: A Symposium on Urbanization and Cultural Development in the Ancient and Near East.* Chicago: University of Chicago Press, 1960.

Labour Department Report, 1938-1939. Gold Coast: Government Printing Office.

Labouret, Henri. "La Main-d'œuvre dans l'ouest-africain," *Afrique Française* (May, 1930).

———. *Paysans d'Afrique Occidentale.* Paris, 1941.

———. "Sur la main-d'œuvre autochtone," *Présence Africaine,* no. 13 (1952), pp. 124-136.

"La Haute Volta," *Magazine AOF,* XVII (Nov., 1955).

Lartilleux, H. *France Lointaine: Géographie des chemins de fer français.* Part 4. *Géographie universelle des transports.* Paris: Chaix, 1950.

Lebeuf, J. P., and A. Masson-Détourbet. *La Civilisation du Tchad.* Paris, 1950.

Ledange, Paul-Louis. "Une Colonie nouvelle, la Haute Volta," *La Revue Indigène,* XVII (1933).

Leith-Ross, Sylvia. "Development of a Middle Class in Tropical and Sub-Tropical Countries," in *Record of the XXIXth Meeting,* International Institute of Differing Civilizations. Brussels, 1956.

Le Moal, G. "Un Aspect de l'émigration: La Fixation de Voltaiques au Ghana," *Bulletin de l'IFAN,* XXII (July-Oct., 1960), 436-454.

"Le Rythme de vie indigène et les migrations saisonnières dans la colonie du Tchad," *Annales de Géographie,* LII-LIV (Oct.-Dec., 1945).

"Les Premiers Fondements historiques de l'urbanisme Yoruba," *Présence Africaine,* n.s., no. 23 (Dec., 1958-Jan., 1959), 22-40.

Lewis, W. A. *Report on Industrialization and the Gold Coast*. Accra: Government Printing Department, 1953.

Levy, Marion. "Some Sources of the Vulnerability of the Structures of Relatively Non-Industrialized Societies to Those of Highly Industrialized Societies," in *The Progress of Underdeveloped Areas*. Ed. Bert Hoselitz. Chicago: University of Chicago Press, 1952.

Little, Kenneth. Introduction to "Urbanism in West Africa," special issue of *Sociological Review*, VII (July, 1959).

——. "Structural Change in the Sierra Leone Protectorate," *Africa*, XXVI (1955), 217-233.

——. "The Urban Role of Tribal Associations in West Africa," *African Studies*, XXI (1962), 1-9.

Lloyd, Peter C. "Craft Organization in Yoruba Towns," *Africa*, XXIII (Jan., 1953).

——. "The Yoruba Lineage," *Africa*, XXXIII (July, 1955).

——. "The Yoruba Town Today," *Sociological Review*, VII (July, 1959), 45-63.

——. *Yoruba Land Law*. London: Nigerian Institute of Social and Economic Research, 1962.

Lombard, J. "Le problème des migrations 'locales': Leur rôle dans les changements d'une société en transition (Dahomey)," *Bulletin de l'IFAN*, XXII (July-Oct., 1960).

——. "Les Bases traditionnelles de l'économie rurale bariba et ses fondements nouveaux," *Bulletin de l'IFAN*, XXIII, no. 1-2 (1961), pp. 179-242.

——. "Un Système politique traditionnel de type féodal: Les Bariba du Nord-Dahomey," *Bulletin de l'IFAN*, XIX (1957).

Londres, Albert. *Terre d'Ebène (La Traite des Noirs)*. Paris: Albin Michel, 1929.

Mabogunje, Akin. "The Growth of Residential Districts in Ibadan," *Geographical Review*, XII (1962).

McElrath, Dennis C. "The Social Areas of Rome: A Comparative Analysis," *American Sociological Review*, XXVIII (June, 1962), 376-391.

Maine, Sir Henry. *Ancient Law*. London: J. Murray, 1861. 15th ed., 1894.

Maitland, Frederick W. *Township and Borough*. Cambridge: The University Press, 1898.

Malgras, R. P. D. "La Condition sociale du paysan Minyanke dans le Cercle de San," *Bulletin de l'IFAN*, XXII, no. 1-2 (1960).

Mangin, Eugene P. *Les Mossi*. Paris: Augustin Challamel, 1921.

Manshard, Walther. *Die Geographischen Grundlagen der Wirtschaft Ghanas unter Besonderer Berücksichtigung der Agrarischen Entwicklung*. Wiesbaden: Franz Sterner, 1961.

——. "Verstädterungserscheinungen in Westafrika," *Raumforschung und Raumordnung* (1961).

Marris, Peter. *Family and Social Change in an African City*. Evanston, Ill.: Northwestern University Press, 1962.

Martindale, Don. Preface to Max Weber, *The City*. Trans. and ed. Don Martindale and Gertrude Neuwirth. London: Heinemann, 1958.

Mason, P. "Inter-Territorial Migrations of Africans South of the Sahara," *International Labour Review*, LXXVI (Sept., 1957).

Mathews, A. "The Kisra Legend," *African Studies*, IX (1950).

Mayer, P. "Migrancy and the Study of Africans in Towns," *American Anthropologist*, LIV (June, 1962).

Mercier, P. "L'Affaiblissement des processus d'intégration dans les sociétés en changement," *Bulletin de l'IFAN*, XVI (Jan.-April, 1954).

Meyerowitz, E. L. R. *Akan Traditions of Origin*. London: Faber and Faber, 1952.

Miller, R. "Katsina, A City of the Desert Border," *Geography*, XXII (1937).

Miner, Horace. "The Folk-Urban Continuum," *American Sociological Review*, XVII (Oct., 1952), 529-537.

————. *The Primitive City of Timbuctoo*. Princeton: Princeton University Press, 1953.

Mitchell, J. Clyde. "Migrant Labour in Africa South of the Sahara: The Causes of Labour Migration," *Bulletin of the Inter-African Labour Institute*, VI (Jan., 1959). Also in *African Abstract*, XI (April, 1960).

————. *The Kalela Dance*. Manchester: Manchester University Press, 1956.

————. "Urbanization, Detribalization and Stabilization in Southern Africa: A Problem of Definition and Measurement," in *Social Implications of Industrialization and Urbanization in Africa South of the Sahara*. Prepared under the auspices of UNESCO by the International African Institute, London. 1956.

Monteil, Charles. "Les Empires de Mali," *Bulletin du Comité d'Etudes Historiques et Scientifiques de l'AOF*, XII (1929).

Moore, Wilbert E. *Industrialization and Labor*. Ithaca: Cornell University Press, 1951.

Moore, Wilbert E., and Arnold S. Feldman, eds. *Labor Comitment and Social Change in Developing Areas*. New York: Social Science Research Council, 1960.

Morazé, Charles. "Dakar," in *Annales de Géographie*. Paris: Librairie Armand Colin, 1936.

Morgan, W. B. "Farming Practice, Settlement Pattern, and Population Density in South-Eastern Nigeria," *Geographical Journal*, CXXI (1958).

————. "The 'Grassland Towns' of the Eastern Region of Nigeria," in *Institute of British Geographers Transactions*, no. 23. London: George Philip and Son, 1957.

Mumford, Lewis. *The City in History*. London, 1961.

Niven, Sir Rex. *A Short History of the Yorubas*. London: Longmans, Green, 1958.

Oliver, Roland, and J. D. Fage, *A Short History of Ghana*. Harmondsworth, 1962.

Palmer, H. R. *Sudanese Memoirs*. Lagos, 1928. 3 vols.

Parsons, Talcott. Introduction to Max Weber, *The Sociology of Religion*. Trans. Ephraim Fischoff. Boston: Beacon Press, 1963.

Parrinder, E. G. *West African Religion*. London: Epworth Press, 1949.

Pauvert, J.-C. "Migrations et éducation," *Bulletin de l'IFAN*, XXII (July-Oct., 1960).

Pedler, F. J. *Economic Geography of West Africa*. New York and London: Longmans, Green, 1955.

Peterec, Richard J. *The Port of Saint-Louis-du-Sénégal*. New York: Columbia University, 1961.

————. *The Position of Kaolack (Senegal) and Other Ports of the Saloum Estuary in West African Trade*. New York: Columbia University, 1961.

Piault, M. P. "Migration des travailleurs en Afrique de l'ouest," *Bulletin of Inter-African Labour Institute*, VIII (Feb., 1961).

Piggott, Stuart. "The Role of the City in Ancient Civilizations," in *The Metropolis in Modern Life*. Ed. Robert Moon Fisher. New York: Doubleday, 1955.

Pirenne, Henri. *Medieval Cities*. Princeton: Princeton University Press, 1946.

Portères, Roland. "Berceaux Agricoles primaires sur le continent africain," *Journal of African History*, III, no. 2 (1962).

Powell, Elwin H. "The Evolution of the American City and the Emergence of Anomie," *British Journal of Sociology*, XIII (1962), 156-168.

Prothero, R. Mansell. "Land Use at Soba, Zaria Province, Northern Nigeria," *Economic Geography*, XXXIII (1957), 72-86.
——. "Land Use, Land Holdings and Land Tenure at Soba, Zaria Province, Northern Nigeria," *Bulletin de l'IFAN*, XIX (1957).
——. "Migratory Labour from North-Western Nigeria," *Africa*, XXVII (July, 1957).
——. "The Population of Eastern Nigeria," *Scottish Geographical Magazine*, LXXI (1955).
Proudfoot, L. "Mosque Building and Tribal Separatism in Freetown East," *Africa*, XXIX (1959), 405-415.
Radcliffe-Brown, A. R. *Method in Social Anthropology*. Chicago: University of Chicago Press, 1954.
Raulin, H. "Changes in the Socio-Economic Structure of Family Groups." Unpublished manuscript. Niger Republic.
——. "Mission d'étude des groupements immigrés en Côte d'Ivoire." Part 3. "Problèmes fonciers dans les régions de Gagnoa et Daloa." Document du Conseil Supérieur des Recherches Sociologiques Outre-Mer. Mimeographed. Paris, 1957.
Read, Margaret. "Migrant Labour in Africa and Its Effects on Tribal Life," *International Labour Review*, XLV (June, 1942).
Redfield, Robert. *The Folk Culture of Yucatan*. Chicago: University of Chicago Press, 1941.
——. "The Folk Society," *American Journal of Sociology*, LII (Jan., 1947).
Reports of the Detroit Area Study. Ann Arbor: University of Michigan, 1952.
Richard-Molard, Jacques. *L'Afrique Occidentale Française*. 3d ed. Paris: Berger-Levrault, 1956.
Richards, A. I., ed. *Economic Development and Tribal Change: A Study of Immigrant Labour in Buganda*. Cambridge, Eng.: Heffer, 1954.
Rodwin, Lloyd, ed. *The Future Metropolis*. New York, 1961.
Rostow, W. W. *The Stages of Economic Growth*. London: Cambridge University Press, 1960.
Rouch, Jean. "Migrations au Ghana (Gold Coast)," *Journal de la Société des Africanistes*, XXVI, no. 1-2 (1956), 33-196.
——. "Problèmes relatifs à l'étude des migrations traditionnelles et des migrations actuelles en Afrique occidentale," *Bulletin de l'IFAN*, XXII (July-Oct., 1960).
Rougerie, G. "Le Port d'Abidjan," *Bulletin de l'IFAN*, XII (1950).
Ruel, M. J. "Labour Migration among the Banvang." Report to the Colonial Social Science Council, London, 1956. Unpublished manuscript. Abridged version is in Edwin Ardener, Shirley Ardener, and W. A. Warmington, *Plantation and Village in the Cameroons*. London: Oxford University Press, 1960.
Sahlins, Marshall. *Evolution and Culture*. Ann Arbor: University of Michigan Press, 1960.
Savonnet, G. "Une Ville neuve du Sénégal: Thiès," *Les Cahiers d'Outre-Mer* (1956).
Schapera, Isaac. *Migrant Labour and Tribal Life*. London: Oxford University Press, 1947.
Schwab, W. B. "Continuity and Change in the Yoruba Lineage System," *Annals of the New York Academy of Sciences*, XCVI (1962).
——. "Growth and Conflicts of Religion in a Modern Yoruba Community," *Zaïre*, VI (Oct., 1952).
——. "Kinship and Lineage among the Yoruba," *Africa*, XXV (1955).

———. "The Terminology of Kinship and Marriage among the Yoruba," *Africa*, XXVIII (Oct., 1958).

Séré de Rivières, E. *Le Sénégal et Dakar*. Paris: Editions Maritimes et Coloniales, 1953.

Sharp, Harry, and Morris Axelrod. "Mutual Aid among Relations in an Urban Population," in *Principles of Sociology*. Ed. R. Friedman, A. Hawley, and W. S. Landecker. New York: Holt, 1956.

Simmel, Georg. "The Metropolis and Mental Life," in *The Sociology of Georg Simmel*. Trans. Kurt Wolff. Glencoe: Free Press, 1950.

Sjoberg, Gideon. "Folk and 'Feudal' Societies," *American Journal of Sociology*, LVIII, no. 3 (1952), 231-239.

———. "The Preindustrial City," *American Journal of Sociology*, LX (March, 1955), 438-445.

———. *The Preindustrial City: Past and Present*. Glencoe: Free Press, 1960.

Skinner, Elliott P. "An Analysis of the Political System of the Mossi," *Transactions of the New York Academy of Sciences* (June, 1957).

———. "Christianity and Islam among the Mossi," *American Anthropologist*, LX, no. 6 (1958).

———. "Integrational Conflict among the Mossi: Father and Son," *Journal of Conflict Resolution*, V, no. 1 (1961).

———. "Labour Migration and Its Relationship to Socio-Cultural Change in Mossi Society," *Africa*, XXX (Oct., 1960), 375-399.

———. "The Diffusion of Islam in an African Society," *Annals of the New York Academy of Sciences*, XCVI (Jan., 1962).

———. "The Mossi *Pogsiouré*," *Man*, LX (1960).

———. "Traditional and Modern Patterns of Succession to Political Office among the Mossi of the Voltaic Republic," *Journal of Human Relations*, VIII, no. 3-4 (1960).

Sklar, R. L. *Nigerian Political Parties*. Princeton: Princeton University Press, 1963.

Smith, M. G. "Exchange and Marketing among the Hausa," in Paul Bohannan and George Dalton, *Markets in Africa* (Evanston, Ill.: Northwestern University Press, 1962).

———. *Government in Zazzau*. London: Oxford University Press, 1960.

———. "History and Social Anthropology," *Journal of the Royal Anthropological Institute*, XCII, Pt. 1 (1962), 73-85.

———. Introduction to M. F. Smith, *Baba of Karo*. London: Faber and Faber, 1954.

———. *The Economy of Hausa Communities of Zaria*. London: Stationery Office for the Colonial Office, 1955.

Smythe, Hugh, and Mabel Smythe. *The New Nigerian Elite*. Stanford: Stanford University Press, 1960.

Southall, A. *Social Change in Modern Africa*. London: Oxford University Press, 1961.

Spitz, Georges. "L'Ouest Africain Francais: AOF et Togo," *Société d'Editions Géographiques, Maritimes et Coloniales* (1947).

Steel, R. W. "Land and Population in British Tropical Africa," *Geography*, XL (1955).

———. "The Population of Ashanti: A Geographical Analysis," *Geographical Journal*, CXII (1948).

———. "The Towns of Ashanti: A Geographical Study," *Comptes Rendus du Congrès International de Géographie* (1948).

Summary of the Report of the Commission for the Socio-Economic Development of the Bantu Areas within the Union of South Africa. Pretoria, 1956.

Suret-Canale, Jean. "L'Industrie des Oléagineaux en AOF," *Les Cahiers d'Outre-Mer* (1950).

Tauxier, Louis. *La Noir du Soudan Pays Mossi et Gourouns: Documents et Analyses*. Paris: Emile La Rose, 1912.

Teixeira da Mota, A. *Guine Portuguesa*. Lisbon: Agencia Geral do Ultramar, 1954. 2 vols. Summaries in English and French.

Thomas, Benjamin E. "The Legend of Timbuktu," *Journal of Geography*, LV (1956).

———. "Railways and Ports in French West Africa," *Economic Geography*, XXXIII (1957).

———. *Transportation and Physical Geography in West Africa*. Washington: National Academy of Sciences, 1960.

Thomas, L. V. "Esquisse sur les mouvements de populations et les contacts socioculturels en pays Diola (Basse-Casamance)," *Bulletin de l'IFAN*, XXII (1960).

Thompson, Virginia, and Richard Adloff. *French West Africa*. Stanford: Stanford University Press, 1958.

Trewartha, Glenn T., and Wilbur Zelinsky. "Population Patterns in Tropical Africa," *Annals of the Association of American Geographers*, XLIV (1954).

Tricart, J. "Développement économique récent du Liberia," *L'Information Géographique* (1959).

Trimingham, J. S. *A History of Islam in West Africa*. London, 1962.

Urbanization in Asia and the Far East. Proceedings of the joint UN/UNESCO Seminar, Bangkok, August 8-18, 1956. Delhi: Research Center on the Social Implications of Industrialization in Southern Asia, 1957.

Urvoy, Y. *Histoire de l'Empire du Bornou*. Paris, 1949.

Vansina, Jan. *De la Tradition orale*. Tervueren, 1961.

Vanter, Warner. "The War against Ignorance in Northern Nigeria," *Oversea Education*, XXXII (1961), 174-177.

Van Velsen, J. "Labor Migration as a Positive Factor in the Continuity of Tonga Tribal Society," *Economic Development and Cultural Change*, VIII (April, 1960). Abridged version in A. Southall, ed., *Social Change in Modern Africa*. London: Oxford University Press, 1961.

Varley, W. J., and H. P. White. *The Geography of Ghana*. London: Longmans, Green, 1958.

Von Grunebaum, G. E. "The Structure of the Muslim Town," in *Islam: Essays in the Nature of a Cultural Tradition*. American Anthropological Association Memoir no. 81. London: Routledge and Kegan Paul, 1955.

Wallerstein, I. "Class, Tribe and Party in West African Politics." Proceedings of the Fifth World Congress of Sociology, held in Bari, Italy, in 1962.

———. "Ethnicity and National Integration in West Africa," *Cahiers d'Etudes Africaines*, III (1960), 129-139.

Watson, William. *Tribal Cohesion in a Money Economy: A Study of the Mambwe People of Northern Rhodesia*. Manchester: Manchester University Press, 1958.

White, H. P. "The Ports of West Africa: Some Geographical Considerations," *Tijdschrift voor Economische en Sociale Geografie*, L (1959).

White, Morton, and Lucia White. "The Intellectual versus the City," in *From Thomas Jefferson to Frank Lloyd Wright*. Cambridge: Harvard University Press, 1962.

Whittlesey, Derwent. "Dakar and the Other Cape Verde Settlements," *Geographical Review*, XXXI (1941).

———. "Dakar Revisited," *Geographical Review*, XXXIII (1943).

———. "Kano: A Sudanese Metropolis," *Geographical Review*, XXVII (1937).

Wilks, Ivor. "A Medieval Trade-Route from the Niger to the Gulf of Guinea," *Journal of African History*, III, no. 2 (1962).

———. *The Northern Factor in Ashanti History*. Legon: Institute of African Studies, University College of Ghana, 1961.

———. "The Rise of the Akwamu Empire, 1650-1710," *Transactions of the Historical Society of Ghana*, III (1957).

Willett, Frank. "Excavations at Old Oyo and Ife," *Man* (1959).

Wilson, Godfrey. "Economics of Detribalization in Northern Rhodesia," *Rhodes-Livingstone Papers*, no. 5 (1941).

Wirth, Louis. "The Urban Society and Civilization," *American Journal of Sociology*, XLV, no. 5 (1940).

———. "Urbanism as a Way of Life," *American Journal of Sociology*, XLIV, no. 1 (1938).

INDEX

INDEX

Abeokuta, 45; population of, 25
Abidjan, 31, 33, 138; population of, 25, 31; railway, 31
Abomey, 5, 195 n. 3
Accra, 36; population of, 25, 31; port at, 31, 37
Achievement: status assignment and, 107; as norm, 149-150
Adaptation: migrant labor as "efficient," 161; migration as natural, 164
Administration: migration and, 150, 152, 154
Age-sex balance, 153-154
Agriculture, 71; urbanization and, 23; as base of economy, 41, 85, 108, 110; cycle of, 67, 68, 168; surpluses in, 96, 112; revolution in, 111, 177-178; organization of, 169; development of, 177. *See also* Crops
Aku, 140
Alkali, 117
Ancestor worship, 92-93
Anchau village: education and, 118, 119; district affairs, 123
Apartheid, 161
Arabs: influence of, 3, 50; writings of, 40; language and, 53, 56
Archaeology: chronology and, 39; towns and walls and, 45
Ascription, 107
Ashanti, 25, 56, 62; Mossi attitude toward, 71; Asantehene of, 77; women and migrants, 155
Associations, 64, 108; Temne Young Men's, 57; tribal, 57, 193 n. 26; development of, 86, 102-103; bases of organization of, 102-103, 107, 171-172;

entertainment societies as, 141-142. *See also* Clubs; Companies; Voluntary associations
Atoaja, 91
Axes: as lines of historical migration, 42; as trade route, 42-44; and walled cities, 44-46; traditions and, 46-49; transverse, 188 n. 6

Bamako, 34, 35; population of, 25, 33; inland trade and, 33; railway at, 35; growth of, 38
Bassa, 141
Batak, 134
Begho, 43
Benin, 40; walls of, 6, 44, 45; power struggles in, 20; population of, 25; Ife and, 45; traditions of origin of, 46, 47
Bicycles: migrants and, 68; district council and, 124; in Takalafiya, 128-129
Blacksmiths, 168
Bobo-Dioulasso, 34, 64; population of, 25, 33; as trade center, 33; as Dioula settlement, 43; Mande traders in, 43
Borgu, 45, 47; tradition and, 46; Kisra and, 48
Bornu, 45; as walled city, 44; Sefawa and, 46; Kanuri in, 53

Cameroons, 173, 174
Chiefdoms, 88
Chiefs: in South Africa, 15-16; Mossi, 17, 61, 62, 63, 65, 68, 73, 75-79, 82, 83, 158; of Benin, 20; and migrants, 69, 76; Oshogbo, 89-91, 93, 97-98, 101; Hausa, 115; of Kong, 149; Dahomey, 154. See also *Oba*

Children: per cent in school, 119; and migrants, 157; production and, 170

Christianity: South Africa and, 12; Mossi and, 80, 81, 83; influence of, 97, 103; prestige of, 97, 110; lineages and, 106; Creoles and, 140-141; Kru and, 141

Cities, 20, 26-27, 50, 111, 131, 178; medieval European, 3, 7; industrial, 3, 12, 16; preindustrial, 3, 112; in savanna, 5; twin cities, 5, 43, 45; West African, 7, 21-22, 26-27; Yoruba, 11, 44, 50, 51; elite and, 19. *See also* Towns

City, 21, 27, 112, 139, 146, 149; concepts of, 1-2, 4, 7, 11, 194 n. 6; preindustrial, 3, 110; industrial urbanism and, 13; and village, 13-15; West African, 15-17, 131-147 *passim;* colonial administrative, 149. *See also* Walled cities

Civilization: ideas of origin of, 6; in Sudan, 41; external influences and, 41-42; elites of, 110; Temne and, 142

Clan: Yoruba, 95; identity and, 145

Cleavages: types of, 14; in Rhodesian towns, 15; in West African towns, 16

Clubs: bereavement, 141-142; savings, 144

Colonial administration: African participation in, 112

Colonialism: effects of, 3, 27, 86, 97-98; language and, 9, 53-54, 58; and migration, 63, 149, 150-151, 152, 156; and Hausa, 112

Commercial centers: Hausa and Yoruba towns as, 45; characteristics of, 85, 111

Commercial expansion: of Dioula, 42-43

Commercial influences: trans-Saharan, 41

Companies: Young Men's, 141-144; Temne, 142-143. *See also* Voluntary associations

Competition: values stress, 108; urban life and, 135

Compound: characteristics of, 89, 95, 115

Conakry: population of, 25; physical characteristics of, 30, 38

Conflict, 16, 105; interpretations of, 13; political, 79, 105; of loyalties, 86; social change and, 132

Consensus: concept of, 131; common

values and, 132; social change and, 132

Contractual relationships, 101, 107; and status, 1; in market system, 99

Convention People's Party, 78; Mossi and, 158

Copperbelt, 134, 140; structural opposition and, 133

Cotonou, 151; population of, 25, 31; port at, 31

Cotton production: migration and, 70-71, 83; as cash crop, 125-126; Cotton Marketing Board and, 126; food crops and, 126

Council: Oshogbo, 91, 95; district, 121-125

Cowries, 62-63

Crafts: of Hausa men, 116; of Hausa women, 116; training for, 119

Craftsmen, 26; in Zaria City, 113; migration of, 166

Creole language, 8, 54, 59

Creole people: in Freetown, 16, 135-147; lack common culture, 135; tribesmen and, 136, 140; identity problem, 137; political power of, 137, 146; solidarity of, 138, 147; and Christianity, 140-141

Crime: social change and, 132

Crops, 18, 70, 172; migration and, 17, 70, 168-169, 170, 172; labor and, 18; production of, 36, 99, 110, 173; and subsistence farmers, 71; introduction of, 99, 100; consumption and, 116; of Hausa, 116; and taxes, 116; specialization of, 126; area of, 126, 152, 153, 155, 163; and urban expansion, 128; transportation and, 128-129; men and, 168, 169

Cults: Oshogbo, 93; heads of, 193 n. 28

Culture: European imported, 27; in Sudan, 41; migration and, 72; transmission of, 157

Customs barriers: migration and, 63, 68, 80, 151

Dagomba, 61

Dahomans, 152, 158

Dahomey, 25, 151, 152, 161; Mossi and, 61; migration in, 172

Dakar, 30, 55, 161; population of, 25

Descent: cohesion and, 90; agnatic, 96;

Ghana, 25, 61, 152, 155, 162, 164, 165, 173, 174; ancient, 42; Soninke and, 42; Mossi migrations and, 61-82 *passim. See also* Gold Coast

Gluckman, Max, 14, 133, 134, 187 n. 28

Gold Coast, 62, 63, 150, 151; customs tolls and, 68; mines and, 77; Mossi political leaders and, 78

Goods and services: exchange of, 93; agricultural surplus and, 96; migration and, 166

Guilds: merchant, 102; craft, 102, 110

Guinea, 161, 174; emergence of states in, 39; written sources in, 40; urbanization in, 40, 41; myths of origin of, 42

Group alignment: structural approach and, 132; identity and, 133; in Copperbelt and West Africa, 133-134; and social change, 146-147

Groups: occupational, 2-3; political, 55, 109; and language, 55-59; tribal, 57, 136, 147, 154; kin, 60, 62, 99, 101, 107, 108, 115; color, 85; corporate, 90, 95; coöperative work, 167, 171. *See also* Ethnic groups

Handicrafts, 18; migration and, 166, 168, 169, 172

Harbors, 29, 30-31, 34, 37

Hausa language: and Kanuri, 53; spread of, 53; as lingua franca, 53, 55; learning of, 56; official recognition of, 58; classes in, 119

Hausa people, 90, 97; walled cities and, 3, 44, 45; slavery and, 6; as traders, 42, 152; origin myths, 47; rural, 110-130 *passim;* colonialism and, 112; as middlemen, 116, 125; economy of, 125-129

Headman: of *zongo*, 76; of district, 121, 122, 124, 125; in Freetown, 136

Heterogeneity: in Timbuktu, 11; absent in Yoruba cities, 11, 96; stratification and, 11-12; defined, 13; ethnic, 50; migration and, 50; linguistic, 51; Rhodesian town and, 85

Hinterland: of Conakry, 30; of Abidjan, 31; and ties to urban center, 57

Homogeneity: linguistic, 51; cultural, 51, 87; ethnic, 108

Houphouet-Boigny, Félix, 78

Ibadan, 36, 37, 105, 109; contrasts in, 3; as old urban center, 23; population of, 25; walls of, 44-45; settlement of, 45

Ibo, 12, 52, 113

Identity: language and, 10, 55-58; kin, 12; social, 132-147 *passim;* immigrant and, 133; and self-conception, 133; ethnic, 133, 134, 135, 138; in Copperbelt, 134; of educated tribesmen, 137; problem of Creole, 137; Islam and, 139; voluntary associations and, 139; Temne, 143; class, 145

Ife, 46, 87; population of, 25; walls of, 44; and Benin, 45; relative age of, 45; and Yoruba origin myths, 47; mythical features of, 87

Ikara District: elections in, 121-122

Immigrants, 14; politics and, 20; wall building and, 45; industrial urbanization and, 113; incorporation of, 131, 132, 133, 136, 146, 147; Creoles and, 136; settlement patterns of, 138; perception of other groups by, 140; involved in oppositions, 145; second generation, 153; occupations of, 155; as "supertribalized," 155

Imports, 180; across Sahara, 25; coast and, 26; cost of, 26; manufactured, 113; through migration, 172

Incest, 93

Income: desire for cash, 100; sources of, 100; status and, 100; migrants and, 165, 166, 169, 173; money, 169, 173; of villager, 172; growth of, 178

Independence, 19, 99; migration after, 157-159

Indians: North American, 134; West Indians, 153

Indirect rule: Mossi chiefs and, 76; Hausa and, 114-115

Industrial centers, 2, 82

Industrialization, 21; process of, 1; and urbanization, 13; urban centers and, 15; change and, 16, 86; Oshogbo and, 109; and colonial elite, 111

Industrialized societies, 85; characteristics of, 111, 193 n. 4

Industrial revolution, 19, 21

Industrial urbanization, 109; characteristics of, 2; and tradition, 4; concomitants of, 12, 129; lingua franca and, 52-53; urban development and, 107, 109-110; immigrants and, 113. *See also* Urbanism; Urbanization

Industries, 111; types of, 37

Intergroup relations: lingua franca and, 52; in Freetown, 138

Islam, 20, 80, 81, 82; introduction of, 5; as urban religion, 12; Jenne rulers and, 43; prestige of, 57, 140, 141, 144, 145; Mossi resistance to, 62; Mossi converts and, 83; elites and, 110; Freetown converts to, 139; interpretations of spread of, 139; social aspect of, 141; role of, 143. *See also* Muslims

Ivory Coast, 61, 64, 152, 158, 159, 162, 165, 174; Mossi labor and, 61, 64; railroad, 64, 190 n. 19; Mossi chiefs and, 76; export crop production and, 162

Jakpa, 43

Jenne, 42, 43

Jihad, 5, 62, 114

Kanem, 48; as state, 41; as walled city, 44; Sefawa and, 46; Kanem-Bornu, 46, 47

Kano, 34, 117; walls of, 6, 44, 45; as old urban center, 23; as inland trade center, 33; railways at, 34

Kanuri, 9, 53; as lingua franca, 53; population described, 53

Katsina, 44

Katanga: labor force in, 175-176

Kayes, 34; railway at, 35; road transport and, 35; Kayes-Niger railroad, 64

Kinship, 10, 93, 95, 101, 102, 193 n. 29; and Oshogbo, 12, 92-109 *passim;* matrilineal, 75; lineage and, 92; as system of norms, 92; characteristics of, 92, 109; and economy, 93, 100, 102, 171; bilateral, 102, 115; societies and, 110; stratification and, 145

Kisra: traditions of, 47-49

Kru, 138; in Freetown, 136; employment of, 138; Christianity and, 141

Kubau, 10; railroad and, 113, 114; Zaria City and, 117; education in, 118; and

elections, 121-122; markets in, 126

Kumasi, 66, 73, 74, 79, 155, 168; population of, 25

Labor: unskilled, 16, 20, 162, 165; demand for, 18, 63, 65, 163, 165; recruitment of, 60, 65, 76, 167; markets for, 60, 62, 68, 156, 160, 161, 162, 163; *corvée,* 65, 82; forced, 65, 66, 71, 76, 81; slave, 115; racial division of, 133; sexual division of, 169; stabilization of, 174-176 *passim;* exporting of, 178. *See also* Labor migration

Labor migration: seasonal, 17, 63, 162, 164, 165-167; emigration and, 18; characteristics of, 60; and Europeans, 60; history of, 61-66; patterns of, 63, 161, 165-166; taxes and, 65, 195 n. 1; motives for, 66, 154, 176, 195 n. 1; attitude toward, 67; effects of, on society, 69-71, 73, 173; women and, 75; religious changes and, 80-82; and adjustment to change, 84; employer prestige and, 155-156; criticisms of, 160, 176; economic aspects of, 160-181 *passim;* economic change and, 163-164; temporary labor migration, 164; impact of, on village economy, 164-173; costs involved in, 165; short-term, 168-172; and village output, 172-173; tenacity of, 173-176, 181; economic growth and, 176-181; restriction of, 178-180; and permanent migration, 195 n. 1. *See also* Migrants; Migration

Lagos, 36, 88, 105, 109, 113; contrasts in, 3; population of, 25, 31-32; harbor at, 31, 34; kin ties in, 193 n. 29

Land, 163; alienation of, 15, 85; Oshogbo, 88, 92, 100; rights to, 92, 100, 114, 115; competition for, 100, 156; usufruct, 114; communal, 126; renting of, 126-127; *fadama,* 126-128; vacant, 154

Languages, 8, 9, 50-59 *passim;* and social identity, 7, 10, 55; number of, in Africa, 8, 51; influences on, 9, 51, 58; spread of, 53; pidginized, 54; continuity of, 56, 57; assimilation and, 56-57; nationalism and, 59. *See also* Lingua francs; Pidgins

Leaders: traditional, 15-16; and towns,

21; nationalism and, 132; of immigrant communities, 136. *See also* Chiefs

Legends, 6; in Guinea, 42; in Hausaland, 47. *See also* Myths; Traditions

Limba: in Freetown, 135, 136, 137, 141; and Islam, 141

Lineage: Oshogbo, 12, 89-108 *passim*, 192 n. 13; royal, 61; Mossi, 61, 62, 66, 73; economic activity and, 62, 73, 93, 96; mother's, 66, 95; principles of, 92; segmentary, 92; and *omole*, 95-96; flexibility of, 105; associations and, 106; education and, 106

Lingua francas, 8, 9, 51-55, 56-59 *passim;* characteristics of, 8, 52; political dominance and, 9; spread of, 52-53, 54; European languages as, 54; tribal languages and, 56; attitudes toward, 57

Literacy: industrialized society and, 111, 129; Zaria City and, 113; Zaria Province and, 118; literacy campaign, 120; in Kubau, 120; and status, 120

Maine, Sir Henry, 11, 132, 134, 185 nn. 1 and 13, 193 n. 24

Mali, 27, 33, 45, 53, 161; Mossi migrations to, 61; Federation of, 159

Malinke, 53, 54

Mande: early commerce and, 41; traders, 42, 43; and Bono, 43; Jakpa and, 43; and Kong, 43; Akan states and, 44; Hausa and, 45; on east-west axis, 188 n. 6

Mandinka, 135, 140; associations, 57, 142; attitude toward Temne, 141, 142; Temne companies and, 142

Marriage: intertribal, 56, 136, 138, 153; Mossi, 62; rules of, in Upper Volta, 73-74; effects of migration on, 73-74, 83, 160; Oshogbo, 92, 96; Muslim converts and, 97; education and, 144

Market relationships, 108, 109

Markets: control of, 2; local, 62; wives of migrants and, 75; town, 116; weekly, 117; cotton and, 126; outside, 179; potential, 179

Market system, 86, 99, 102

Mende: in Freetown, 135, 136, 137; out-

marriage rates among, 138; Islam and, 141

Merchants, 43, 46; Mande, 43; Syrian-Lebanese, 153

Migrants: as commodities, 18; language and, 51, 55; Mossi, 60-84 *passim;* numbers of, 61, 161; death rates for, 65; ages of, 67, 162; occupations of, 67-68, 136, 164; earnings of, 68, 172; per cent on farms, 69; and wives, 75, 162; attitude of, toward Nkrumah, 77; traditional values and, 77; politicians and, 79; attitude of, toward Catholics, 81-82; attitude of, toward migration, 82, 176; in Freetown, 134, 135; ties of, with villagers, 137; educated as, 152; rights of, in foreign country, 158; defined, 160, 161; and pressure to return, 167; Europeans as, 196 n. 16; as subversives, 197 n. 28. *See also* Labor migration; Migration

Migration: defined, 2, 17; urbanization and, 2, 17, 19, 50; explanations of, 2, 151-152; environment and, 4; periods of, 19; psychological aspects of, 19; political aspects of, 19-20, 148-159 *passim;* alliances and, 20; axes as lines of, 42; precolonial, 50, 148-149; linguistic isolation and, 55; of Mossi, 60-84 *passim;* nonfarming roles and, 129; Freetown and, 134, 135; restraints on, 149-150; and transportation, 150; universities and, 151, 159, 196 n. 15; permanent, 152-153; temporary, 152-153; function of, in colonial era, 153; local, 154; nationalism and, 157; after independence, 157-159 *passim;* of politicians, 158; of elite, 159, 196 n. 15; of Europeans, 196 n. 16. *See also* Labor migration

Mines, 60, 163, 174; importance of, 37; Mossi and, 61, 77, 82; and Copperbelt, 133

Missionaries: influence of, on language, 58; Mossi view of, 81; imitate Muslims, 82; Western values and, 86; in Oshogbo, 97; activity of, limited, 117; Creoles and, 135, 137

Mobility: occupational and political,

107; social, 112-113; and education, 120; international, 162

Mogho Naba of Ouagadougou, 65, 76, 78, 79

Monrovia: population of, 25, 31; port at, 31

Moslem Association Party, 78, 158

Mossi, 9, 10, 17, 60-84 *passim*, 150, 151, 159; language and, 55; and Ashanti women, 56; labor migration and, 60-84 *passim;* viability of, 61; village population, 61-62; household, 62; "local urbanism" among, 155; and local politicians, 158; in Ghana, 166; communal labor, 172

Muslims, 43, 53, 111, 140; advantages of Mossi, 80-81; Oshogbo and, 97; and lineages, 106; British policy toward, 117; as association officers, 141

Myths: of Guinea origin, 42; of state origins, 46-48; of Yoruba origin, 87. *See also* Traditions

Nakomcé, 75, 76

Nationalism, 20; language and, 58, 59; and African elite, 112; education and, 122, 151; learned abroad, 132; and local quarrels, 156; and migration, 157, 159

Native Quarter, 89, 103

Neutralism, 159

Niger, Republic of, 61, 161

Nigeria, 47, 113, 152, 161, 173, 174; political ferment in, 112

Nigerian Tobacco Company, 127

Niger River, 30, 33, 34, 41, 42, 113; transportation and, 34-36

Nkrumah Kwame, 77-79 *passim*

Nobles: Mossi, 62; and migrants, 75

Norms, 105, 136; as fluid, 86; kinship as, 92; changes in, 106-107; adoption of, 109; traditional, 109; literacy and, 121; in companies, 144; Creoles and, 147; and achievement, 149-150

Northern House of Assembly, 121, 122

Northern People's Party, 158

Nuatsi, 44, 45, 46

Oba, 10, 89, 91, 98

Occupations, 197 n. 26; social relation-

ships and, 10, 96; lineage and, 93; of women, 93; government and, 98; new, 98; craft, 98-99; change in, 107; of Hausa men, 116; elections and, 122; and tribal affiliation, 138

Omole, 102; compound and, 95; functions of, 95; basis of authority of, 95-96

Omolebi, 102; lineage and, 95. *See also* Clan

Oral traditions: and historical reconstruction, 5; and language, 7; and historian, 39; town origins and, 40

Orisha, 93, 192 n. 13

Oshogbo, 10, 12; population of, 25, 88; as Yoruba town, 85-109 *passim;* land and, 88, 93, 100; traditional social system in, 90-96; similarities with other towns, 108; value system in, 108

Oshogbo Progressive Union, 102

Ouagadougou, 63, 64, 71, 75; population of, 25, 33; railway to, 33; Mossi and, 72, 79, 155

Oyo, 88; walls of, 6, 44, 45; population of, 25; age of, 45

Pagans, 80; number of, in Oshogbo, 106; views of, 139; influence of, 193 n. 28

Pan-Africanism, 159

Peasants: and preindustrial cities, 3; and elite, 110; characteristics of, 111; urbanization and, 111, 129; and land rights, 114; mobility of, 114; and kinship, 115; as shrewd farmers, 128; movements of, 148

Perfect market: characteristics of, 18, 162

Pidgins, 8, 9, 52, 59; relationship of, to Creole, 54; denigration of, 55; and illiteracy, 55

Plantations: labor migration and, 60, 61, 65, 82; started by migrants, 164

Pluralism, 16

Po, 63, 67, 71

Pogsiouré, 62; outside country, 75; between chiefs, 77

Political change: in Upper Volta, 79-80; in Zaria, 121-125

Political diversification, 100-102 *passim*

Political office: patrilineage and, 91; recruitment to, 91, 192 n. 3

Political parties, 21, 77-79

Political power, 19; struggles for, 20, 145; of *atoaja*, 91; and lineages, 91; city as center of, 112; ethnic communities and, 131; shift of, in Freetown, 137; of Creoles, 146. *See also* Power structure

Political system: Oshogbo, 90-91; Hausa, 129; groups and, 147; migration and, 148-159 *passim*

Politics: characteristics of, 20; and Mossi, 158

Polygyny, 62

Population: centers of, 23; of urban centers, 25

Port Harcourt, 34; population of, 25

Ports: as colonial capitals, 26; as trade centers, 26; nature of, 29-33; industries in, 37; site and situation of, 37; and urbanism, 50

Power structure: migration and, 148, 153, 155

Prestige, 143, 147; Islam and, 57, 140-141; African languages and, 58; of Temne, 142, 143; in companies, 144; occupational, 144

Public works, 63, 64

Racism, 15, 16

Railroads, 26, 30, 31, 33, 35, 98, 113; importance of, 34; ports and, 37; lingua francas and, 54; labor supply and, 64; Oshogbo and, 88, 98; and industrialization, 113; cash crops and, 128; and intercolonial migration, 151

Redfield, Robert, 11, 134, 186 n. 20

Relatives: of migrants, 68, 69; of chiefs, 75; maternal, 101-102; unemployed, 154

Religion: urban, 12; Mossi and, 62, 83; and labor migration, 80; *atoaja* and, 91; Yoruba and, 92-93, 97; political rank and, 96; pagans and, 106; and group membership, 139; social significance of, 141. *See also* Christianity; Islam

Repatriation, 158-159

Residence: and cohesion, 90; Yoruba rules of, 92; basis of, 95

Rhodesian Copperbelt. *See* Copperbelt

Roads: interior, 34-36, 88, 128; and lingua francas, 54; as source of work, 68; effect of, on migration, 151

Roles: of chiefs, 76-77; economic, 100-101, 106, 107, 108; differentiation of, 107, 108, 129; bases of assignment of, 111, 129, 130, 193 n. 4; and development, 129; specificity of, 129; political, 130; educated tribesmen and, 137; prestige and, 144

Rural areas: relative growth of, 50; interdependence with urban areas, 110, 113; power structure and, 155

Rural-urban continuity, 133

Sabon Gari ("Newcomers' Town"), 113

Sahara: as trade route, 25; early commerce and, 41

St. Louis, 34-35; population of, 25, 30; as port town, 30; site and situation of, 30

Sanctions: migration and, 73-74; Yoruba, 93; and emigration, 150

Savanna belt: states in, 4-5; precolonial trade centers in, 25; climate in, 34; transportation problems in, 34; labor supply and, 163; underemployment in, 164

Sefawa, 46

Schools: missionaries and, 97; enrollment in, 118; koranic, 118; in Takalafiya, 118-119; utility of, 119-120

Secularization, 12, 110

Senegal, 161, 162, 174

Senegal River: physical nature of, 30; transportation and, 34-36

Sierra Leone, 132, 152; diamond seekers and, 158

Sierra Leone River, 31

Sissosé, 69, 70

"Site," 29, 30; defined, 28

"Situation," 29; defined, 28

Sjoberg, Gideon, 3, 110, 193 n. 1

Slaves: wall building and, 6; and Hausa, 53, 115, 121; pidgin of, 54; in Mossi village, 62

So: towns of, 45, 46; traditions of, 46

Social change: and functional inter-dependence, 13; and urbanization, 13; migration and, 17, 61; factors causing, 86; in Yoruba towns, 86; evidence for, 89-90; education and, 97, 121; isolation and, 113; and Hausa, 124; relationship of, to consensus, 132. *See also* Structural change

Social class: Creoles and, 136; distinctions, 145; class alignment, 146; rural middle, 153; and ethnic group, 155; class consciousness, 156

Social identity. *See* Identity

Social relationships, 10; underlying towns, 85; changing in Yoruba towns, 87-109 *passim*; ecology and, 96

Social stratification, 19, 54; in West and South Africa, 17; and tribal proletariat, 143; and companies, 143, 144; nonethnic basis for, 149; and immigrants, 155

Social structure, 20, 150; and spatial configuration, 89; as kin-bound, 96; Hausa traditional, 114-115; solidarity and, 132. *See also* Social system

Social system, 13, 133; society as integrated, 16; of African towns, 86; traditional Oshogbo, 90-96; present Oshogbo, 97-106; basis for complexity of, 110; and land tenure, 163

Sociolinguistics, 51; approach of, 7; aspects of, 59

Sokoto, 53; as walled city, 44; urban growth and, 129

Solidarity, 132, 141; lingua franca and, 57; paramount chief and, 91; weakening of corporate, 108; Batak and, 135; and class alignment, 146

Songhai, 61; wall building and, 45; and Timbuktu, 50; as lingua franca, 53, 56; on east-west axis, 188 n. 6

States, 5; emergence of, in Sudan, 39, 40, 41; emergence of, in Guinea, 41; named after cities, 44; and walled capital cities, 44

Status: assignment of, 100, 107; changes in, 100, 107-109 *passim*, 153; ambiguity of, 107; and literacy, 120. *See also* Roles

Structural approach, 132-133

Structural change: economic development and, 163; migration and, 176

Structural opposition: and urban consensus, 132; on Copperbelt, 133; model of, 133, 147; and group definition, 147

Subcontracting, 174

Subsistence output: migration and, 167; and quantity of effort, 173. *See also* Crops

Sudan: origin of urban settlements in, 39-49 *passim*; data on history of, 40; Nilotic influence on, 41; urbanization in Guinea and, 41

Sultan of Sokoto, 114

Supply, 162

Swahili: as indigenous lingua franca, 54; recognition of, 58

Tado, 45; earthworks at, 44; in legends, 44; and emigration line, 46

Takalafiya, 114; market at, 117; and district government, 118; school at, 118-119; funds spent in, 123; tobacco market in, 127; energy sources in, 128

Takoradi, 25, 31

Talakawa, 114

Taxes, 71, 116; and migration, 62, 63, 65, 82, 83, 150, 151-152, 178, 180; as obligation to chief, 114; manipulation of, 125; cotton and, 126; considered as persecution, 151; and emigration, 154

Tema, 31

Temne, 135, 141; and linguistic passing, 57; tribal strength of, 57; association, 57, 142; numbers of, in Freetown, 136, 137; outmarriage rates among, 138; prestige of, 142

Tenkodogo, 63, 67

Thiès-Kayes railroad, 64

Timbuktu, 29, 33, 36, 42, 61; characteristics of, 11; urban elements in, 11; lingua franca in, 11, 53; as old urban center, 23; population of, 33; roads and, 34; Kabara as port for, 35; ethnically heterogeneous, 50; "stable bilingualism" in, 56; Mossi traders and, 62

Togo, 61, 62, 151, 158, 161

Tönnies, Ferdinand, 11, 134, 186 n. 20

Toucouleur, 55

Town: concept of, 1-2; Oshogbo as pre-colonial Yoruba, 85-109 *passim*

Towns, 14, 115, 152; and migration, 2; politically centralized, 2; elements of geographic relevance to, 4, 28; growth of agricultural, 5; in forest regions, 5, 41; South African, 15, 175; as centers of progress, 21; planning of, 21; of savanna, 25; location of large, 26; growth of, 26, 178; as heterogeneous, 27; in Mali, 27; port towns, 30-33; interior towns, 34; of French influence, 36; of British influence, 36, 37; market industries in, 37; emergence of, in savanna, 39, 41; and Egyptian influence, 41; emergence of, in Guinea, 41; as commercial centers, 45; antiquity of, 45; traders in, 60; in Rhodesia, 85; of Yoruba, 85-86; Oshogbo, compared with other towns, 108; weekly markets in, 117; population far from, 163. *See also* Walled cities

Trade, 62; in Sudan, 40, 41; in Guinea, 41; and language, 53; migrants and local, 71-72; change of basis for, 98; rural men and, 116

Trade centers: in savanna, 25; growth of cities and, 26; importance of ports as, 26; inland location of, 26, 33

Traders, 45, 53, 60, 116, 150; Mande, 43; complex societies and, 60

Trade unions, 156-158

Traditions, 4; character of formal, 39; of Hausa walls, 45; of Benin origin, 46; of Ewe and Ga, 46; of Sefawa, 46; of So, 46; of state origins, 46; of Kisra, 47; of Yoruba origin, 47. *See also* Oral traditions

Transportation, 179; and rise of trade centers, 26; cost of, 26, 67, 167; effect of seasons on, 34-36, 164; and migration, 67, 150-151, 167; in labor-intensive economy, 111; and energy sources, 129; growth of facilities for, 178

Tribalism, 57, 58

Tribal unions, 57. *See also* Associations

Tribe: as reference group, 19; defined by language, 55; and ethnic group, 57, 195 n. 19

Tuareg, 50; and language, 53, 56

Upper Volta, 10, 78, 79, 151, 159, 161;

Mossi of, 60-84 *passim*; migration as problem in, 61; political change in, 79

Urban: "urban" and "folk," 11; as concept, 11, 87, 135

Urban centers, 2, 71, 132; industralization and, 15; number of, 23; growth and, 23, 37-38, 50, 111-112; population of, 25; urban geography and, 27-29; inland, 33-34; in Sudan, 41; walled, 44; and migration, 50, 61, 111, 155; language and, 51, 54; and ties to hinterland, 57; and taxes, 82. *See also* Cities; Towns

Urban community: components of, 21; Oshogbo as, 85-109 *passim*; interdependence with rural, 110; and American experience, 131; immigrants incorporated into, 132, 136, 139, 146, 147

Urban industrialization. *See* Industrial urbanization

Urbanism, 12, 22, 23-26, 51; and ethnic heterogeneity, 11; Western industrial, 13; precolonial, 50, 53; and traditional forms, 86; as uniform process, 86; "local urbanism," 155

Urbanization, 21, 25, 50, 84; and social change, 13; as process, 13; and industrialization, 13; in South and West Africa, 16; potentials for, 23; in Sudan, 40; in Guinea, 41; present and precolonial, 50; rate and intensity of, 86; peasant participation in, 129; analysis of, 134; in North Sumatra, 134; consequences of, 140; tribal ties and, 145

Urbanizing influences: of colonialism, 112; listed, 128

Urban settlement: types of, 5, 42; Dioula, 43; on axes, 44

Urban society, 10, 13, 131; principles of, 13; ecology and, 96

Values: retained by migrants, 77; as fluid, 86; introduction of Western, 86; change of, 86, 107, 109, 129; uniform, 108; incompatibility between, 109; industrialization and, 109; and education, 129; consensus and, 132; and solidarity, 132

Village: concept of, 1; and city, 13-14; output, 18, 166-173 *passim*, 177; population and, 25; Mossi rulers of, 61;

headman of, 114, 123-125, 127; economy of, 163-181 *passim*; capital formation in, 166, 167; proportion of males absent from, 170-171

Virilocal residence, 62, 92, 171

Voluntary associations, 103, 105, 158; and lineage control, 105; spread of, 139; and institutional change, 141; officers of, 141; functions of, 142-144; nature of, 142-144

Wages: and emigration, 18; Ivory Coast Railway and, 65; low, 65, 160; effect of change in, 162; and labor demand, 165; seasonal, 168

Walled cities: and Hausa, 3, 45; development of, 5; distribution of, 44; Kano and Katsina as, 44; northeast axis and, 44; terrain and, 44-45; north of Yorubaland, 45; reasons for building, 45-46; of Logone-Shari, 46; as result of political impulse, 49; Oshogbo and, 88

Wards: and traders, 60; headmen of, 76; and Native Quarter, 89; and British, 91; as local grouping, 91; as village division, 114

Weavers: migration and, 72, 168

Weber, Max, 11, 21, 186 n. 20

Wirth, Louis, 11, 12, 134, 186 n. 20

Wives: inheritance of, 62; runaway, 73; of migrants, 75, 162; commercial activity of, 116; education of, 144

Wolof, 55, 152

Women: taken by migrants, 66; runaway, 66, 73; migration of, 75; treatment of, 75; occupations of, 93, 116, 169, 170

Work force: difficulties in developing, 163; stabilization of, 174-176 *passim*. *See also* Labor

Work organization, 170, 171; of Mossi, 70; composition of, 93; of Hausa peasants, 115; in traditional agriculture, 169. See also *Sissosé*

Yoruba, 23, 57, 88; cities, 11, 44, 45, 50, 51; traditions, 46, 47; Oshogbo as Yoruba town, 85-109 *passim*; per cent of town dwellers among, 87; number of, 87; history of, 87-88; new groups of, 103; in Zaria City, 113; subdivisions of, 191 n. 3

Zaghawa, 47, 48

Zagon Katab District, 122

Zaria City: Kubau District and, 14, 117; population of, 25, 113; characteristics of, 113; and cotton gins, 126; rail junction at, 128

Zaria Province, 10, 112; Hausa of, 113-130 *passim*; education in, 117-121; governmental changes in, 121-125

www.ingramcontent.com/pod-product-compliance
Lightning Source LLC
Chambersburg PA
CBHW031129270326
41929CB00011B/1553